WORDSWORTH'S
Historical Imagination

WORDSWORTH'S
Historical Imagination

THE POETRY OF DISPLACEMENT

David Simpson

METHUEN *New York and London*

First published in 1987 by
Methuen, Inc.
29 West 35th Street, New York NY 10001

Published in Great Britain by
Methuen & Co. Ltd
11 New Fetter Lane, London EC4P 4EE

© 1987 David Simpson
Printed in Great Britain
at the University Press, Cambridge

*Library of Congress Cataloging in
Publication Data*

Simpson, David, 1951–
    Wordsworth's historical imagination.
    Bibliography: p.
    Includes index.
    1. Wordsworth, William, 1770–1850 –
Knowledge – History.   2. Wordsworth,
William, 1770–1850 – Political and social
views.   3. Historical poetry, English.
4. Politics in literature.   5. Social problems
in literature.   I. Title.
PR5892.H5S56   1987   821′.7
86-23921

ISBN 0 416 03872 7

*British Library Cataloguing in Publication
Data*

Simpson, David, 1951–
    Wordsworth's historical imagination: the
    poetry of displacement.
    1. Wordsworth, William, 1770–1850 –
    Criticism and interpretation
    I. Title
    821′.7   PR5881

ISBN 0 416 03872 7

Contents

Acknowledgements   vii

Citations and abbreviations   ix

Introduction: writing in history and theory   1

1   'Gipsies'   22
    Minding the poet's trade   25
    The travelling people   43

2   Wordsworth's agrarian idealism: the case against urban life   56

3   Another guide to the lakes   79
    The real state of sublunary nature   79
    The real language of men   97

4   'In single or in social eminence'? The political economy of
    The Prelude and *Home at Grasmere*   108
    Forced hopes and proud rebellion   108
    The world of all of us   121

5   'By conflicting passions pressed': 'Michael' and 'Simon Lee'   140
    The poetry of property   141
    The poet as patron   149

6   Poets, paupers and peripatetics: the politics of sympathy   160
    The uses of poverty: 'The Old Cumberland Beggar'   162
    Versions of relief: 'Beggars' and 'Alice Fell'   175

7   Structuring a subject: *The Excursion*   185
    Talking through the rural life   187
    Education and religion   196
    'A species of ventriloquism'   200

    Postscript: 'The star of eve was wanting'   209

    Notes   217

    Bibliography   225

    Index   236

Acknowledgements

This study was carried out during an idyllic year spent at the National Humanities Center in North Carolina. My warmest thanks go to the staff and fellows for all their various contributions, and to Northwestern University for granting me a second year's leave to work on this project. In particular, I have profited from the advice and expertise of Emilia Viotti da Costa, Morris Eaves, Donald Greene, Stuart Marks and Jack Wilson. The hospitality and knowledge of Mark Reed have informed what I hope are some of the best parts of what follows. I am also grateful to Rodney Baines, John Barrell, Clifford Darby, Sarah Maza, W.J.T. Mitchell and Regina Schwartz for various important insights and perspectives. I owe a very great debt to my colleague Wallace Douglas, whose unpublished dissertation on the social and economic features of Wordsworth's Lakeland environment deserves greater recognition than it has had. I have drawn heavily upon it in my second and third chapters. The reader for Methuen made careful and pertinent suggestions that have, I hope, improved the final version of this manuscript. Jeffrey Robinson also gave generously of his time and concentration. It is a pleasure to thank the staff of the various libraries I have used: the British Library, Cambridge University Library, Duke University Library, Northwestern University Library, and the library of the University of North Carolina at Chapel Hill. Finally, I want to thank Caroline Cahan, Georgia Eaves, Mona Frederick, Pat

Kucker, Wayne Pond, Val Rogers and Joe Viscomi for the constant pleasure of their company; and Joe, Mike, Brennan and Wendy, who almost
taught me to keep to the rhythm. They will understand that whatever is
incoherent here was probably written on Thursday mornings.

Citations and abbreviations

Most references in the body of the text are to author and date of edition. The bibliography should be consulted for full details.

The following abbreviations have been used for frequently cited works:

PW	*The Poetical Works of William Wordsworth*
PrW	*The Prose Works of William Wordsworth*
EY	*The Letters of William and Dorothy Wordsworth: The Early Years*
MY	*The Letters of William and Dorothy Wordsworth: The Middle Years*
LY	*The Letters of William and Dorothy Wordsworth: The Later Years*
Prelude	*The Prelude: 1799, 1805, 1850*
LB	*Lyrical Ballads*
1807	*Poems, in Two Volumes*
B	*The Borderers*
BW	*Benjamin the Waggoner*

DS	*Descriptive Sketches*
EW	*An Evening Walk*
HG	*Home at Grasmere*
RC	*The Ruined Cottage*
SPP	*The Salisbury Plain Poems*
PL	John Milton, *Paradise Lost*

Introduction: writing in history and theory

For many lovers of poetry, Wordsworth is the great Romantic, and his greatness is founded upon his identity as the poet of nature and of solitude. Nature and solitude, it is often said, are the primary sources of the Wordsworthian imagination and the creative energies of his mind and heart. This imagination has thus passed into the tradition as an essentially private faculty, one whose very existence is premissed upon the absence of other people.

This established view of Wordsworth is amply supported by many of his writings, both in poetry and in prose. It responds adequately enough to a great deal that Wordsworth himself makes explicit. But it has failed to recognize and explain another dimension of the poet's argument, whereby the very possibility of privacy is dependent upon social circumstances. As these circumstances vary, so the experience of privacy may be creative or uncreative, genuinely imaginative or hopelessly alienated. There is, in Wordsworth's writing, no such thing as a private or individual imagination capable of complete and entire self-determination. His exposition of the nature and exercise of the most essential faculty in human nature makes constant reference to limiting or enabling conditions of time and place.

As the Wordsworthian imagination is thus social, and defined even in its isolation by its relation to others, so it is also historical, defined in relation to particular others and at specific moments. It is historical in at least three mutually interdependent ways. First, as I have said, the creative imagination is significantly both formed and maintained by empirical circumstances, human and geographical. This model of determination affects the imagination of the poet and that of his readers, and Wordsworth was unsure of both. Even as he hoped to appeal to the common sympathies of all readers, he argued, at times obscurely but nevertheless coherently, that the habits of mind necessary for the full comprehension of his poems were not already in place for most potential readers, but were determined by particular conditions of time and place that were themselves disappearing.

Second, many of Wordsworth's poems address themselves to fairly precise events and circumstances: the French Revolution, the condition of England, the plight of the poor, and so forth. He selects, that is to say, a historical subject matter, the details of which often appear lurking within the very poems that seem to want to avoid them. The following study makes no attempt to deal with all of these topics, but rather pursues a thematic argument that seeks to explore and explain another sense in which Wordsworth's imagination is historical.

This third sense includes aspects of both of the above, and describes the way in which Wordsworth's own imagination is historical, and apparent as such in the details of his writing. This writing, at least in the early Wordsworth, transcribes a subject in conflict, a subject defined by a condition of acute alienation, both vocational and social. It is a writing that continually falls short of what it aspires to be, but reveals in that falling short its greatest intelligence and its most coherent messages. When this writing is understood for what I think it is, it should become almost impossible to cite Wordsworth as the exemplum of any organicist reconstruction of Romanticism and any unitary discursive energy, whether it involve the relation of mind to nature or that of mind to body, or self.

This study seeks to show that Wordsworth set out to address some conscious and urgent questions to his contemporaries about the critical issues of his times. The private resolutions that so many of his poems seem to propose had a recognizable public import, against which privacy became variously a triumph and a defeat, at times something of both. At the very moment that Wordsworth positions his poetry as a polemical commentary upon the condition of England, he theorizes as part of that condition the circumstances that will prevent his poetry being usefully understood. His writing thus strives for self-respect, for recognition as a productive medium in the social order, often imaged in the language of work and property; but it also undercuts or displaces itself, as in its propensity for the vocabulary of idleness and vagrancy. Even when the private moment is the apparent outcome of these narrative anxieties, it is a moment most often expressed in a language that presumes some public visibility.

There is thus, and in a primary way, an explicit public discourse in Wordsworth's poetry. Although he is well known as the poet of private experience, he is hardly known at all as moralist and political economist. To say that he held 'views' on these subjects is of course to say nothing new, but I shall argue a much stronger case: that his writings contain a sophisticated (if often implicit) reformulation of the traditional defence of civic or public virtue against the dangerous effects of a commercial and industrial economy. His comments on the changing relations of town and country, and the consequent transformations of the nature and balance of work and leisure, are coherently worked into his negative analysis of the uncreative forms of thought and perception expressed in an incrementally alienating language. The fact that Wordsworth's argument is never formally set out in the form of a treatise, taken together with literary criticism's institutional reluctance to examine the historical energies of both poetic and theoretical language, has meant that we do not yet have in place a proper understanding of the integrity and scope of Wordsworth's case against what he saw as the course of English society. In this particular blindness we have all been the willing subjects of Coleridge's revisionary magic, most obviously of his rewriting and negation of Wordsworth's ideas about the exemplary value of the language of ordinary men in a state of vivid sensation. Part of this study must then be taken up with expounding the nature and coherence of those ideas, and of the polemical framework within which they make sense.

To take up this task is, however, to produce an over-coherent reading of Wordsworth. In my second chapter I take that risk in order to make clear that a hitherto unnoticed coherence is there; but it seldom emerges in the forms of sustained arguments or achieved aesthetic wholes, whether in prose or in poetry. Because of this, few critics have hitherto tried to argue that the political or sociological (a better term would be 'psycho-sociological') themes in Wordsworth's writing might constitute anything resembling a centre or major rhetorical strategy. I seek to demonstrate that they do constitute such a major strategy, one that holds together a number of otherwise disconnected gestures; but it must be traced in the forms of its displacement, as much in its radical incoherence as in its life within the tidy language of propositional argument. There is no simple, unitary, public Wordsworth, a persona masterfully commanding the kind of tried and true view of the world that might reciprocally make possible an efficient habit of self-endorsement and self-consolidation. Nor is there a simple conflict or tension between the private and the public. Each of these terms is created only in terms of the other, so that each bears the marks of frustration, hesitation, hyperbole and incompletion. Thus it is that Wordsworth so often seems to be engaged in an obfuscation of or falling from the positions that his polemic, as previously explained, would seem to entail. While being very clear about what is wrong with the world, one might say, he is very unclear about exactly how to set it right. I do not here see an individual mind engaging in various degrees of hypocrisy or bad faith, nor indeed the deep and abiding logic of a constitutional conservative who only ever 'dallied' with egalitarian ideals. Others have read Wordsworth this way, and not without some good evidence. But I have found it most productive of insight to regard the Wordsworthian subjectivity as a particular medium (and entity) that was, by virtue of its openness to the energies of language and experience, extraordinarily articulate about the pressures and tensions that we may with hindsight regard as central to the culture at large. Few writers can match Wordsworth in his representation of the creative mind as the site of errors, conflicts and uncertainties. He is, *par excellence*, the poet of self-consciousness, writing out at once his impressions, and his impressions of his impressions. By this *critical* imaging of the poetic subjectivity (and his own), he allows for the articulation and objectification of those elements of the personality that are intersubjective; that is, his genius enables him to discover for his personal anxieties the very language that renders them objects of public inspection and subjects of public concern.

The significantly historical aspect of the Wordsworthian selfhood does not then so much reside in its coherence as in its incoherence. He was subject, as many others must have been, to a series of fairly standard conflicts accompanying the passage from a counter-cultural youth to a middle-class maturity. We will see that he worried about property, both actual and imaginary; about work and labour, and whether the writing of poetry could ever be considered a respectable form of such; and about achievement – about finishing things (for himself) and displaying them as products (for the approbation of others). These are ordinary enough concerns. But Wordsworth's articulation of these tensions and anxieties takes place in a language that so fully images and alludes to the public and political dimension that it becomes profoundly representative. In its social and political resonances, and in its command of the literary and theological inheritance, Wordsworth's language stands as an essential and luminous part of the archive of his culture.

Take, for example, the presence of Milton in Wordsworth's writing, a presence about which I shall have much to say in what follows. Harold Bloom and Geoffrey Hartman, in particular, have made sure that all readers of Romantic poetry will be vigilant in their expectation of the Miltonic dimension, a dimension that is in no sense covert or embarrassed when it is as clearly and literally invoked as it often is. Now, there may be a certain potential in viewing Milton as some sort of anxiety-provoking father-figure in the Wordsworthian psyche; but such a universalizing approach does little to explain satisfactorily the complex level at which *Paradise Lost* functions in Wordsworth's writing as the major setting-forth of the cultural and theological syndrome that Wordsworth too continues to inhabit. There is in the persona of the Wordsworthian speaker a recapitulation and recuperation of the tripartite drama of Milton's poem, as enacted by Satan, Adam and Messiah. Satan and Messiah are mutually constituting antitypes – reference to one invokes awareness of the other as cause and consequence in the cycle of damnation and redemption – and Adam is caught awkwardly in the middle. In calling up and employing this precedent, Wordsworth is not simply engaged in a gesture of literary or even theological self-positioning. For in the spectrum contained within the limits of Satan and Messiah, and most often centring around the unstable Adam, Wordsworth explores and delineates his own being in the world, his identity as a social and historical individual. Adam's fall, in Milton's poem, brings about a world in which work has become painful rather than pleasurable, in which darkness and cold appear as the climate of paradise is replaced by the weather of northern Europe, and in which suffering plays an unprecedented part in human experience. These details were not just concepts or tropes for Wordsworth; they were the discursive formulations within which he seems to have described his everyday life, within which he expressed his experiences. If this process at times clearly depended upon a high level of false consciousness, then there were other times when it did not. It is indeed in the play between the imaginary and what we may call the 'real' anxieties, thus described, that we may begin to trace the generic and individual profiles of Wordsworth's writings. The Miltonic rhetoric of his poems speaks for a seriously maintained insecurity about being in the world. Evidence for this assertion is plentiful in the rest of this study; suffice it to say here that Wordsworth's Milton should not be reduced to an idealist father-figment with which the rebellious son struggles in his quest for a place on some imaginary Olympus.

Wordsworth's imaging himself as an inconsistent blend of the three figures of Satan, Adam and Messiah is then one prominent example of the degree to which the poet's subjectivity is not a thing made and finished, a bold front for or against things as they were, but a medium constantly open to patterns of deconstruction and reconstruction. Moments of sheer confusion interact with the rhetoric of firm persuasion, neither ever quite displacing the other. The case of Wordsworth is thus a good example of the way in which the more general debate about freedom and determination, whether carried on by literary critics or by social scientists, is not much furthered by recourse to ungainly extremes. Subjectivity is neither a 'historically' created automaton, passively reproducing its imprinted culture, nor an exclusively individual entity governing itself by choice and free will. It is, awkwardly, something between the two, seeming to partake of each extreme to various degrees at different times and in different ways. Biologists are fond of the metaphor of the template as a way of explaining the interaction of 'self' and 'world'. We come into the world perhaps in part with genetically determined programmes for development and behaviour, but also with a 'potential' for development along certain general lines that can only become specific when the environmental, contingent factor is present. The organism, that is to say, requires an external (and perhaps cultural) input in order that its genotypes shall develop at all. The question of the degree to which subjectivity as a whole may be determined by innate rather than contingent factors thus becomes impossible even to formulate clearly when it is postulated that the self as we know it is always a composite organism (phenotype) in which both these forces have *already* interacted with each other to produce that self.

Application of this general syndrome to particular cases produces differently emphasized explanations. Some areas of human behaviour, such as sexuality and aggression, are highly contested and unclear. To adjudicate how much of each is determined by genetic or cultural forces is to venture into a region where hard science and political persuasion can be hard to disentangle. Perhaps it might be suggested, at least, that to commit oneself to *language* is to move further into the realm of intersubjective behaviour than is the case with many other forms of action. Sex and aggression are also open to explanation in historical–objective terms, as the analysis of different cultures can demonstrate. But language seems culture-specific to a particularly high degree. It seems most plausible, at this early stage in the science of genetics, to assume that what we bring into the world is the capacity *for* language; and that it will be developed in different ways at different times and places. This does not of course produce univocity among speakers in common cultural slots: Wordsworth does not write the same language, exactly speaking, as Blake or Coleridge. But when we look closely, we must realize that at the most specific level there is *no totally common* cultural slot. Biographical experience remains to a degree genuinely individual, both genetically and phenotypically. It is not then surprising that the symbolization of such experience in language should take the form of particular formulations of *general* discourse; formulations that remain recognizably specific to one writer but at the same time draw heavily upon semantic residues that are verifiably objective. What makes a poet's voice most convincingly individual may in fact be the degree to which it is exemplary of these common semantic resonances. Given the likelihood of these resonances sounding in the unconscious as well as the conscious ear, we cannot be guided in our interpretations by a poet's declared intentions, but neither can we ignore them entirely. Poetic language, partly by virtue of its standing outside the constraints of conventional exchange, where gesture, intonation and avowed context all help to specify the limits on allusion, is particularly open to the complex interplay of possibilities for meaning.

If these observations pertain to poetry in general, then they are especially pertinent to Wordsworth's poetry, for he is, as I have said, engaged, in a seemingly conscious (or at least highly coherent) way, in the problematization of subjectivity, of perception and of expression. At times, as in 'The Thorn', this is done by conscious exploitation of the dramatic method, where we are clearly told not to miss the poet's critical distance from his speaker. At other times, the dramatic method is not declared, although it seems necessary or useful to invoke it. And on still other occasions, Wordsworth seems to slip in and out of a potentially dramatic method, reporting the actions and thoughts of the narrative ego in such a way as to invite a critical response without quite demanding it. This is one of the formal manifestations of Wordsworth's ideological openness or insecurity. Even as he asks his readers to make their own tales, as he does at the end of 'Simon Lee', thus subscribing to a consciously anti-authoritarian imperative very popular in his generation, he also 'suffers' or lives through passively the impossibility of being clear and conclusive. In other cases it is his overemphatic closures that call into question the nature and possibility of doctrinally coherent positions; in 'Gipsies', for example, the poet too much affirmeth, and it is in the hyperbole itself that we must look for alternative clues to the poem's allusions.

It would be hard to bring forward a poetic ego that occupies a greater range of positions than Wordsworth's. At times he celebrates an aesthetic of amorphous undecidability, 'alive to all things and forgetting all' (*LB*, 218), only to query it; at times he speaks out in the voice of didactic self-confidence, also often held up for critical inspection. Some patterns seem to emerge with the passing of time. Most famously, the later Wordsworth is construed with some justice as a more didactic poet than the younger. But a great deal of Wordsworth's poetry is best approached as if it were a core sample of an especially contorted geological substrate. One works with a rough prediction of how the layers ought to relate one to another, but there are continual local deviations and surprises. Keats was, I think, superbly intelligent in describing Wordsworth as the poet of the 'egotistical sublime' (1958, 1: 387). For Wordsworth is indeed at once thrilled and frightened, master and slave to the object of his attentions; and that object is himself, his own ego, that is, a part of the self that is at times engrossing and at other times open to representation from a position of difference. As has been explained already, this self is not exclusively individual, so that its prominence entails an effacement of the 'world' – a thesis that is probably the hoariest of all latterday constructions of Romanticism – but is a medium in which the world is already *there*, and open to inspection. The hermeneutic ironies that suggest the necessary imperfection of such moments of inspection are themselves part of the programme of Wordsworth's poetry, and they too are implicated within a historical–ideological syndrome.

Wordsworth is thus the poet of displacement or alienation in the same sense that Blake's poems are *of* innocence or *of* experience. That is to say his poems expound and occupy a range of positions pertaining *to* alienation. It may be imaged critically, or reproduced passively, whether in the self or in others; and, in the case of a dramatic speaker, the self may be presented as an other. But whatever point on the spectrum the poem seems to occupy, the element of *pertaining to* is preserved. Even visionary epiphany experienced as a desired extinction of the social self, is given life and thought by what it replaces and what it returns to.

I hope I have given some sense of the general questions that this study seeks to explore, as well as of the methodological assumptions that I am making. I hope that these assumptions will be seen to be inductively sensitive, rather than prioristically conceived; for, like most introductions, this one was written after the rest of the book. It is now appropriate to say something about the material content of what follows, for it will surely strike Wordsworthians as an odd choice of poems, and a small number of poems at that. A long chapter on *The Excursion* needs no apology, though it will surely sink the spirits of many readers. It is the longest published poem of Wordsworth's lifetime, and it was written at an important 'transitional' stage in his career. It was intended as a major public statement, a long poem addressing topics of great public concern. Obviously, it must figure significantly in any study such as mine, as must *The Prelude* and *Home at Grasmere*. The case for a detailed attention to Wordsworth's prose will already be clear; we have to understand the integrity of his case against the directions being taken by English society and the national economy, and much of this is articulated in prose. Few would contest that 'Michael' and 'The Old Cumberland Beggar' are in different ways major poems; the first is an acknowledged masterpiece, the second a notorious challenge which most students of Romanticism choose to face up to. Here, my reader is less likely to be puzzled at my choice than to wonder whether I can possibly say anything new. To discuss 'Simon Lee' is also to stand within a well-established tradition, if not quite so centrally – for this poem has troubled many readers since it troubled Coleridge. But 'Gipsies' has hardly been noticed, except with embarrassment, by even the most dedicated readers, and 'Alice Fell' and 'Beggars' are not much better known.

My decision to begin this study with a detailed reading of 'Gipsies' did not emerge from an ambition to set the canon on its head, for it happens that this poem reproduces, with great precision and density, the terms of the syndrome that I intend to examine. Wordsworth's anxieties about poetry, property and labour, and the relations between them, are here set forth in sophisticated detail, and they are the leading themes in what I am calling the poetry of displacement. Once seen at work in 'Gipsies' they may be traced elsewhere in the 1807 *Poems*, and beyond. Given the range of Wordsworth's poetry, and the sheer amount of it, it seems likely that canons are going to be forming and reforming for some time to come. The history of this process is worth analysing, but such analysis is another project and not a task that can be undertaken here. Matthew Arnold faced the problem of presenting a coherent Wordsworth, and solved it by making an intuitive distinction between the good and the bad poetry. As an editor seeking to redeem Wordsworth from inherited stigmas about decorum, he saw his task to be that of sorting out and omitting the 'flat and dull' poems that Wordsworth himself seems to have been able to produce with apparent 'faith and seriousness' (1935, 96).

Arnold disavowed a philosophical coherence to Wordsworth's poetry in order to highlight its truth to nature, and the urgency of its invitation to share in nature's 'joy' (108). Prefigured by Coleridge, and further assisted by John Stuart Mill's contention that the best of Wordsworth has 'no connexion with struggle or imperfection' and teaches the 'permanent happiness of tranquil contemplation' (1969, 89), Arnold produced a selection that privileges the spiritual over the intellectual, the natural over the social, and the resolved statement over the transcription of crisis or struggle. Selective and extrinsically motivated as such a species of canonization may be, it does yet respond to something in Wordsworth's poetry that we should not lose sight of in explaining the role of its anxieties about poetry, property and labour. The mistake occurs, however, when we take the part for the whole, and fail to set the one against the other. Wordsworth's poetry does include a spiritual, organicist aspiration; but this too has to be set within a material history. If he was himself never the tranquil sage of popular reputation, as the most casual perusal of Dorothy's journals will tell us, then no more are his poems to be reified as doctrinally conclusive or otherwise immune from the signs of struggle and conflict. In the editions now being published by Stephen Parrish and his team of editors, the transcriptions and details of those struggles are more apparent than ever before. Many latterday readers of poetry have followed Coleridge and Arnold in demanding some experience of moral, formal or aesthetic integration before they will bestow upon a piece of writing the judgement that it is 'good'. The play of history in writing is however far too complex to be apprehended in such judgements about aesthetic quality.

I shall not, in other words, pay much attention to the 'standard' conventions about what it might be that constitutes a 'good' or a 'bad' poem. Poems that do resolve themselves into formally harmonious structures are interesting indeed, and for that very fact; they give us clues about those themes or questions that Wordsworth does appear to have been able to fashion into finished or untroubled statements. Poems that do not achieve such 'resolution' are interesting for their evidence about the other themes – the ones I am largely concerned with here. These themes, despite the existence of a considerable body of criticism, have not yet had their share of close attention. Careful understanding of them might indeed have the effect of reopening the casebook on some of the more familiar 'good' poems. The 'Tintern Abbey' poem, for example, is sometimes understood and much more often received as a masterpiece. But very few students or critics who read it as such have been able to explain exactly how the many eminently memorable passages hang together and amount to a narrative. Recent scholarship, to which I shall refer in due course, has been busy recovering some of the less evident references that the poem makes, or fails to make. As a result it seems likely that its argumentative identity, its status as a 'finished' piece, will also be revised. Having functioned in the Wordsworth canon largely as a poem of affirmation, it may well come to appear as a poem of negation. And so on. Many readers celebrate the 'Immortality' ode without quite knowing why; here, we need to appreciate the precision of the poet's vagueness. My point is not that we will thereby convert good into less good or bad poems, or vice versa, but that we will come to see such terms as useless for anything but an appeal to unexamined standards of 'taste'.

I must now explain why it is that I have written upon such a small number of poems – so few, indeed, that it must seem that this study can have no claims to represent the 'whole' of Wordsworth. Indeed it does not, for reasons that will be apparent already. But it does claim to be a serious interpretation of some poems, and one that could be extended to others, even as it might be qualified by new evidence. This calls for some preliminary discussion.

Writing this book has helped me to understand how Wordsworth might have felt about *The Recluse*, for my original fantasy was to produce a comprehensive account of the political dimensions of his career, each part of which would be sufficient unto itself, with the whole resembling some modern equivalent of a Gothic church. The reader's sense of awe at the grand structure would have been softened by a familiar appreciation of the detailed workmanship of the lesser parts, and so forth. The reasons for my failure to produce such a book have, I hope, less to do with the Casaubon syndrome – the conventional pedantic inability to see the wood for the trees – than with what I have come to see as the nature of the critical task facing poetic language as a medium existing in history. The historical element in language is, as I have said, not just a 'context' – something that we may, if we choose, advert to as a means of asserting the relevance or timeliness of art – but an integral part of the medium, and an inescapable part of its meaning. Thus I have found the references and allusions of Wordsworth's language to be far more substantial and complicated than has for the most part been hitherto admitted. A literary criticism that is committed to a historical method must, it seems to me, do more than offer allegorical or referential translations of images that can be simply substituted into the poem. It must recognize also the significance of silences – the things that a poet does not mention but which we must believe his audience to have been familiar with – and the frequent subtlety (or crudeness) of the poet's particular inflection of the medium, whether it be that of historical facts or discursive debates (so often assuming the status of facts). There is no *essential* complexity to poetry, whereby it necessarily and by definition expands upon or questions things as they were, or as they have been said to be by historians. The belief that there is such a complexity is especially strong in the British tradition of literary criticism, which has for clear historical and cultural reasons (which I shall not here explore) seen fit to constitute itself as the 'central' discipline within the humanities, able to adjudicate the limitations of historians, philosophers, anthropologists and others by reference to something thought of as 'truth to life'. Such an assumption has absolutely no place in the approach I take here; and, in fact, one might point to any number of poems or works of fiction that *reduce* the complexity of history to some relatively manipulable format. In looking closely at the historical energies apparent within poetic language I am not, then, seeking to establish anything in the way of a general truth about 'poetry', nor do I accept that there is any such thing. We are faced with particular poems, the conditions of whose production vary to a degree that no theory, whether of ideological determination or individual creativity, can convincingly prescribe. In the analysis of specific texts, different degrees of both subjective and intersubjective energies will be attributed to elements of their language; neither can be usefully discussed without the recognition of the other.

The complexity that I try to address, and that requires such an obsessive commitment to detail, is not then that of 'poetry', or art, but that of language in history; or, better, particular languages in history. The species of materialist analysis that is here undertaken is intended as an alternative to the more theoretically contextualized approaches that obtain within what we might roughly think of as the 'Marxist' tradition, which tends to work with pre-established causal vocabularies that, ironically enough, often pre-empt a sense of the need to recover the precise features of a historical moment. This is of course not a fair summary of *all* criticism in the Marxist tradition, nor is it intended as such.[1] But it does describe a strong tendency within that tradition, a tendency perhaps all the more powerful for a generation that is so clearly responsive, as ours is, to the temptations of what is called 'literary theory'. This too is a beast with many heads, not all nodding benignly at each other. But it seems fair to say that, thanks to the powerful influence of especially the American academic establishment over both material rewards (jobs, salaries, reputation) and spiritual initiatives (what we 'see' as exciting and important), we live in a 'theoretical' time. If this commitment to theory has assumed a hegemonic form – a shifting form, it must be said – then it is one often characterized by an aspiration toward *totality*; something that can pronounce upon all poetry, all language, all criticism. The totalizing aspiration remains latent even within the antagonistic but still canonical celebrations of relativism, or agnosticism, of which poststructuralism provides the best-known examples, as well as within the more embattled prophecies of various forms of idealism or objectivism. My suggestion is that, if we want to discover something about how intersubjective motives operate in language, we had best do away with theories of ideology (except perhaps as a propaedeutic clearing of the head) and acquaint ourselves with the materials familiar to the social historians.

To free ourselves from the restraints of theory, understood in its most totalizing and therefore inadequate form, is not, however, to fall back into an even more untenable faith in the complete uniqueness of every poem. Just as no critic can completely clear his or her head of all expectations and preconceptions, being forever distanced from this most radical form of innocence, so no writer, or series of writings, need be posited as totally unique. Once again, it is the belief in an achieved totality itself that must be restrained. There can be meaningful patterns of continuity between the works of the same or different authors, but these patterns, thanks to what seem to be the biologically inevitable facts of individuality (these facts themselves belonging to the materialist dimension) in combination with the considerable (though not absolute) refigurings of historical circumstances when viewed as minute particulars, are best regarded as inabsolute even as they are admitted to be constitutive and perhaps determining. Edward Said has, for example, found in Swift many of the features of instability, incoherence and occasionality that I here discover (always of course set against the aspiration *toward* wholeness) in Wordsworth.[2] At the same time, there are many differences between the two writers. What they share, I suspect, is a common sensitivity to the predicament of the bourgeois experience of authorship: radical uncertainties about readership, affiliation and determination. At this level, we should expect to discover some limited forms of coherence, some patterns, that can be seen to characterize the writings of various eighteenth- and nineteenth-century authors. To erect these patterns into indiscriminately and irresistably powerful causal syndromes that extinguish and overwhelm all idiosyncratic energies would be to render materialist analysis absurdly reductive; but it would be equally reductive to pretend that these patterns are not there at all. A leading sense of the forms of indecisiveness affecting the profession and practice of authorship in the period marked by the coming into being of what we sometimes call 'modernity' should provide us with ways of reading that are not just useful but essential to any serious historical method. At the same time, we must preserve a very large space for the filling out of particular details – the details of disposition and empirical contingency that explain why Coleridge, or Keats, responded differently to pressures very similar to those felt by Wordsworth. Culture is only ever composed of subcultures, none of them able to claim discursive comprehensiveness even as some are more powerful than others. We would be better served for our analysis of poetic language by imaging this situation as one characterized by struggle and constant mutual redefinition rather than by passive submission before some monolithic discourse. And within subcultures, we must also leave room for individuals.

This nervousness about the aspiration toward totality, combined as it is with a definite commitment to some level of 'scientificity', explains a good deal about my choice of subtitle. A number of variously technical or theoretical terms presented themselves as candidates for titular status: alienation, divided labour, property, industry, urbanization, civic virtue and so forth. Ultimately, none of them seems as accurate as the humbler word 'displacement'. The whole range of the above terms is of course implicated in the approach taken in this study; but I wished to avoid a vocabulary that has been already reified within and between various theoretical traditions. Perhaps 'alienation' comes closest to being adequate for a title word; and, in the Hegelian *Entfremdung* and *Entausserung*, and the Marxist-Brechtian *Verfremdung*, there lie a whole series of social–psychological models and aesthetic strategies, none of which are irrelevant to what I have to say about Wordsworth. But 'alienation' is too contentious a term, and implies a greater degree of scientific or theoretical exactitude than I wish to pretend to. Thus my preference for a coyly commonplace term like 'displacement' is not intended as a plea for yet another addition to the theoretical vocabulary, but rather as a recourse to a word that can, it is to be hoped, remain outside that vocabulary, drawing from it but never settling within it. If the term should remain tinged by an association with psychoanalysis, so much the better, for it seems to me impossible to look closely at the historical identity of a poet's language without also calling forth the question of the relation between conscious and unconscious representation, and the historical position of that relation.

The term 'displacement' is not new to Wordsworth criticism. It figures, for example, in Geoffrey Hartman's account (e.g. 1977, xix, 64, 65), where it describes a condition of the psychological self with disruptive formal and aesthetic consequences. Much more centrally it is deployed by

Jerome McGann (1983, 84–90) to describe an apparently conscious strategy whereby the unpleasant or challenging details of a real landscape are excluded or decentred from the poem, a process attended by a further displacement of the natural scene to the spiritual plane of attention. My use of the term here excludes neither of these precursors; indeed, it seeks to put them together by locating the argument at a level that is perhaps best described as that of the historical unconscious. I share McGann's sense of the empirical locus of the phenomenon of displacement, though I detect in his account a residual tendency to read Wordsworth's poems as unified and achieved instances of successful displacement, rather than as transcriptions of conflict. In his reading of 'The Ruined Cottage', for example, he is surely convincing in his case that there is an 'ambiguation' or decentring of the political theme; but in failing to explore the possible tensions between the personae of narrator and poet, whereby the 'happiness' of the one is not clearly endorsed by the other, he renders the poem more of a 'whole' than I think it is.[3] To make the Wordsworthian subjectivity so efficient in its avoidance of uncomfortable social pressures is to present yet another version of an organically coherent personality, this time held together not by its incorporation into nature but by its ability to deny and to negate. By contrast, I think that the phenomenon of displacement occurs not just as an effect wrought *by* Wordsworth *upon* the world, but also as a feature of the language of subjectivity itself. To say, as McGann does, that Wordsworth 'lost the world merely to gain his own immortal soul' (88) seems to make the assumption that he successfully displaced that world. Close inspection of the poet's language seems to me, however, to make clear that it very seldom manages to repress efficiently the traces of whatever most threatens its ideal or other-worldly aspirations. We can admit that there is in many poems an attempt to establish an alternative (displaced) consolation beyond the empirical–historical; but the language of such attempts very often contains the terms of its own undermining. If we are looking to judge Wordsworth as a moral agent, we must then entertain the possibility that displacement is something that he experienced and perhaps even suffered as much as he achieved.

If my reluctance to theorize the term 'displacement' in a more specific way risks angering those who seek exact and exclusive significations, it will cause greater offence to others who are opposed to *any* methodological approach to literature. In my wariness about committing myself to 'theory', I do not intend any approval of the intellectual amateurism that speaks out against any reflection upon formal implications, assumptions and procedures, and that claims for itself Edmund Burke's privilege 'to throw out my thoughts, and express my feelings, just as they arise in my mind, with very little attention to formal method' (1976, 92). There is nothing that says that such an approach to criticism cannot produce great insights; but it is too impatient and unpredictable a procedure for my purposes here. It too resists, much more passionately indeed than any literary theorist, the task of inductively examining as best we can the historical identity of particular items of language.

As I have said, this identity is not a consistent thing, nor can it be assumed that an approach that bears interpretative fruit for one item of language will necessarily work for another. This is so not only because of the variability of the finer details of the 'objective' archive – what happened, to whom, how often, and so forth – but also because of the equally if not more various subjective energies that determine the poet's selection of a language from the possible range of public (intersubjective) significations. It is not always, though it certainly can be, a matter of an author consciously choosing to activate certain of these significations at the expense of others. As often as not, the others cannot be avoided. When we accept fully the problematic status of the unconscious, then it becomes impossible to be precise about where subjectivity begins and intersubjectivity ends; the very terms come to seem like elements of an ideological debate, rather than descriptively accurate concepts. When Wordsworth, in the poem 'Alice Fell', uses the word 'relief' to describe an individual's emotional state, does he consciously intend to invoke the specific, public sense of the term, describing the provision of parish welfare? Is the intention unconscious; still subjectively motivated, but not realized? Or does the association reside in the language pool, so that its place in the poem, though inevitable, is coincidental rather than subjectively selected? It is hard to make these sorts of decisions, without the kind of evidence that comes from a poet's own explanations; and even these are not definitive. What remains is the sense that the public signification of 'relief' provides some coherent interpretative potential for the poem, enough to assure us that its relevance is verifiable. But there is nothing scientific or prioristically guaranteed about such assurance; nor is there any sure way of distinguishing between the conscious, the unconscious, and the contingent kinds of determination. We are left with a language that is inescapably and at once both general and particular; the public vocabulary is organized in a specific, individual way, but there is no way of defining an individual subjectivity in language that is not also and always general and intersubjective. As the same time, the conditions of determination that are traceable in language will differ in different cases. To insist on constant close attention is to recognize that both objective and subjective energies must vary along with and in terms of each other, and that language is a medium governed by both, each within the other.

It must again be emphasized that the appeal for such attention, and for the admission of a good deal of variability in the conditions that appear to have affected the coming into being of poetic language, has nothing to do with the traditional literary–critical celebration of some mythologized 'human' complexity or creative myriad-mindedness. On the contrary, the forms of explanation available to us are always materialist, in a broad sense that is also rather specific. For the structures of continuity that do emerge from reading closely are not always, or only, continuous in autonomously individualist ways. They emanate from intersubjective (and thus effectually objective) discourses and experiences, in this case those of property, labour, and the urban and rural life. Our estimation of the precise ways in which these preoccupations emerge in the writing of a particular poet is not merely to be declared, in a magisterial way, as a necessary determination deduced from a prior sense of the general features of a historical condition; it must be traced in detail in the writing, and in such biographical information as we can collect. The biographical approach has all too often been assumed to provide evidence for a creative personality that is outside or beyond material determination; but it is in fact in the small details of everyday life, as well as in its major tragedies and epiphanies, that the individual orientation toward the intersubjective world must also appear. It matters to know that Wordsworth was staying on the Beaumonts' estate when he wrote 'Gipsies', and living at Alfoxden when he composed 'Simon Lee'. These are not incidental details; they are essential to an understanding of how the general features of a historical moment register upon a particular consciousness, and form its language. Without such an understanding, we will be left with some vague model of the *Zeitgeist* as somehow able to inscribe itself upon the mind. We need to know what Wordsworth might have read in the newspapers, indeed; but also where he was when he read them.

In the dimension of language, it may finally be impossible to answer the question of the precise degree to which we are made by it, and it by us. Logically speaking this is a paradoxical question, since it seems to demand a perspective outside the language system if it is to be answered. It may also be a false question, since it presumes, as I have said before, that there is in this context a 'we' and an 'it' to begin with, which then come into mysterious conjunction. In place of this, it is perhaps more apt to think of a synthetic self, one that is both originally and always 'we' and 'it', self and other. This is not an idealist synthesis, of the sort that has preoccupied so many phenomenologists, but a material one, open to constant redefinition and redetermination by intersubjective energies and empirical pressures, and never settling into the framework of an inevitable human nature. Or at least, we may say this much of language, which is the part of the synthesis of self and other with which literary criticism has to deal, and which is constantly pointing beyond itself to the public sphere in which it has its place.

A materialist literary criticism must, then, rely always upon an argued objectivity for its forms of analysis, but it must always resist the temptation to present them as total, or finished, or beyond modification. Traditionally established terms like 'ideology' and 'alienation' will be useful only as class terms requiring precise definition, if they are useful at all; at worst, they are monsters gone out of control, proto-idealist categories in some critique of pure historicism, *into which* all forms of evidence must necessarily subside.

Given these convictions, it seems to me a waste of time to worry over making distinctions between 'art' and 'ideology', between what is creative and what is reproductive; in so doing, we merely flounder with conceptual problems of our own making. Something of a model for displacing such questions is to be found in Raymond Williams's *Marxism and Literature* (1977), which employs the openness of Marx's own writings to break down the oppositional rigidity of those critical vocabularies that present the personal and the social as in some sense antithetical. We should perhaps observe with relief rather than regret that the Marxist founding fathers themselves left behind them no systematic aesthetic theory, whether of creation or response.

The materialist approach here deployed is not then to be feared as a dry, doctrinal obsession of the Gradgrindian species. On the contrary, it is not only conducive to enhancing the excitement of reading poetry, but offers the added incentive that such excitement might be explained in ways that are not just matters of opinion or intuition. Of course, hermeneutic ironies always threaten such assertions, and it may well be true that certain readers (like me) can only understand Wordsworth in the way that they do because of their own positions in the world. But this neither proves nor disproves anything about Wordsworth's poetry; it is merely an enabling (or disabling) coincidence. The enjoyment of, or despair about relativism has proved too easy an alternative to the more ossified forms of objectivism; neither is at all helpful in trying to understand the historical identity of writing.

I hope I have explained why a materialist literary criticism should beware of committing itself to an all-embracing theory, and why I have chosen to write about such a small number of poems. If I have laboured the point, then my excuse must be that a large number of readers and critics now approach literature from the perspective of theory. I am not of course trying to dissuade anyone from being educated in theoretical procedures, and from acquiring the forms of special alertness that such an education can at best produce. But I should be disappointed if I did not upset those readers who think that there is an entity called 'literature', and that it is useful to have a 'theory' about it.

The materialist tradition in literary criticism, and particularly Marxist criticism, has in general been much more interested in the novel than in poetry. This is partly because poetry has been typified as 'high' art, the property of an élite rather than of the bourgeoisie or the 'people'. Furthermore, Marx's own generation is often thought to have inhabited an age of prose. For these and a host of other reasons, the literary criticism of poetry has developed to a very high level of formal and philosophical sophistication without achieving a correspondingly sophisticated historicization. This is especially true of Romantic poetry, which so often seems to seek to persuade its readers to move beyond the limits of time and place, beyond the material world at large. Pedagogic constraints inside the universities also contribute to placing poetic language outside history. It is, quite simply, easier to teach poems as 'words on a page' than to put a student in the position of reconstructing the discursive and historical archive within which poetic language came into being. And it may also be true that poetic language seems to operate at a more complex level than other forms of language; so much so, that its formal ingenuities might appear to be beyond a historical–materialist explanation.

For these and perhaps other reasons, poetry has not yet been the focus of the *major* efforts of materialist criticism. And the prevailing formalist tradition does have an integrity in its commitment to close reading and to the finer details of language operating in local and purposively artificial contexts. Materialist criticism must not ignore this tradition, but must, in the Hegelian sense, supersede it. That is, it must preserve the accuracy and detail of the best of the formalist traditions of literary criticism as part of its own method. It must not ride roughshod over detail in order to expound its themes, and must not abuse what it regards as 'superficial' in order to establish what it thinks is 'real'. Both New Criticism and poststructuralist criticisms have popularized exemplary standards of close reading. The first has long since freed us from regarding the tale as always at one with the teller, but the formal coherence that was no longer required of the author's 'self' was displaced and required of his or her poem. Only well-wrought poems were discussed with any pleasure; others were regarded as prototypic or simply 'bad'. A poem like 'Gipsies' would never make it into the canon that a New Critic would have constructed. Pleasure, for such a critic, consists in the explanation of antithetical voices or themes that are then reintegrated, balanced and reconciled into a greater whole. Finally, it is the reader-critic's subjective integrity that is appeased and reconstituted. In its purest form, for example in some of the writings of I.A. Richards, there is offered an amoral balancing of impulses attendant upon the successful reading of a good poem; we are reconciled to our mistress the world by the working through of an experience of language.

Poststructuralist practices, in most cases, have challenged the tradition formed by New Criticism by refusing or negating this return to the self as the end of reading. The most fashionable American criticisms, legitimating their convictions by a reading of modernism and of some French theorists, have resolutely insisted upon language as a mere surface which is yet all that we have of depth. The healthy result of this challenge has been to disrupt the old continuity between poem and reader, and to disestablish art as any kind of alternative to the psychically disturbing quality of the rest of experience. Art no longer heals or reconstitutes, but takes away whatever assumptions of integrity the reading subject might have retained. This commitment to the anarchic superficiality of language has presented a necessary countervoice to what was arguably untenable in the traditional practices of interpretation. But it offers little assistance to a materialist methodology, whose aspirations it often regards as embroiled in some epistemological contradiction. The materialist approach must always insist on going beyond and behind the surface of language to discover a system of energies that are not to be conjured away into merely additional fictions and substitutions. Mirror upon mirror is *not* all the show.

It is appropriate at this point to acknowledge the existence of a distinguished body of criticism that pertains to my argument. The terms of the challenge are most fruitfully set forth in Geoffrey Hartman's great book, which I first read rather more than five long years ago, and which continually reminds me of its centrality and importance. Hartman's thesis is constantly cited as the one primarily responsible for taking the poet *out* of history. But it articulates, in a more exact and sophisticated way than almost any other of its kind, all the major syndromes that a historical method must account for. In its focus on Wordsworth's 'vital schizophrenia of decentering' and his 'poetics of error' (1977, xvii, xix), Hartman's book brings out the formal and psychological terms of the Wordsworthian displacement; and its sense of the *tension* between imagination and nature offers an important qualification of the traditionally positive or celebratory reading of that relation. My aim here is not to negate this tension, but to explain it in a new way, arguing for its place as a symptom of social as well as theological or psychic alienation. That place is, I suggest, understood by the poet's own writings. Hartman sees in Wordsworth a problem of reification resulting from the apocalyptic imagination's tendency to produce 'a too-human or super-human image, and so fix the person to one self-image' (290). The mode in which nature may correct that self-image is not always, I argue, autonomous, but related to a model of man-in-nature whose ideal existence is at once affirmed and severely questioned or compromised by the poet. The solution to Wordsworth's sense of displacement is thus itself a displaced ideal – and in this we may see the true depth of his alienation.

There are other studies that more directly apply some version of a historical method to the explanation of Romantic poetry. The recent and wide-ranging accounts by Aers, Cook and Punter (1981), Barrell (1983), Goldstein (1977), Heinzelman (1980), McGann (1983) and Sales (1983), along with established studies by Brinton (1926), Erdman (1977) and Woodring (1970), have created a 'field' that one might think of as a collective project. Marilyn Butler (1982) has written a fine account of the period in which her strong sense of the historical identity of consciousness and language far outperforms her title's implication that history is a 'background'. Further studies of Wordsworth by Chandler (1984), Friedman (1979), Jacobus (1976), Kiernan (1975), and E.P. Thompson (1969), among others, have demonstrated the need for a consideration of the political positions touched upon in the poetry of the longest-lived major Romantic. I mention here also the forthcoming study by Marjorie Levinson (1986/7). Predictably, these studies both agree and conflict in various ways, making clear once again the need for considerable care and patience in producing a 'history' that is adequate to the finer details of Wordsworth's poetry. It is a large and even unwieldy body of writing, produced over a great many years, and Kiernan has wisely remarked that Wordsworth's interpreter requires an 'Ariadne's thread' to plot a way through 'such a span of history' (1975, 205). Raymond Williams has said of Cobbett, another figure of the times whose politics are very difficult to unravel, that he 'cannot be said to have produced any connected and systematic set of ideas, though he undoubtedly achieved, in his mature work, a coherent and powerful body of positions' (1983, 28). Wordsworth's positions, it must be said, always move toward accumulation in systematic sets of ideas, though not in all ways at all times. But much (not all) of the political and historical texture of his poetry is highly implicit. Its allusions need to be recovered carefully, and they often depend upon our knowing what is not said. Thus John Jordan (1976, 128f.) has shown very convincingly what the *Lyrical Ballads* were *not*: not patriotic poems, not anti-war poems, not about major public figures, or the slavery debate, or the condition of Ireland; not sonnets, odes or blank verse. This does not make them completely 'original' (see Mayo, 1954; Jacobus, 1976), but it does mean that we have to understand their failure or reluctance to decide between or among the variously available models for clear 'political' statement.

All of the studies I have so far mentioned deal with the broad, thematic energies of Wordsworth's poems, and they have all been useful to me in clarifying my own thoughts. Equally if not more important for the precise adjudication of the effects of such energies on Wordsworth's creative mind is the information gathered into Mark Reed's two chronologies (1967 and 1975) of the poet's life up to 1815. I have found them continually crucial in confirming or qualifying my intuitions about the kinds of interaction happening between the poet and his world. These volumes, more than any, have convinced me that when we speak of 'history' we must include the falling of a sparrow as well as that of an empire; and that we must be aware of the potential, in languages such as Wordsworth's, for the emergence of analogies and homologies between the two.

1
'Gipsies'

Life in Revolution is camp life. Personal life, institutions, methods, ideas, sentiments, everything is unusual, temporary, transitional, recognizing its temporariness and expressing this everywhere, even in names. Hence the difficulty of an artistic approach.

Trotsky (1960), 77

Oliver Goldsmith published *The Deserted Village* in 1770, only four years before he died at the age of (probably) 44. It was a popular poem, going quickly through five editions, and it has remained a very famous poem. Even after such a success, the career of man of letters was never to prove financially or psychologically comfortable for the author, who may have died as much as £2000 in debt. A displaced and impoverished traveller for much of his life, he had been variously actor, physician, flautist, reviewer and translator; even this does not exhaust the list of vocations he had to touch upon. Besides working in poetry, drama and the novel, he wrote histories and lives of eminent men, and a popular (though posthumously published) zoological volume – anything to turn a penny.

The more one learns about Goldsmith's life and environment, the less surprising it seems that *The Deserted Village* should have been a contested poem, as well as a popular one. It is a poem that constantly redefines and unsettles our sense of the relation between the objective and the subjective;

that which we may believe to have been 'what happened', and that which is better read as the poet's own opinions or imaginings. It thus seems to take all sorts of risks, aesthetic and thematic. Objectively, it resides intelligibly if radically within a tradition of eighteenth-century moral poetry, and makes sense as an argument for the precise and deleterious effects of the commercial economy and the process of imparkment upon a rural world inhabited by self-sufficient owner-occupiers. To those ideologically indisposed to accept such a criticism, the poem would have been unpalatable, and the more so because it was implicitly drawn from the poet's early life in Ireland (despite his declared location in England), where the landlord–peasant question was particularly anxious, most of all in the years around the Act of Union of 1800; a glance at some of the periodicals of the time suggests that Ireland was an even more urgent topic of debate than was the course of the French Revolution. Furthermore the idealized nature of Goldsmith's account of life in old Auburn might have caused another class of readers to raise questions about the poem's credibility. If such readers were not predisposed to understand it as a polemically sharpened argument, but more as a 'slice of life', then they might well have been disinclined to confirm a 'realism' that seemed to include no measure of cynicism, and nothing of a complex admission of good and ill in everything. Crabbe, in *The Village* (1783), took up this particular cudgel, with an alternative political agenda at work behind it; an agenda even more explicit in *The Parish Register* (1807).[1]

Goldsmith's poem is thus thematically contentious in its objective dimension, that is, in the historical and discursive events it addresses. It is also significantly unstable in its subjective element, that is, in the moods and gestures of its speaker. For it insists upon raising the question of the poet's place in this ideal village of the past, or rather of the vanishing present. That the poet seems to have lived there as a child immediately compounds the presentation of the actual with that of the imaginary or the mythologically created. And this uncertainty is enhanced when we see that Goldsmith never describes his fantasies as those of a permanent integration. At best, he had hoped to *retire* there, to give up his 'wanderings' and 'die at home at last' (1966, 4: 291). Auburn was recalled as the place of origination, and anticipated as a place to end. In between, Goldsmith is quite explicit about the need to wander and be a man of the world. There might have been a place for the retired author to show his 'book learned skill' among the 'swains'. There was, in other words, never a place for the *working* man of letters, with his peculiarly specialized audience and employment, in this world in which 'every rood of ground maintained its man' (289). And Goldsmith admits as much.

It is then an oddly disjunctive moment when, towards the end of the poem, the speaker claims that 'sweet Poetry' is the 'first to fly where sensual joys invade' (303). There is here a telling refusal to specify the balance of the particular and the general, the subjective and the objective. We are uncertain whether the 'sweet Poetry' is that which he, the man of letters, writes, or whether it describes in a more general sense the poetry of ideal rural life, as experienced by those who have fully participated therein. Obviously both are implied, but in the most literal sense Goldsmith as poet has already fled; what is inhibited is his chance of returning, and of writing poetry about the village, or for the village. His writing can now only register as a criticism of the new order; hence he will gain no patronage from men of power, and remain as poor as he was at first. The potential audience (for his retirement) among the village swains is embarking for the inhospitable world of the colonies; he will be alienated from that which remains by virtue of his disapproval of its behaviour.

By now it is perhaps becoming clear that these two elements in the poem, the subjective and the objective, cannot very comfortably be kept apart. For *The Deserted Village* is a sophisticated expression of the poet's displacement imaged at both these levels at once. Each determines the other, although a hierarchy of determinations is visible. The final lines of the poem, penned by Samuel Johnson, counsel recourse to a 'self dependent power' (304) that is ambiguously economic and spiritual. The second is clear enough – self-reliance as a moral quality. But how is the first to be implemented, when the audience for poetry is disappearing, if it was ever there? And might this not threaten to convert moral self-reliance into hysteria?

In a manner analogous to the refutation of Berkeley by kicking stones, we may rejoin that the poem did find an audience, and has continued to do so. But the dilemma that it transcribes does not anticipate this eventuality; whether Goldsmith himself might have, is not a matter I can adjudicate here. By opting for the vocation of man of letters, Goldsmith has obliged himself to leave Auburn and to seek his fortune in the heart of the very metropolitan economy whose hegemony he deplores in the poem. He is thus a man of the middle ground, in which both shelter and companionship are insecure and unpredictable. What he has left behind could not afford him a living. He wishes for it none the less, but it is disappearing as a result of the doings of the very urban and urbanized readers whose favours he is obliged to depend upon. Enclosure, Goldsmith implies, makes some of the land more productive, so that what remains can be exploited for pleasure and vanity. This trend is further accelerated by the financial revolution enabling fortunes to be made in the stockmarket. The agricultural base of the economy is diminished, and the small man is driven from his holding, for the sake of the rich man's park. But the would-be poet had already gone, aware that there was no market for his wares in a rural subsistence economy. Luxury and art had often, if not always, cohabited, as they mostly did in Goldsmith's times. Between two worlds, he is at home in neither. His moral intelligence forces him to utter the very message that is most likely to deprive him of the patronage upon which writers depend; and those with whom he is most in sympathy are disappearing. They probably never had much money, or inclination, for poetry in the first place. Goldsmith images himself as a man compelled to earn, but destined to remain unpaid.

Thus it is that Goldsmith, as Laurence Goldstein has aptly put it, 'discovers in a historical problem the exact form of his own alienation' (1977, 106). We cannot, I think, choose between the two, because both are always there. We cannot say that Goldsmith fabricates a historical analogue for a personal crisis, because the personal crisis (and to call it just this is to demean it considerably) is at all times historical. No more does he present himself simply as the passive victim of circumstance. Those circumstances are indeed beyond his control – he cannot alter the course of political and economic change. But by seeking to live as a man of letters he has anticipated and perhaps conspired in the very change that he deplores. Before we read this as some kind of logical or moral contradiction on Goldsmith's part, we must understand it as the experienced and transcribed crisis of his life. Read from this perspective, the poem can be seen to document and detail this crisis. Goldsmith was always to be at a distance from his fellow villagers, but he might yet have had his place, within the limits open to a man in retirement. But changing times have destroyed what he once experienced, and wished to retain. The lament that this change inspires *is* personal; but it is also clearly intersubjective, and verifiable in general terms, both discursive (at the level of publicly recognized arguments) and factual (what happened).

Minding the poet's trade

Thanks to the institutionalizing of Goldsmith as an 'eighteenth-century' and Wordsworth as a 'Romantic' poet, these two writers are not often discussed together. And the move which I now make, from *The Deserted Village* to 'Gipsies', might seem particularly odd. The first is an acknowledged masterpiece by a writer usually thought of as minor; the second has generally been judged a terrible poem by a great poet. Few critics have understood 'Gipsies' as anything other than an embarrassment, a poem they might wish had not been written by Wordsworth. Its speaker seems anything but a man speaking to men, and more like a pompous poet all too confident of his own high calling. I shall try to show that there is a strong continuity between the terms in which I have analysed *The Deserted Village* and those which make sense of 'Gipsies'; and, eventually, that those same terms can be traced through some of the more famous and accepted poems in the Wordsworth canon.

I thus begin this study with 'Gipsies', because I find in it a major statement of the preoccupations of Wordsworth's poetic intelligence considered as a simultaneously subjective and intersubjective faculty. Anxieties about labour, poetry and property are addressed here in an especially urgent way, revealing both the historical features of Wordsworth's predicament, and the personal turn that he gives to it. A rather brief poem, it is yet one that demonstrates in a very complex way the degree to which the lyric moment is not simply informed but *constituted* by both literary–historical and social–historical intuitions. Its brevity, together with its traditional status as a 'bad' poem, makes it furthermore an apt example of the kinds of disbelief that I shall be asking my reader to suspend throughout the course of the argument that follows. In response to the question of whether a few lines of verse can 'really mean all this', I offer a case for a high degree of referential density; in response to the standard concern about whether Wordsworth himself could have 'intended' so much, I offer a reading of the poem's language that seeks to transcend the limits associated with the conscious control of its transcriber; and in response to the almost universal assumption that this is a 'bad' poem, I offer the kind of reading that aspires to render judgements of good and bad comparatively uninteresting.

For ease of reference, here is the poem entire, in its first published version of 1807 (*1807*, 211–12):

Yet are they here? – the same unbroken knot
Of human Beings, in the self-same spot!
  Men, Women, Children, yea the frame
  Of the whole Spectacle the same!
Only their fire seems bolder, yielding light:
Now deep and red, the colouring of night;
  That on their Gipsy-faces falls,
  Their bed of straw and blanket-walls.
– Twelve hours, twelve bounteous hours, are gone while I
Have been a Traveller under open sky,
  Much witnessing of change and chear,
  Yet as I left I find them here!

The weary Sun betook himself to rest.
– Then issued Vesper from the fulgent West,
  Outshining like a visible God
  The glorious path in which he trod.
And now, ascending, after one dark hour,
And one night's diminution of her power,

Behold the mighty Moon! this way
  She looks as if at them — but they
Regard not her: — oh better wrong and strife
Better vain deeds or evil than such life!
  The silent Heavens have goings on;
  The stars have tasks — but these have none.

It must seem a formidable task indeed, after reading this poem, to argue
for a benign Wordsworth, the poet of wise passiveness, sympathy for the
meanest flower that blows, and understanding of the subtle details of
ordinary life. Here, it seems as if there is no attempt to disguise or
complicate what has appeared to many readers to be an odious and
morally repugnant complacency on the speaker's part. So it seemed to
Coleridge, whose criticism must remain the starting point for any reading
of the poem. He finds in it an exemplary instance of '*mental* bombast':

Whereat the poet, without seeming to reflect that the poor tawny
wanderers might probably have been tramping for weeks together
through road and lane, over moor and mountain, and consequently
must have been right glad to rest themselves, their children and cattle,
for one whole day; and overlooking the obvious truth, that such repose
might have been quite as necessary for *them*, as a walk of the same
continuance was pleasing or healthful for the more fortunate poet;
expresses his indignation in a series of lines, the diction and imagery of
which would have been rather above, than below the mark, had they
been applied to the immense empire of China improgressive for thirty
centuries.

(1983, 2: 137)

As if to make matters worse, Wordsworth adds these final lines for the
1820 edition, as follows:

Yet, witness all that stirs in heaven and earth!
In scorn I speak not; — they are what their birth
  And breeding suffers them to be;
  Wild outcasts of society!

(*1807*, 212)

The expression of cultural relativism — they cannot help it, they were born
that way — only makes us the more uneasy with the speaker's self-
righteousness. He disavows scorn only to introduce an equally unsettling
condescension.

Coleridge was not the only one to pick on the poem. Hazlitt, in a note
to his essay 'On Manner' in *The Round Table*, also published in 1817,
thought it a quite shocking statement from one 'whom we had considered
as the prince of poetical idlers, and the patron of the philosophy of

indolence', and found in it more than a hint of 'Sunday-school philosophy' (1930–4, 4: 45–6). John Keats in turn reacted to both Hazlitt and Wordsworth in a letter of the same year. He found both right, but Wordsworth 'rightest', for Wordsworth 'had not been idle he had not been without his task'. At the same time, Keats opines, Wordsworth might not have written the poem if he had 'though[t] a little deeper at that Moment', which seems to have been marked by 'one of the most comfortable Moods of his Life' (1958, 1: 174).

It is interesting that three such distinguished contemporaries should have commented in such detail on the poem, for it has received little subsequent attention. Barron Field was happy enough with the idea that gypsies are 'naturally loitering basking idlers' (*LY*, 1: 645, note), but those among Wordsworth's admirers who do not subscribe to this view have usually opted for tactful silence. David Ferry is almost alone among modern critics in trying to fit the poem into a reading of Wordsworth's major preoccupations. He argues that the poet 'blames the gypsies for their mortality, for not participating sufficiently in the eternal'. His mood is not one of 'trivial irritability' but of 'sublime arrogance'; the common-sense considerations voiced by Coleridge are pushed aside by the poet's desperate desire to participate in infinity and eternity (1959, 9). Ferry is right to focus on the speaker's longing for a kind of immortality, and to emphasize the drama of the speaker's entire posture. Wordsworth himself first signalled this in including the poem in the category of 'Moods of my own Mind' in the 1807 edition. Only in 1815 did it become one of the 'Poems of the Imagination'. We may usefully begin to read this poem by seeking to understand the terms of this 'sublime arrogance', even as we must not, as Ferry tends to, forget its empirical base.

Michael Friedman, one of the few other critics to attend to 'Gipsies', attributes Wordsworth's unease to the presence of 'alien social forces' (1979, 168).[2] What might this alien society have meant to him, and how is it related to his sublime enthusiasm? The degree to which the 'poet' identifies himself with the heavenly bodies is extravagant even for the Wordsworthian speaker. Like Vesper, he is following in the 'glorious path' of the sun, and like the sun he has proceeded through a twelve hour cycle. He too is 'weary' and entitled to his rest. The speaker inscribes himself within the natural cycles of the heavenly bodies obeying the eternal laws of cosmological harmony, and ensuring the proper interchange of day and night through the mediations of the morning and the evening stars, Lucifer and Hesperus (Vesper).

This is obviously a hyperbolic posture on the speaker's part. What is troubling, however, is that there are no technical signals in the poem to suggest that it might be a conscious, dramatic hyperbole, whereby we are *expected* to question the speaker's good faith. Wordsworth does write poems in which he rebukes himself for allowing an enthusiastic mood to perpetrate hurtful misunderstandings of others: examples would be 'Anecdote for Fathers' and the 'Point Rash-Judgment' poem. But 'Gipsies' does not seem to be such a poem, in that there is no clear formal directive or moment of reversal; there is only the excess of the sublime mood itself. Stephen Parrish has persuasively argued that many of Wordsworth's poems seem to require the assumption of a dramatic speaker even when we are not told to be alert for one (1973, 115–48), although readers have managed to ignore the clues even when they are provided, as they are by the note to 'The Thorn'. Is 'Gipsies' one of these poems, where a dramatic speaker must be assumed to make sense of the rhetoric? Why should we be expected to supply evidence that Wordsworth does not provide for us, if he meant the poem to be read as a dramatic utterance in a character not his own?

The answer is, I think, that 'Gipsies' is both dramatic and not dramatic. Coleridge and Hazlitt were hardly naïve readers, and they each chose to interpret the poem as a flagrantly self-righteous statement to a public that was, as we shall see, all too willing to endorse negative judgements about gypsies and about all such socially displaced persons. There can be no reasonable way of denying the justice of this interpretation, based as it is on a plausible reading of the poem in itself, and on a credible estimation of its effect on a readership. At the same time, and at quite other levels, there are many signs that the speaker of this poem is not to be received as the single or authoritative Wordsworth. How then might he be received? Hartman (1977, 3) has aptly noted that the criticial literature on Wordsworth 'does not provide a consensus that effectively separates his mental or emotional bombast from appropriate lyrical effusion'. There are good reasons for this, and not the least of them is that the poems themselves are indecisive and often mutually incommensurable in this respect. How does this poem articulate a distinction between emotional bombast and lyrical effusion, if at all? We must begin by trying to suspend the language of praise and blame, in order to examine the speaker's diction in some detail.

First, we may note that the roundly disciplinary tone of the speaker's judgements in the second stanza seems to place him in the company of other Wordsworthian protagonists who are clearly ironized. In failing to recognize Leonard Ewbank, for example, the vicar of 'The Brothers' chides him as one who

Will look and scribble, scribble on and look,
Until a man might travel twelve stout miles,
Or reap an acre of his neighbour's corn.
(*PW*, 2: 1)

Leonard has indeed changed, and the vicar touches a half truth in casting him as extrinsic to the life of the vale; but his pious self-esteem is quite at odds with the truth of the situation, whose tragic details he learns only much later. The speaker of the 'Point Rash-Judgment' poem delivers similarly casual verdicts on the integrity of the old fisherman, only to feel ashamed thereafter. The speaker of 'Gipsies', then, belongs in this kind of company, but he is not ironically contextualized in any explicit way.

The clues are implicit. His reference to the 'weary Sun' is only mildly arresting in its bland attribution of human feelings (and his own at that) to the major heavenly body. But the following line, 'Then issued Vesper from the fulgent West', seems highly untypical of Wordsworth's standard poetic language. It reminds me of another line in Wordsworth's writings: 'And reddening Phoebus lifts his golden fire'. These two lines contain similar classical epithets and similarly ornate noun phrases. They have the same declamatory authority, surely not that of a man speaking to men, but more that of an author trying to impress upon his readers 'a notion of the peculiarity and exaltation of the Poet's character' (*PrW*, 1: 162). But this is exactly what Wordsworth objects to in the standard poetic diction; and the second line cited above is not by Wordsworth, but by Gray. Wordsworth quotes Gray's sonnet in order to go through it and pick out the five valuable lines. 'And reddening Phoebus lifts his golden fire' is not one of them – it is therefore implicitly consigned to what is 'curiously elaborate' (*PrW*, 1: 132) but essentially redundant.

Can we then detect here an apparently unconscious faltering, or slip, on Wordsworth's part? Is he himself an exponent of poetic diction, or does this hyperbole bespeak, by its very overemphasis, an underlying insecurity or lack of conviction? Why does Wordsworth deploy, in what seems to be his own voice, the very language he criticizes elsewhere? We cannot say, of course, that he never uses classical epithets. Lane Cooper's *Concordance* notes five occurrences of 'Phoebus' and four of 'Cynthia' (as the moon). By 1807, Wordsworth is, moreover, already moving away from the commitment to simplicity of diction that characterizes the majority of the *Lyrical Ballads*, though he never gives it up entirely. Nevertheless, both 'fulgent' and 'Vesper' are unusual words for Wordsworth, and neither they nor the other classical terms occur elsewhere in such a strident and histrionic context as that of 'Gipsies'. It is not simply our reconstruction of the canon that makes 'Fair Star of Evening' (*1807*, 155) a more typical locution than 'Vesper' (cf. *PW*, 3: 274–5).

In this extravagant diction, so perilously close to that Wordsworth had criticized only seven years earlier, we can trace, I suggest, an anxiety that is both idiosyncratic and intersubjective (i.e. social–historical). This may be brought out by recognizing the literary antecedents of the poem. These antecedents and allusions are scientific and Christian as well as literary, and they relate in interesting ways one with another. In his address to the celestial bodies, Wordsworth is remembering a long tradition of eighteenth-century poems versifying Newton's laws. Planetary and sidereal motions would probably have been familiar to Wordsworth from his Cambridge education; and if not from there, then from Thomson's *Seasons*, or Savage's *The Wanderer*, or Mallett's *The Excursion*. At this level, the movements of sun, moon and stars might have appealed to the travelling speaker as emblems of immortality, of the diurnal round of the universe. In invoking them, he casts himself as part of nature, and of a world wherein there need be no concern about death, or about moral decisions; he projects himself into an abstract and mechanical existence, with rocks, stones and trees.

But 'Gipsies' is also packed with echoes of *Paradise Lost*, and thus of an entirely different, symbolic cosmology from that intimated by a deistic interpretation of celestial motion. It is at this point that the poem becomes most complex and informative. I begin somewhat at a tangent, with a passage in *The Prelude* (1805, 10: 466ff.) that is especially dense in Miltonisms.

Here, Wordsworth recollects gazing at the 'fulgent spectacle' (line 486) of a glorious sky that seemed never to pass away or change. This 'fancy' is the 'more alive' (line 488) because he has just visited the grave of one of his old teachers, who *has* passed away. On this same day, he has heard of the death of the Satanic Robespierre, the leader of the 'atheist crew' and the 'foul tribe of Moloch' (lines 457, 468) of post-revolutionary France. Robespierre is a Satan figure because of his attempt to abolish Christianity, and because of his gestures toward immortality in the form of an eternal reason. In traditional Christian terms, as Satan makes us doubt salvation so he makes us fear to die, and want to live forever, disobeying God's law. Thus Satan makes us like himself. Wordsworth here associates two deaths, one desired (Robespierre) and one regretted (the teacher), together amounting to a powerful reminder of the fact that mortality makes no such distinctions. This gives the dramatic context to his own minor echo of the Luciferic ambition in the vision of a 'fulgent spectacle' that 'neither changed, nor stirred, nor passed away' (line 487): a moment of time that seemed eternal and immortal.

The poet's own recollected fantasy of a world of immortal things is hardly blasphemous or critical, but it is none the less a quiet repetition of the Satanic gesture; the same gesture that appears at the other end of the moral spectrum in Robespierre's destructive ambition. In its subtle reincorporation of the speaker within the mentality that he has condemned, and in its allusion to the events in France, this passage is a telling prefiguring of the drama of 'Gipsies'. Most of this poem's Miltonic allusions are to Book Four of *Paradise Lost*. First, there is the setting sun that signals Satan's first view of paradise:

> for the sun
> Declined was hasting now with prone career

To the Ocean Isles, and in the ascending scale
Of heaven the stars that usher evening rose.
                        (4: 352–5)

Satan ends his journey through space, as Wordsworth returns from his. The sun continues to descend as he wanders about trying to plot the boundaries of paradise – 'Through wood, through waste, o'er hill, o'er dale, his roam' (line 538) – in a peregrination not dissimilar from that of one Wordsworth in his rambles under open sky. Milton reports Uriel seeing him 'Alien from heaven, with passions foul obscured' (line 571), and Uriel's own departure from the scene is accompanied by the second moment 'recalled' in Wordsworth's poem, the rise of the evening star followed by the moon:

Hesperus that led
The starry host, rode brightest, till the moon
Rising in clouded majesty, at length
Apparent queen unveiled her peerless light,
And o'er the dark her silver mantle threw.
                        (lines 605–9)[3]

Neither of these allusions that Wordsworth makes to *Paradise Lost* would be convincing in themselves, were it not for the third echo. Immediately after Uriel's departure, Milton reports Adam's sermon on prelapsarian labour. It is now time to sleep, since

God hath set
Labour and rest, as day and night to men
Successive . . .
            . . . other creatures all day long
Rove idle unemployed, and need less rest;
Man hath his daily work of body or mind
Appointed, which declares his dignity,
And the regard of heaven on all his ways;
While other animals unactive range,
And of their doings God takes no account.
                        (lines 612–22)

Not only does Wordsworth thus echo the onset of night as Milton describes it, with the sequence of declining sun, evening star, and moon; he also invokes ('The stars have tasks – but these have none') the Adamic censure of idleness and unproductive time. It is as if the gypsies are, in these terms, 'animals inactive', made bestial because they are not at work; if they are indeed ignored by God, then they are all the more justifiably upbraided by the Wordsworthian speaker, for whom even 'wrong and strife' and 'vain deeds or evil' would be better than such a life. This assertion seems at first sight very odd indeed. Is it better to sin, or fall from innocence and grace, than to sit at peace around a campfire? Who could claim this with any sincerity?

The answer, of course, is Satan. And here the subtlety of Wordsworth's allusion to Milton becomes clear. If the speaker casts himself as one with the sun, the light of heaven, abroad for 'twelve bounteous hours', then he is also the light of heaven fallen, the Luciferic spirit bitterly exiled from a community he can only behold from outside, and which he must therefore hate and resent. The speaker's hyperbolic rhetoric in fact sustains his comparing himself simultaneously with divine and infernal energy. Only this, I think, explains the preference for 'vain deeds and evil' over self-contained inertia. The poet may after all not be a productive (let alone prelapsarian) labourer, working hard by day and earning his rest at night; he may be a Satanic figure, already guilty of vain and evil deeds. The word 'vain' thus asks to be read as both 'self-aggrandizing' and 'futile', both perhaps areas of concern for a poet anxious by personal and historical destiny about his relationship to society in general, to a wider reading audience, and to a particular, local community.

Hazlitt was then perhaps being especially astute, in his verdict on this poem, in denominating Wordsworth the 'prince of poetical idlers', a Lucifer among poets. And as with Lucifer, so with the Wordsworthian speaker; the self-righteous bombast that he speaks forth is implicated in a whole litany of retractions. The dramatic preference for vanity and evil over idleness suggests the Satanic consolation that it is better to reign in hell than serve in heaven; even failed rebellion is better than passive acceptance. This reflexively locates the gypsies as a paradisal society; they occupy the same position for the speaker as do Adam and Eve for Satan. The sight of the 'harmless innocence' (4:388) of the first couple causes a complex attraction and repulsion in the archfiend, who claims to have to do 'what else though damned I should abhor' (line 392). Looking again at the opening of Wordsworth's poem, we may now read behind the mood of outrage to notice that the gypsies are an 'unbroken knot' of human beings – a society self-contained, integrated, paradisal. Wordsworth too thus implies both a contempt for and an envy of a community wherein there is no sign of restlessness, vaulting ambition, or change. The gypsies are made into an image of the infernal, with their fire now *seeming* (a key word?) bolder, and its light 'deep and red'. But the truly infernal predicament may well be that of the peripheral narrator, looking from outside at a social gathering whose unambitious integrity he can neither take part in nor emulate elsewhere. For him, the knot is broken, and the distance constantly increasing. The heavenly bodies with which he aspires to be at one may thus occupy a threateningly empty space; dead to all human fears, they neither hear nor see.

The speaker is alone, a 'traveller under open sky', the same 'open sky' beneath which Adam and Eve turn to adore their maker, their 'appointed work' complete for the day (*PL*, 4: 721, 726). But Wordsworth has no partner, is not adoring his maker, has not clearly performed any tasks, and is alienated from the gypsies who are here cast as part of a theatrical exhibition or landscape painting, a 'Spectacle' within a 'frame'. He is also, implicitly, alienated from himself, unsure of the value and integrity of what he does, and driven thereby to a spectacular hyperbole. Adam had allowed that authentic labour might be 'daily work of body or mind' (4: 618). The poet's work is obviously that of the mind, even as it takes the form of strenuous walking. But to what end, and by what divine command? Wordsworth's poetry is constantly posing the question of its status as authentic labour. If the voice of *The Prelude* is sure that Shakespeare and Milton are indeed 'labourers divine' (5: 165), it is far from sure of its own relation to those high standards. The poem, which famously opens with an allusion to the expulsion from Eden – making Wordsworth begin, with Adam, where Milton's poem ends – is structured around the play between infinite possibility, the heart 'not scar'd at its own liberty' (1: 16), and necessary limitation and application to a theme 'Single and of determined bounds' (1: 668). In *Home at Grasmere*, the unpublished poem that is perhaps more than any other riddled with anxieties about community and poetic labour, as well as with wishful hyperbole, Wordsworth again starts out by describing himself in the third person and in a state of Satanic isolation: 'Alone and devious, from afar he came' (*HG*, 39). And it is by labour that he seeks to redeem himself:

> But 'tis not to enjoy, for this alone
> That we exist; no, something must be done.
> I must not walk in unreproved delight
> These narrow bounds and think of nothing more,
> No duty that looks further and no care.
>
> (*HG*, 94)

There is a Luciferic confidence in his assurance of an 'internal brightness' that 'must not pass away' (94), which is thus also an over-confidence, undermined by itself. The sententious and embarrassingly urgent involvement in the labour cycle that the speaker of 'The Idle Shepherd Boys' projects may also be related to an anxiety about the nature of poetic work. The admonition to the boys to 'better mind their trade' (*LB*, 167) comes from a figure who has been momentarily and unpredictably elevated to the status of heroic participant (for labour is also this, participation), and who is far less sure than John Keats that 'Wordsworth had not been idle he had not been without his task' (1958, 1: 174). Looking back to 'Gipsies', we notice that the heavenly body that is in many ways most closely identified with the speaker is not the sun or the evening star (though both are so identified) but the moon. Like the speaker, the moon *looks* at the gypsies, who ignore it as they ignore the passing poet. The moon is indeed 'mighty', but her power is on the wane. And, as the symbol of inconstancy and madness, the moon is the deity of the lunatic, the lover and the poet; it is the feminine counterpart of the masculine sun. In sharing the perspective of looker-on with the moon, Wordsworth again undercuts the confident hyperbole of his earlier identifications with sun and evening star. He has, like the sun, done his day's 'work', but the appearance of the waning muse of poetry serves to question the nature and integrity of that work.

Anxieties about the business of poetry, and its place in the labour cycle and in the 'respectable' world, in fact occur throughout the 1807 *Poems, in Two Volumes*, the collection in which 'Gipsies' first appeared. At the time of its writing, February, 1807, Wordsworth had been living since the previous autumn on a farm on the estate of the temporarily absent Sir George and Lady Beaumont, at Coleorton in Leicestershire (Reed, 1975, 348). The farm had been lent to him by Sir George, so that he and his family were living by the charity of others, rather than by the fruits of his own labour. But as a counterbalance to any awkward feelings of dependence, Wordsworth could assure himself that he had indeed been 'working'. He was well along with the composition of the volumes, and had already sent several sheets to the printer. The particular walk during which he met the gypsies was to Nottingham, to obtain plants for the estate's winter garden. Then as now, there is nothing like gardening to give the man of sedentary vocation the glow of honest labour. All of these special circumstances seem to me to find their way into the mood and rhetoric of the poem, and its parading of a self-importance that is also insecure.

Besides these immediate circumstances, there were two other biographical factors that must have rendered Wordsworth extremely anxious about the dignity of poetic labour. For his vocation had been significantly enabled by two deaths, those of Raisley Calvert and of Wordsworth's brother John, the most obviously 'working' member of the family whose expressed ambition had been the consolidation of the family fortunes.

Calvert had died in 1795, but the sonnet to his memory was not composed until seven or eight years later, and it too was to appear in the 1807 *Poems*. It is to Calvert that Wordsworth owes his 'many years of early liberty', for Calvert had left him a legacy of £900. It is thanks to Calvert's 'wasting, root and stem'

> That I, if frugal and severe, might stray
> Where'er I liked.
>
> *(1807, 152)*

The 1805 *Prelude* had similarly stressed the degree to which the same benefactor's untimely death had left the poet able to 'pause for choice/ And walk at large and unrestrained' (13:358–9). He who walks at large to

Nottingham has been freed to do so by a dead friend's legacy and a rich man's charity. But this is a mixed blessing and Wordsworth's writing registers it as such. For if labour is a punishment and a burden, it is also traditionally one tinged with the pleasure of sociability and mutual endeavour; unless, that is, you are a poet. Wordsworth in 1807 lived both with the embarrassment and guilt of dependence, and with the insecurity of his vocation as an unestablished writer.[4]

That Wordsworth's poetry does thus register these tensions should, I think, cause us rather to admire than to dispraise it. One of the most complex incarnations of such tension is to be traced in the little-noticed poem on the fir grove, begun as early as 1800 and substantially complete by 1805, but unpublished until 1815, when it appeared as the sixth of the 'Poems on the Naming of Places'. One can imagine why its appearance was delayed, given the depths of fraternal feelings that it plumbs, difficult enough for Wordsworth to face without John's tragic death in 1805. I have written on this poem elsewhere (1982a, 31–4, 37–8), so will not here undertake a lengthy exposition. The poem tells the story of Wordsworth's ceasing to frequent a favoured spot, a grove of fir trees, because it was so thickly planted that he could not find a place to walk within it. Walking is described as necessary to the work of making poems; as so often, the poet seeks a constrained and protected space within which he may yet indulge in some degree of wandering and deviation. Moving forward in time, the poet goes on to recount his surprise at revisiting the grove and discovering a well-worn path, not seen before. The conjecture is that his brother John might have worn this path when home on leave from his ship, as a result of an obsessive, occupational behaviour pattern, an 'habitual restlessness of foot' (*1807*, 565) acquired by ceaseless pacing across the limited deck-space of a ship at sea.

The point to note here is that the poet's habit of limited wandering is held in common with that of the brother, affording them an unspoken sharing and commonality. But John's behaviour is explicitly defined in terms of occupational alienation, whereas that of the poet is not. At the same time, the poet declares that there was little else that the brothers had in common, besides those things demanded by nature, the 'common feelings of fraternal love' (570). It is thus significant that the various drafts of the poem are somewhat at variance on the question of whether John really did wear the path through the trees. The first draft is emphatic:

> for at once I knew
> That by my Brother's steps it had been trac'd
> (565)

In 1815, this becomes a 'conviction … flashed upon my mind'; and in 1827 'Pleasant conviction flashed upon my mind' (569). The Fenwick note

(677) has Wordsworth declaring quite simply that John *did* wear the path, though a pencilled note, perhaps in Mary's hand, asks the question: 'If *newly* come, would he have traced a visible path?' (677). As Wordsworth revised the passage, he makes a slight gesture toward turning a 'fact' into a hypothesis, and thus turns attention to his own mood and motives. For if John's occupational alienation, his 'habitual restlessness of foot', was indeed the cause of the newly apparent footpath, then he can be (gently) implicated as responsible for the fact that there was 'little other bond' between the brothers than those 'common feelings of fraternal love'. This, we assume, was much; but Wordsworth does declare that the two, 'conversing not', hardly knew each other (570). If, however, John's reported behaviour is a fantasy of William's, no more than a 'pleasant conviction', then it is perhaps William who must bear some of the responsibility for a relationship left unachieved, and now tragically beyond development. The fir grove can now be celebrated as a symbol of fraternal affection, and one moreover convenient for the poet's own creative needs, his 'easy and mechanic thoughtlessness'; but it is one based on death and perhaps on covert guilt. After John's death, the recollection of the degree to which his own vocation as solitary poet had kept him sequestered from his brother must have been extraordinarily painful to Wordsworth. It is entirely typical of his writings on such subjects that he should be at once implicating John and himself in a rhetoric of reflection that is finally impossible to disentangle unambiguously. When the poet claims to love the fir grove 'with a perfect love', it is the *symbol*, and not the person imaged by it, that he is attached to. The attachment is in no sense criminal or improper, but it is tinged with the same hint of fetishistic contingency as is the mood transcribed in 'A slumber did my spirit seal' (*LB*, 154). It is all he now has, but it is not a convincing substitution for the living relationship now never to be consummated. Perhaps that is why it is a *perfect* love: unchanging because founded in death, and thus beyond challenge or modification. At the beginning of the poem, Wordsworth abandons the grove, because he can find in it no 'length of open space' suitable for his habit of ambulatory composition, 'without concern or care' (568). The 'habitual restlessness of foot' that is attributed to John is, again, also his own. And the work that is done on the grove to produce the 'length of open space' has an explicitly Adamic dignity. Adam describes how dawn must find the first couple risen

And at our pleasant labour, to reform
Yon flowery arbours, yonder alleys green,
Our walk at noon, with branches overgrown,
That mock our scant manuring, and require
More hands than ours to lop their wanton growth:
Those blossoms also, and those dropping gums,

That lie bestrewn unsightly and unsmooth,
Ask riddance, if we mean to tread with ease.
                                    (*PL*, 4: 625–32)

John's alienation, imagined or actual, thus has the Miltonic *imprimatur*,
and it emphatically provides a place for the poet to write, to do *his* work,
if such it be; for the opening of the poem describes his life as one of
'studious leisure' (567). John's absence at sea, perhaps with the purpose of
freeing William from financial concerns and allowing him to write, must
have seemed like a prefiguring of death; when the imaginary became the
literal in 1805, the shock to the poet must have been profound. Wordsworth had previously been preoccupied with this relationship, as 'The
Brothers' demonstrates; after 1805, one can only marvel that he had the
courage (or the innocence) and the insight to work on this poem about the
fir grove, whose irresolution of the self–other question is precisely its
deepest meaning.

Raisley Calvert and John Wordsworth are both, then, writ large in the
poetry worked on in the years around 1807, and published in the volume
that includes 'Gipsies'. These lived experiences must have significantly
informed Wordsworth's anxieties about whether poetic labour was a properly accountable pursuit. In a poem written to Coleridge in 1802, also
unpublished until 1815, he describes the two poets in the third person:

There did they lie from earthly labour free,
Most happy livers as were ever seen.
                                    (*1807*, 583)

It is left open whether they are engaged on spiritual or divine labour, or
just sitting around. It is not insensitive to read 'Resolution and Independence', one of the central poems of the 1807 volumes, as another meditation upon poetic labour. Here again the poet is a 'traveller … upon the
moor' (*1807*, 124), and one whose freedom from engrossing tasks allows
him to wander between moods of joy and fits of melancholy. For

how can He expect that others should
Build for him, sow for him, and at his call
Love him, who for himself will take no heed at all?
                                    (125)

The poet has lived a life of 'pleasant thought', as if 'life's business were a
summer mood', and as if 'all needful things would come unsought' (124).
Knowing what we know of his career up to this point, we can read into
these lines the awkward awareness that others *have* built for him –
Calvert, Beaumont and John Wordsworth. He lacks the independence
without which true resolution may well be impossible; he may thus fear

'Solitude, pain of heart, distress and poverty' all the more because he is not properly responsible for himself, and therefore has never cultivated the habitual stoicism that would enable him to cope with such challenges, as the leech gatherer has. This figure, who is almost refigured by the poet's self-projecting mood – 'Like one whom I had met with in a dream' – not only corrects this habit of misappropriation by imagination that is a prominent feature of Wordsworthian poetic labour, thus in itself incipiently improper; he also suggests, by example, that true resolution comes from an occupational obligation to absolute concentration and full-time labour, of precisely the kind from which the poet has been *freed*. The Spartan ideal of full-time subsistence labour is imaged by the poet as the only available vocation for the emergence of psychological (and thus civic) virtue, but he himself is cut off from it. Wordsworth is much more explicit about admiring the leech gatherer than he is about envying the gypsies; for the gypsies are not 'workers', and thus allow him the luxury of self-esteem. But the two encounters speak forth the same insecurity, and the same division within the self. As he elsewhere almost wishes himself impoverished, or 'frugal and severe' (*1807*, 152), in order that a virtuous independence might ensue, so he admits that he has already been denied that experience, partly by the generosity of others, and partly by the choice of the poetic vocation itself. For poetry could never provide anything akin to the leech gatherer's 'honest maintenance' (128). Wordsworth was not a peasant poet, like Burns, who walked 'Behind his plough, upon the mountain-side' (125); and even if he had been, the equation of poetry with full-time subsistence labour is unlikely ever to have been convincing. 'Resolution and Independence', read as the record of a profound historical and individual displacement, becomes a true companion poem to 'Gipsies'.

Both together, along with the general priority of this concern in the 1807 edition, also serve to render a poem like the 'Ode to Duty' a rather less rigidly doctrinal utterance than it has often been taken to be. Searching for a 'second Will more wise' (*1807*, 107), in a telling pun upon his own name (and that of Shakespeare: the same pun figures in the sonnets), Wordsworth is admitting that he cannot license his impulses by claiming for them an innate moral propriety. He cannot, any longer, be one of those who do God's, or duty's work 'and know it not' (105). This harks back to the careful qualification that the 'spontaneous overflow of powerful feelings' that characterizes authentic poetic creativity can only be proper if the poet has also 'thought long and deeply' (*PrW*, 1:126). Thus, when he obeys his impulses 'blindly and mechanically' he is in fact projecting a cultured and organized behaviour pattern. In both the preface to *Lyrical Ballads* and in the 'Ode to Duty', Wordsworth is alluding to a very famous argument which he could hardly have failed to be aware of through Coleridge: that concerning the 'beautiful soul' (*schöne Seele*). In answer to what he saw as Kant's rigid separation of ethical from intuitive behaviour, Schiller had posited certain circumstances under which the two might be identical.[5] In the preface, Wordsworth makes use of a similar model to explain how spontaneity may also be meditated and accountable; and in the 'Ode to Duty' he addresses the ethical question directly. If such a synthesis were achieveable, he would be able to appeal to a conscious and public standard of accountability for his otherwise apparently casual labours:

> Me this uncharter'd freedom tires;
> I feel the weight of chance desires:
> My hopes no more must change their name,
> I long for a repose which ever is the same.
> *(1807, 106)*

Like many other poems of this period – including 'Gipsies', as we shall see – the 'Ode to Duty' is shot through with allusions to the demise of Britain and Europe in the aftermath of the French Revolution. The 'glorious ministry' (104) that duty might provide is of the sort not to be found in parliament, and least of all in Napoleonic France, which was itself frequently regarded as the regrettable outcome of an 'uncharter'd freedom'. Similarly, in opting for the traditional restrictions of the sonnet form over other options, Wordsworth is responding to 'the weight of too much liberty' (133), and a liberty that is political–historical as well as individual.

A further account of these wider historical allusions will come later. For the moment, we may see in the 'Ode to Duty' another version of Wordsworth's anxiety about meeting public and visible standards, whether in the form of a moral code or of productive labour. The desire to be placed beyond the demands of choice and mutability, and to achieve a 'repose which ever is the same', is also very slightly tainted by the blasphemy of a death-wish. And it is, almost precisely, the state of passive continuity for which he upbraids the gypsies. It is *repose*, not labour, that he seeks, in a gesture that promises both relief and guilt.

The paradoxical nature of Wordsworth's feelings about effort and indulgence, closed and open spaces, and patronage and independence, is aptly evident in the letters of the Coleorton period. They are full of discussions of gardening. Wordsworth himself, always a reluctant penman, writes no less than nine pages to Lady Beaumont (*MY*, 1: 112–20) about his plans for the estate; he calls it, indeed, 'the longest Letter I ever wrote in my life' (120). He plans for a fence of evergreen shrubs and cypress, to give the garden 'the greatest appearance of depth, shelter, and seclusion possible' (112). In fifty years, with the proper nurture, Wordsworth predicts that this garden may be a 'paradise' (119); but it is really a garden for life after the fall, a place to hide rather than one affording the 'prospect large' of Milton's paradise (*PL*, 4: 144). It seems to provide Wordsworth with a quite rhapsodic sense of purpose, and a promise of *work done*; feelings that came only occasionally from the writing of poems, if at all. The other striking feature of the Coleorton letters is the frequent mention of the splendid sunsets, of which the Wordsworths had been robbed by the high mountains of Grasmere. It is very typical of Wordsworth that he is at once responding to the appeal of open space, so aptly inscribed into the poem 'Gipsies', and to the instinct or inclination to protect himself from it, and from the outside world, with some horticultural facsimile of the vale, or veil, of Grasmere.

We have established, then, that the author of 'Gipsies' is a poet acutely anxious about his dependence upon others, and about the public status of his 'work' as a poet. This goes some way toward explaining the peculiar superimposition of over-confidence upon insecurity that a careful reading of the poem can support. It is time now to explore a further telling detail in the poem's rhetoric, in which the speaker's dual status as at once divine (in aspiration) and Satanic (if aspiration fails) is once again unfolded: that of Vesper, the evening star. Geoffrey Hartman has accurately noted the appeal of the evening star as the image of a 'continuity that persists within apparent loss'. It is a threshold, a passage between the separate states of day and night; as such, any appeal to it tends to suggest a 'fear of discontinuity, of a break in personal or cultural development; but also a vatic overestimation of poetry which, putting too great a burden on the artist, made this break more likely' (1972, 90, 123).[6] We have seen something of these fears, and of the compensatory 'vatic overestimation', in 'Gipsies'. The morning star and evening star are cosmologically identical, hence their (its) convenience as an image of the identity of endings and beginnings; in the first of the 'Essays upon Epitaphs' Wordsworth wrote eloquently of the way in which 'origin and tendency are notions insepar- ably co-relative', and of how any curiosity about either must lead to 'nothing less than infinity' (*PrW*, 2: 51).

The superimposition of origin upon tendency works also for Milton, who uses the Old Testament chronology whereby the onset of darkness is technically the beginning of a new day. The evening star has a mythologi- cal as well as a temporal instability: in the non-Christian tradition, it is the planet Venus (evening and morning star) that is sacred to earthly love. The evening star proper does not occur in the Bible, and it is only in the New Testament that the morning star is appropriated to Christ (*Revelation* 22: 16), so suspicious were the Hebrew authors of any hint of idolatry. Christ thus supplants the ruling presence of Lucifer, the fallen 'son of the morning' (*Isaiah* 14: 12; cf. *PL*, 5: 708–9, 7: 133). For Milton too the birth of Christ will break the dominion of Satan over the sidereal elements (see 'On the Morning of Christ's Nativity', lines 69ff.), just as his peregrination through the wilderness in *Paradise Regained* is a redeeming repetition and annulment of Satan's through and around paradise, and a prospective alternative to the same Satan who is, like Wordsworth, 'roving still/ About the world' with 'large liberty' (1: 33–4, 365).

Milton is very purposeful in his presentation of the 'identity in differ-ence' of endings and beginnings, both temporal and spiritual, by way of the image of the evening star. Messiah's creation of the world ends with sunset on the sixth day (*PL*, 7: 581f.), and it is at twilight that Hesperus heralds Satan's return to the task of temptation (9: 48–52). As a Messiah-figure, Wordsworth claims to have done his work; but as a Satan-figure, it may be just beginning. The 'twelve bounteous hours' that he has been abroad echo the identical duration of the fall of Mulciber, who 'with the setting sun/ Dropped from the zenith like a falling star' (1: 744–5) – at least, according to the pagan tradition that Milton seeks to subvert. Among the various associations of the evening star, the only one that seems not to be relevant to 'Gipsies' is that pertaining to earthly love and the erotic; Wordsworth's bracing hike admits little time or space for such thoughts.

I turn again to that intriguing line, 'Then issued Vesper from the fulgent West'. As has been noted, both *Vesper* and *fulgent* are uncommon words in the poet's vocabulary, so that to see them occur together is especially striking. The image of sunset might be, and often is, one of peace and repose; but the associations of *fulgent* are rather more energetic and challenging, suggesting a sky shining brightly, glittering and splendid. Wordsworth uses the word to describe the sky in that passage from *The Prelude* (10: 466f.) already discussed, when he recollects hearing of the death of Robespierre. Satan has a 'fulgent head' when he returns to hell to recount his exploits (*PL*, 10: 449), but it is 'false glitter' (line 452), as well as a remnant of what was 'left him' since his fall. Recounting again the details that Mark Reed has recorded (1975, 348) of the walk to Notting-ham, it may now seem more significant that Wordsworth implies, in the poem, that he is *alone*, whereas in fact he had the company of Craig, the gardener. It would have been perfectly easy to have written the poem with an acknowledgement of Craig's presence; it is hard to believe that Word-sworth could not have managed the necessary change in the rhyme (I/sky), had he wished to suggest an alternative to the gypsy camp that offered community instead of solitude. But he did not. To include his companion in the poem would have weakened the image of alienation, and of the poet's Satanic dimension. The longer and the more closely one looks at this poem, the more it comes to seem weighted toward the Satanic and away from the divine. The gesture of self-apotheosis that is first apparent is only the start of a cycle that turns back upon itself.

This inversion becomes clearer still when 'Gipsies' is read together with the other 'evening star' poem of the 1807 edition, 'It is no Spirit who from Heaven hath flown' (1807, 216–17). This opening line tells us what the evening star is *not*; no more is it a 'Traveller gone from Earth the Heavens to espy'. It is simply Hesperus, with 'his glittering crown' – another image faintly tinged with associations of vainglory. But the sight of this star with the sky all to itself, and thus 'most ambitious', inspires an 'inquest' in the poet and a fantasy that he too might 'step beyond' his 'natural race', treading 'some ground not mine . . . / with steps that no one shall reprove'. The poem declares an obvious aspiration for poetic immortality, but also images a Satanic desire not to die. Thus the expression of eternal life is one conditioned by earthly habits, a continued treading forth that pre-figures the theme of 'Stepping Westward'. Wordsworth seems to want to preserve the expectation of movement and desire in this imagined afterlife. The wish that no one should 'reprove' his steps of course seeks to lay aside the accusation of blasphemy or impropriety, but it also suggests that his steps on *this* earth, and the desires that motivate them, may well be open to such reproof. The speaker's Satanic wish to 'step beyond my natural race' is a direct contradiction of Milton's angel's advice to 'be lowly wise' (*PL*, 8: 173). As such, he implicitly lines himself up with the Satanic Robespierre whose fall and death we have seen described in *The Prelude*. But Wordsworth's desires are for an afterlife, and for a place in the gallery of immortal poets, rather than for the leadership of any earthly revolution. Milton's great poem had explicitly cast Satan as the user of republican rhetoric and the language of civic virtue. Satan pretends to speak out against 'tyranny' on behalf of 'public reason' (*PL*, 1: 124; 4: 389), and casts himself as a 'Patron of liberty' (4: 958). The 'glory' that he seeks (e.g. 2: 427; 4: 853) is to be seen as a pagan preoccupation with visible dignity at the expense of inward worth, and this is exactly how Wordsworth casts Robespierre and his followers in their dependence upon revolutionary *gloire*. The Wordsworthian speaker's own assumption of the Satanic post-ure thus both repeats and refutes that of the Jacobin precursors. I shall return at the end of this chapter to the rhetoric whereby Wordsworth seems to be trying to come to terms with the energies of the French Revolution, a process that commits him to a series of substitutions, refus-als and displacements.

The travelling people

The exposition of the 'subjective' element in 'Gipsies' has taken several, I hope bounteous, pages, and we are getting somewhere near an understand-ing of its complexity. In order to reconstitute another aspect of this subjectivity, it is now necessary to discuss the 'objective' dimension of the poem. Why is it important that this band of vagrants was composed of gypsies, rather than discharged soldiers, itinerant labourers, or some other class of vagrants? What were the associations of gypsies for Wordsworth and for the readers of his generation?

Manifold, as usual. Gypsies had always been imaged as in a tense and contested relation to the rest of society. True gypsies had once been banned from Britain, by a statute of 1530, and according to Hale, thirteen gypsies were executed under this law in the mid-seventeenth century (Burn, 1800, 4:452; Blackstone, 1979, 4:166). By Wordsworth's time this law had relaxed, and gypsies were mostly lumped together with other public nuisances. Thus Arthur Young (1770, 563) refers in general to 'beggars, vagrants, gypsies, thieves, pickpockets' as the 'non-industrious poor'. But there seems to have been a common assumption that most gypsies were not true Romanies but 'wandering impostors', the original populations having been swelled by 'idle proselytes, who imitated their language and complexion, and betook themselves to the same arts of chiromancy, begging, and pilfering' (Burn, 1800, 4:452). The anonymous author of *The Laws Respecting Women* (1777) describes them as 'a counterfeit kind of rogues, that being English or Welch people, accompanied themselves together, disguised in the habit of Egyptians' for the purposes of fraud and felony (104). Whether or not this kind of deception really was common in the eighteenth century is hard to adjudicate; but one can see the convenience, at a time when the whole question of vagrancy was in crisis, of treating a significant class of such vagrants as if they were conniving malingerers. Gypsies were all the more powerful a threat to the stability of conventional society because they seemed to have *chosen*, rather than to have been exiled to a life of wandering and displacement. Along with their refusal of a fixed sense of place, they are a counterimage to the central values of the majority society, those of labour and property. Wordsworth is at least technically correct in invoking, in 1820, their 'birth/ And breeding' as explanations of their way of life (*1807*, 212).

We can see why, then, gypsies would have been an alternately attractive and repellent image for the writers of the period. With a complicated case like Wordsworth's, we can almost assume a measure of both. Sometimes they are merely an ingredient in the rural picturesque, as in Wordsworth's *Descriptive Sketches* (*DS*, 56–63). But more often they are clearly evaluated, either as emblems of liberty and commonality, of an ideal society in which all is shared by all; or as examples of the criminal and antisocial element in human nature. Langhorne points the paradox when he says that

The Gipsy-Race my Pity rarely move;
Yet their strong thirst of Liberty I love
(1774–7, 1:19)

Fielding has Tom Jones visit a gypsy camp, in order to learn a few lessons about political organization: most strikingly, that what works well for small societies will not do for large ones. Cowper writes very negatively, in *The Task*, of a race 'Loud when they beg, dumb only when they steal'. Although he does not deny their capacity for mirth and celebration, he asks the question that the Wordsworthian speaker might well have asked, in a less exalted and anxious mood:

> Strange! that a creature rational, and cast
> In human mould, should brutalize by choice
> His nature, and though capable of arts
> By which the world might profit and himself,
> Self-banish'd from society, prefer
> Such squalid sloth to honorable toil!
>
> (1787, 2: 31)

In *The Peripatetic*, a work which influenced Wordsworth in general and *The Excursion* in particular, John Thelwall sets up an important debate between his dramatic narrator and 'Ambulator' on the subject of gypsies (1793, 2: 41–8). The narrator is unambiguous about his disapproval, and especially detailed in his attribution of the polemical exploitation of traditional life by political theorists:

> On every side of them these miserable tribes of wandering robbers behold the fixed inhabitants, the comfortable dwellings, and all the accommodations of settled and regular society; yet these and their allurements they steadily resist, and (with all the inveterate attachment to the prejudices of ancient precedent and ancestral usage, which the political wisdom of our rulers would so piously recommend to our imitation) they persevere to the last in the wretched system with which they began, and set improvement and reformation at defiance. Averse alike to the restraints of civilization and labour, and attached to no community but their own, without either books or established ceremonies, they contrive to perpetuate a language as peculiar as their manners and appearance.
>
> (43–4)

Without Thelwall's dramatic irony, this would not be an untypical opinion. By contrast, we may note the complex analysis offered by John Clare, whose perspicuity is perhaps to be attributed to a personal acquaintance with gypsies, as well as to an alternative political perception of the nature of civil society. 'The Gipsy Song' (1979, 325) is a conventional hymn to 'gipsey liberty', but in 'The Village Minstrel' (1963, 75) he is well aware that the gypsies serve as scapegoats for the societies upon which they impinge:

Though blam'd for many a petty theft you've been,
Poor wandering souls, to fate's hard want decreed,
Doubtless too oft such acts your ways bemean;
But oft in wrong your foes 'gainst you proceed,
And brand a gipsy's camp when others do the deed.

Though their fuel may be 'pilfer'd' – a much gentler word than 'stolen' –
much of what they eat is gathered rather than purloined. Thus the sheep
that Clare pictures died 'of red-water' rather than being stolen from the
flock. In another poem, 'The Gipsy Camp', (1984, 278), Clare delivers a
quite unsentimental portrait of their lives, capturing both their ornamental
or picturesque appeal and the harsh material realities of their existence.
The overall sense he communicates is that of their helplessness before the
aesthetic and legal imaginations of the dominant culture:

'Tis thus they live – a picture to the place;
A quiet, pilfering, unprotected race.

In Jane Austen's *Emma*, this same unprotected race lurks in the lanes
about Highbury to give Harriet Smith and her friend an almighty scare,
from which they are rescued by Frank Churchill's timely appearance (ch.
39). Although Harriet's terror is clearly the object of the author's irony,
nothing is done to suggest that the gypsies are not to be held in suspicion,
and when Mrs Weston's poultry house is robbed of all its turkeys in the
final chapter, Austen does not need to mention the identity of the likely
culprits.

These instances of contemporary representations of gypsy life may serve
as a context for Wordsworth's treatment of the same subject. It is in the
various poems and drafts that have been recently collected as *The Salisbury Plain Poems* that he gives his most detailed account. The text of 'The
Female Vagrant', first published in 1798 (*LB*, 44), is roughly typical of the
other early drafts in its portrayal of gypsies. Here, the woman contrasts
the unfeeling nature of professional charity, its 'service done with careless
cruelty' (52), with the indiscriminate kindness of the gypsy camp, where
'all belonged to all, and each was chief'. But being used to a settled and
legally orthodox life, 'brought up in nothing ill', she is unable to live with
them, since the other side of their 'vagrant ease' involves poaching, thiev-
ing, and the 'black disguise' (53). For the female vagrant, there is thus
nothing between the unpredictable world of occasional charity, 'Now
coldly given, now utterly refused' (54), and a life of illegal self-sufficiency.
The gypsies are both criminal and socially enlightened, and the one fact is
not deployed to discredit the other.[7]

None of this sociological specificity finds its way into the text of 'Gipsies', of course. Here, no empirical details or careful moral meditations are

allowed to impinge upon the speaker's mood. But they are none the less part of the poem's context, because they were current in the society in which both Wordsworth and his readers had their being, and their language. Their absence from the text does not make them irrelevant; it rather signals yet again the degree of anxious compression and repression that the speaker effects. He does not offer, in his image of gypsies, a complex estimate of their moral and sociological role, but he 'assumes' one by his silences. We have seen that the gypsies set going in Wordsworth a highly charged, ambivalent address to the place of poetry on the spectrum that runs between idleness and honest labour. There is another crucial ingredient in this address, which we must now discuss: property.

If labour is one of the primary means by which a person can contribute to and be reaffirmed by the social contract, then property is another. It is indeed often one of the solidified forms of labour, and one of the things for which surplus labour can be exchanged. We will see in the following chapters that Wordsworth had a very sophisticated though often implicit conviction about the human imagination as best thriving in a subsistence, agrarian economy of owner-occupiers. This ideal – for that is what it was – is a fusion of poverty and possessiveness, and work and leisure. One should have enough to live on, but only *just* enough, so that the need to labour is never given over; and with the glow of independence and ownership, work becomes pleasurable and leisure an active concept. Wordsworth's interest in shepherding as an ideal occupation is also to be connected with its intermediary status between the nomadic and the fixed, and thus between two stages of civil society as countless eighteenth-century writers described it. The shepherd has much of a sense of property and place, but is also able to wander and range abroad with his flocks, which have different needs at different times of the year. Shepherding is an image of undivided labour, and of a communal life in which a high degree of solitude and freedom of movement is preserved. Pasturage does not quite have the fixed emphasis on 'permanent property in the soil' that agriculture entails (Blackstone, 1979, 2: 7), but it has enough of it to satisfy Wordsworth's emphasis on the spirit of place.

The details of this Wordsworthian ideal will follow later in this study. For now, we can see how the gypsies might appeal to a certain aspect of Wordsworth's personality, his urge to (or obligation to) wander in a state of freedom and openness, 'Alive to all things and forgetting all' (*LB*, 218). But they would also threaten him by going too far, not only by going beyond the law (perhaps) but by choosing to deny the value, material and psychological, of property. This leads us to notice yet another telling inversion in the poem. Gypsies are by definition constitutional vagrants, wandering across the landscape with no fixed abodes or goals. But in the poem, they are transfixed in a single spot, and seem to be in no hurry to leave. Wordsworth, on the other hand, who has the name and all the addition of a man of substance and perhaps property, is the one who is on the move; and as a man supposedly integrated into ordinary society, he is (imaged as) *alone*, with the 'asocial' gypsies being cast as the 'unbroken knot'. We must of course infer that the speaker will return to a dear perpetual place, but in the poem he is a traveller 'under open sky', without shelter or society. As Coleridge was merely the first to notice, this experience must have been enjoyable *because* temporary; but the way in which the speaker's identifications are with the heavenly bodies does project him into the cold vacuum of celestial physics, well away from the domestic fireside. In so far as he is a Lucifer figure, then his loneliness is the exile of self-despite, able to *witness*, indeed, much of 'change and chear', but not to participate. Even as a solar principle, and thus divine, he is condemned to the same daily round of endless journeying.

Looking through the poems published in 1807, as well as others in the canon, it is striking that Wordsworth so frequently describes himself as a traveller or wanderer, always *between* places, and often with no implied destiny at all. His is a wandering that does *not* appear (in the poetry) to be constrained by property or habitual place; he seldom mentions the termini of his journeys. Wordsworth's displacement thereby takes two antithetical but entirely cognate forms: a strenuous over-identification with places and communities (as in *Home at Grasmere*), and a near-complete remoteness from all human contingencies. Wordsworth is a poet who always wants both to retire to a chosen vale and to sally forth along the roads and over the hills – and wants both at once. He does have a gypsy in his soul, but he also has a longing for the bricks-and-mortar analogue of the 'repose which ever is the same' (*1807*, 106), and for the state of mind that goes with it. With this double focus in mind, it is not irrelevant to review the state of affairs in the Wordsworth household in 1807, on this matter of property.

A month prior to settling in Dove Cottage, in November 1799, Wordsworth had written enthusiastically of building a house by the side of Grasmere Lake (*EY*, 272). Instead, he and Dorothy rented Dove Cottage, for the sum of £8 a year (Reed, 1967, 281–2). This seems to have excited strong feelings of belonging. A small garden was 'enclosed from the road' (*EY*, 295), the orchard was a constant source of proprietal delight, and the Wordsworths kept a small boat (not stolen) upon the lake. But William was not at all the independent owner-occupier whose virtues he would detail in such poems as 'Michael'. In 1803, Sir George Beaumont presented him with a property at Applethwaite (Reed, 1975, 218), and two years later Wordsworth himself tried to buy the Broad How property in Patterdale. But the asking price was £1000, and he was able or prepared to come up with only £800. It was Lord Lowther who made up the difference, in a gesture which, according to Moorman's account (1968, 59–62), caused

Wordsworth a good deal of embarrassment. He accepted the favour never-theless, and the title was transferred to his hands in March 1807, a month or so after the composition of 'Gipsies'. The mortgage was paid off by mid-1809, but Wordsworth never lived at Broad How, nor built there. Instead, he moved to Allan Bank in 1808. While preparing the 1807 *Poems* for the press he was, as we have noted, living on a farm belonging to the Beaumonts. In August of 1806, before moving to Coleorton, Word-sworth had written to Beaumont in response to the latter's advice to build a house. The jocular tone is not entirely light-hearted:

> The *temptation* I like, and I should content myself with the pleasure it gives me, through my whole life (I have at least built five hundred houses, in five hundred different places, with garden, ground, etc.), but I have no house to cover me, and know not where to get one.
>
> (*MY*, 1: 76)

All this is enough to suggest that, along with the anxieties about labour and dependence that we have seen to impinge upon 'Gipsies', we might add thereto a leading preoccupation with the question of property.[8] It was presumably not just a disembodied literary imagination that made Word-sworth project himself into the role of wanderer, and the companion or ambassador of celestial bodies. Poetry was for him a *form* of property indeed, but an especially insecure one in the years before the establishment of comprehensive copyright laws. Moreover, Wordsworth was neither an established nor a particularly visible poet. *Lyrical Ballads* had been written collaboratively and published anonymously; it was neither wholly Word-sworth's, nor did it place his name before a potentially validating public. Neither poetry nor the self that produced it were adequately individuated; Wordsworth had no true freehold upon his work, and no sense of a con-solidated selfhood from which such 'freehold' might have emanated. The copyright of *Lyrical Ballads* had been sold, first to Cottle and then, for the second edition, to Longman. The 'work' that Wordsworth had done was in this further sense not properly his own, so that it is hardly surprising that his poetry should have concerned itself so forcefully with over-strenuous images of individuation. The omission of Craig the gardener is an im-portant symptom of the poet's Satanic self-aggrandizement, but it is also an accurate (if inflated) projection of his psycho-economic condition in the world.

It is not surprising, then, that the 1807 volume was originally to have been introduced by a section titled 'The Orchard Pathway', a phrase aptly expressive of the poet's preoccupation with both property and peregrina-tion. The orchard is a place where nature and nurture combine, and wherein there is a pathway for the limited wanderings that for Word-sworth enabled (as they also imitated) the processes of poetic composition.

This title, and the motto prefaced to it (both apparently cancelled in proof), describes the collection that follows as a 'little lot' – a telling pun upon their quantity, their quality, their identity with a place or plot of ground, and their status as items up for auction in the public sphere. This same motto (*1807*, 63) has the poet going 'to and fro' along his pathway, thus making anticipatory sense of his later return to the 'scanty plot of ground' (133) that is the sonnet form. It seems significant that these introductory motifs were first proposed and then omitted; their absence, I suggest, makes the dominant image of the volume come to be that of the disembodied traveller between earth and sky.

This traveller is incarnate once again in 'Stepping Westward' (*1807*, 185–6), another significant working-through of some of the themes of 'Gipsies'. This poem is the outgrowth of a 'Tour', so that the travellers are already 'In a strange Land, and far from home'. Despite the affirmation that there *is* such a thing as home, Wordsworth appeals to the magnificence of the sunset as an incentive to courage even were 'home or shelter' unavailable. This poem begins in a state of community – 'we, who thus together roam' – but is soon taken over by the first person in his displaced state of solitary wandering. Once again, he is looking for some kind of permission or authority for doing what he is doing; and once again, his search for 'spiritual right/ To travel through that region bright' begs reference not just to his potential apotheosis within the western sunset, but also to his earthly insecurity. Like the 'Tintern Abbey' poem, 'Stepping Westward' has almost no conviction of presence or stability; it is built upon movement and continuing displacement. Looking behind is 'all gloomy'; the 'dewy ground' that is 'dark and cold' threatens to engulf the travellers, who are moving towards the sunset but not at a pace that can match that of the sun itself. The poet's thoughts of transfiguration hold off the prospect of being swallowed by the shades of night. It is the portentous diction of the casual greeting, '*What, you are stepping westward?*', that further stimulates the poet's divine aspirations ('A kind of *heavenly* destiny') as well as providing a 'human sweetness' that keeps him connected to everyday social life. So full of possible superimpositions of beginnings upon endings is this image of chasing the sunset that it becomes empty of all of them, an image of pure process or desire. In the more expansive language of prose, Wordsworth was to write, in the first of the 'Essays upon Epitaphs', a simplified version of this predicament:

As, in sailing upon the orb of this planet, a voyage towards the regions where the sun sets, conducts gradually to the quarter where we have been accustomed to behold it coming forth at its rising; and, in like manner, a voyage towards the east, the birth-place in our imagination of the morning, leads finally to the quarter where the sun is last seen when he departs from our eyes; so the contemplative Soul, travelling in the direction of mortality, advances to the country of everlasting life; and, in like manner, may she continue to explore those cheerful tracts, till she is brought back, for her advantage and benefit, to the land of transitory things – of sorrow and of tears.

(PrW, 2: 53)

In our ends are our beginnings. In 'Stepping Westward', the resolution of the same image is less religiose. The echo of the woman's voice

<blockquote>
enwrought
A human sweetness with the thought
Of travelling through the world that lay
Before me on my endless way.
</blockquote>

The way is *endless*, and it is through the *world*, not the afterlife. As much as he is an Adam exiled from Eden, but offered the chance to work his way back again, Wordsworth is here a wandering Jew, or a Satan 'roving still/ About the world' and compelled to journey thus forever. Adam has his 'wandering thoughts' that are apt to 'rove/ Unchecked' (*PL*, 8: 187–9), but he realizes that a proper discipline is provided by 'That which before us lies in daily life' (line 193). This is the wisdom that is lost or set at naught by the fall of man, whereby Adam's predicament is brought closer to, though of course it is never at one with, Satan's. And Satan's wanderings are almost ludicrously inefficacious, heroic only in his own rhetoric of self-definition. There is no excursive dignity in his being 'alone thus wandering' (3: 667), since he brings hell with him wherever he goes (4: 20, 75, etc.). His search for 'place or refuge' (9: 119) is doomed to fail, and his perception of the 'sweet interchange' of a varied landscape (line 115) can only be in the form of a lamentation. As such, he represents one prospective version of the unredeemed human spirit, one that Wordsworth predictably recalls in the conditional imagination that he too might not have 'home or shelter' (*1807*, 186), as Satan has no 'place or refuge'. The metaphysical, theological and socio-economic dimensions of Wordsworth's imaged stepping westward are, I think, inseparable.[9] And in the absence of any achieved resolution of any of them, the poet is left with the symbolic potential of a casual linguistic exchange. To complete the poem's identity as a parable of displacement, this too is efficacious not so much in itself but as an *echo*. The element of otherness, of public validation, surfaces only retrospectively, moments after the actual exchange. Once again, Wordsworth projects himself into eternal and solitary motion, and the infinite potential thus imagined can only survive in the suspension of fulfilment or completion. Wordsworth's poem is echoed, several decades later, by Tennyson's Ulysses, who also 'cannot rest from travel', who seeks to 'sail beyond the sunset' and to 'follow knowledge like a sinking star' (Tennyson, 1969, 564). Tennyson's poem offers an analysis of the insatiable emptiness that may be at the heart of exploration and empire, the epic ventures of his generation; Wordsworth's, by contrast, seems a sociologically pared-down or abstracted representation of a man trying to keep his feet (and his head) on the surface of a turning world. The desire for the properties of eternal life that is in 'Gipsies' embodied in things (sun, moon, star) is here projected into empty space, into an infinitely receding sunset. The sun itself has dropped from sight; only its last light remains, along with a 'human sweetness' that, instead of restraining the speaker from the urge to travel further, only sends him forth the more assuredly into asocial space.

Further examples could be adduced, but enough has been done to demonstrate, I hope, the incidence of a leading anxiety, especially apparent in the 1807 *Poems*, about the relations between poetry, property, and labour, variously interactive within a general framework that continually superimposes images of exile and wandering, and their Satanic associations, upon assertions of security and propriety. In order to provide what I hope is an incipiently sufficient account of the operation of these anxieties in 'Gipsies', there is one further aspect of the objective dimension of its language that needs to be addressed: Wordsworth's perceptions of the events and aftermath of the French Revolution.

We have noted already the relation between Robespierre, Satan, and the 'fulgent spectacle' that intimates immortality in *The Prelude* (10: 466f.). In the same poem, Wordsworth describes his leaving Cambridge as an embracing of the gypsy life. He was one who

> pitched my vagrant tent,
> A casual dweller and at large, among
> The unfenced regions of society.
>
> (7: 60–2)

His time after Cambridge was much involved with his time in France, and in describing the prospective restoration of an earthly paradise that the early stages of the French Revolution implied, it is again to the imagery of gypsies that he returns. On their walking tour of 1790, the English travellers participated in an unbroken knot of human beings:

> Unhoused beneath the evening star we saw
> Dances of liberty, and, in late hours
> Of darkness, dances in the open air.
>
> (6: 380–2)

At this one time, the image is wholly benevolent, France itself being 'Fresh as the morning star' (9: 392). There are no fallen angels abroad to do mischief, and no evil deeds being plotted by the houseless dwellers under open sky. Wordsworth's image appears to confute the negative scorn of Burke's *Letters on a Regicide Peace* (1797) for the 'gipsy jargon' of the Directory in its renaming of the months (1906, 6: 105). But Wordsworth's account is of course retrospective, and thus presumes knowledge of the darker outcome of the positive moments here recorded. The 'boisterous crew' and 'glad rout' of which he is glad to be a member (6: 420, 422) hint at their identity with Comus' pagan band as well as with the young democracy. Innocence is overlain with knowledge: knowledge of the fall into Satanism with Robespierre and Bonaparte, and of the evolution of community into anarchy and tyranny. A similar if weaker retrospective irony informs the description of the British radical movement as part of a 'caravan' *travelling* toward liberty (10: 216).

The allusion that the poem 'Gipsies' makes to the aftermath of the French Revolution is all the more telling when we recall the highly self-conscious emphasis placed by the pageant masters and legislators of the French Republic upon *open space* as the proper forum for rejuvenated civic, social and political interaction. Mona Ozouf (1976, 149–87) has written well on the reconstruction of urban space in accordance with the emphasis on public visibility and life in the open air. The traditional Spartan ethic was further enhanced by an agrarian Utopianism and a belief in the healthfulness of exposure to the cycles of the seasons – very Wordsworthian priorities, as we shall see. In the words of one revolutionary declaration cited by Ozouf (152, my translation):

> The national festivals cannot have any boundary other than the vault of the sky, since the sovereign – that is, the people – can never again be closed in by a limited and circumscribed space.

It is hard to imagine that Wordsworth would not have been at least unconsciously sensitive to such associations in the image of a band of gypsies who were already and in themselves figured as a threat to the norms of bourgeois ethics – property and labour. Their life as an 'unbroken knot' under 'open sky' makes them images of a prelapsarian state, and the complete availability of their doings to the public gaze in a public space defines them as icons of revolutionary innocence, a condition that Wordsworth both desires and fears. Events in France, and their afterlife in British imaginations, do then stand as an important element in the inter-subjective energies whose presence may be traced in Wordsworth's poem, and in other poems. But Wordsworth was no mere apologist of bourgeois civic virtue, and consequently his transcription is a troubled one. We remember the poem about the fir grove, which chronicles among other things Wordsworth's desire for a protected and sheltered space wherein he might compose his poetry. This seems to represent the opposite of the longing for open space that is also there in the poetry; but, like the longing for open space, it too is compromised and qualified, posited and negated at the same time. We have explored already the ambiguities of the 'easy and mechanic thoughtlessness' that Wordsworth seeks within the 'shady grove' (*1807*, 364). We must further note, along with all the biographical and thematic ironies of this poem, the presence of two telling literary echoes. In the very first stanzas of *The Faerie Queene*, Una and her knight seek shelter in a 'shadie groue':

> And all within were pathes and alleies wide,
> With footing worne, and leading inward farre:
> Faire harbour that them seemes: so in they entred arre.
>
> (I, 1: 7)

The wood, of course, is threatening, and they are soon lost. It has the paths and alleys that Wordsworth seeks, and which his brother is imaged as providing. Error is necessary to poetry, it seems, as is a measure of mobility, or wandering (*errare*). Wordsworth disturbs the birds and animals, and thus suggests that he is violating an innocent space in trying to find a way through the 'perplex'd array' (364); but he is also leaving behind the light of day and perhaps the sight of God. For the other literary predecessor who has a proclivity for shade is Adam, after the recognition of his fall (*PL*, 9: 1086ff.).[10] Both Spenser and Milton play upon the associations of the Greek ῾ύλη, meaning both *wood* and *matter*, and inviting attention thereby as the image of materialism and worldliness. Once again, the immediately intersubjective *and* idiosyncratic associations of Wordsworth's moving between shelter and open space are further informed by major literary–philosophic allusions. Only by admitting the role of all of these inputs, I think, does the full sophistication of his poetry begin to emerge. It is not a matter of choosing between the 'literary' and the 'historical', or between either and the 'biographical' or 'psychological'. All of these components are simultaneously present in and constitutive of the language of poetry. The usefulness of such an approach to the understanding of Wordsworth's poetry of displacement is something that this study can perhaps begin to make clear.

But does such 'making clear' *explain* poetry, and in particular does it explain 'Gipsies'? Does this account amount to a refutation of Hazlitt and Coleridge? We have seen some of the reasons why Wordsworth had the gypsies in his soul, and some of the reasons why this intuition made him very uncomfortable. Wordsworth was not John Clare, a poet able to understand sympathetically the predicament of the wandering tribe and the complexity of their relationship to British middle-class society. And I think it must be admitted that the primary message of this poem is an admonitory one. Coleridge, Hazlitt and Keats were far more familiar with

Milton than I am, yet they saw no ambiguities in or retractions from the rhetoric of self-righteousness. The pressure of the poem's address to its original public must then have been rather straightforward, and in many ways it still is. Much of the complication that this chapter has introduced might then be thought of as secondary. But the question then arises, secondary to what? Even after my account, no reader should feel any reluctance to complain about the inadequacies of Wordsworth's moral intelligence. Wordsworth was surely not alone in experiencing the conflicts and inward violences of middle-class insecurity, but he expressed them, at least in this poem, in a way that other readers have found and surely will continue to find objectionable. My account is not intended as any kind of legitimation of the poet's moral personality. It does however claim that in despite of or along with its primary message, 'Gipsies' contains and projects a sophisticated articulation of an exemplary crisis in the Wordsworthian subjectivity. It is exemplary to the degree that it appears in a coherently intersubjective language which formulates, with remarkable comprehension, one generic reaction to a historical crisis. It would be trite to suggest that the displacement here described within the poet's self-experience 'excuses' his attitude toward gypsies. But it does make clear the pathology of many (not all) such attitudes, and thereby educates us about the covert continuities that often (though not always) underlie hyperbolic assertions of difference. The ethical and psychoanalytic conclusions that might be drawn from my reading – about, for example, the relation between insecurity and aggression, or about the avoidability or inevitability of certain selves deceiving themselves in dangerous ways – are best left to other readers. Wordsworth was always worried that the 'gipsy travel' that he and his companions enjoyed might not be a truly 'blameless pleasure' (*PW*, 4: 150–1). The language of this anxiety is at once personal and interpersonal; it results from the reciprocal determination of his individual insecurities about poetic labour and property and the historical charge, both discursive and empirical, that gypsies (for example) inevitably carried for anyone living and writing around 1800. Reverting to the terms of Trotsky's image that stands as the epigraph to this chapter, we must affirm that the 'revolution' of which Wordsworth seems to be a part is very different from that of Russia in 1917. But Trotsky's invocation of the gypsy life is more than opportunistically relevant. Without the experience, for whatever reason, of an unambiguous political vision, Wordsworth too is a subject in transit, an uneasy wanderer between places and between social roles whose apparent fixity may itself be no more (for him) than a figment, but which it is his personal–historical destiny to both desire and, in a smaller voice, deplore.

2

Wordsworth's agrarian idealism: the case against urban life

Our reading of 'Gipsies' and of its thematic context in the 1807 *Poems* has made mention of Wordsworth's conviction about the socially and psychologically healthful results of rural life, specifically that lived within a subsistence economy composed of owner-occupiers. The place of this conviction has gone largely unremarked, because it was never systematically announced by Wordsworth himself. Like so much else in his writings, it exists everywhere and nowhere. When we understand it, we can make sense of a great deal that is otherwise redundant or incoherent; but in order to make such understanding possible, we are obliged to make those writings more doctrinally assertive than most readers would allow them to be.

Implicit or explicit reference to an ideal of agrarian civic virtue is the major organizational energy that runs through a great deal of Wordsworth's prose and poetry. The purpose of the present chapter is to argue for and demonstrate that energy. In Chapter 3, I shall explore the degree to which both empirical facts and perceived contradictions determined that such a rhetoric could only exist for Wordsworth in a state of stress or extreme ambiguity, with the result that his representations of organicist harmony most be seen as aspirations, rather than as achievements. Much of this exposition is going to seem tedious to those readers who feel that the proper business of literary criticism is literature, in this case poetry. But in order to come back to the reading of poetry, as I shall do thereafter, with a firmer understanding of the issues involved in Wordsworth's poetry of displacement, these chapters are important. One of my ambitions here is thus to focus serious attention on the arguments of Wordsworth's prose writings. At the same time, the decision to open this study with a reading of 'Gipsies' is intended to signal that the arguments of both prose and poetry are inseparably mutual; that the perspectives explored in the one are active preoccupations in the other. I have begun with a poem, to make clear what those preoccupations are, and why they matter to Wordsworth's poetry, and I shall return to poetry in Chapter 4.

Wordsworth himself was never very comfortable with theories. I shall argue for the preface to *Lyrical Ballads* as a very complex polemical essay, but Wordsworth seeks to pass it off as merely 'a few words of introduction' (*PrW*, 1: 120), not wishing to be accused of trying to *reason* his reader into an approval of the poems. The responses to the volume indeed gave him adequate justification for such caution. Countless reviewers were to lament his adherence to a 'system', and the memory of this reaction was sharply enough etched upon his memory to bring forth an explosive annotation to Barron Field's projected memoirs: 'I never cared a straw about the theory – & the Preface was written at the request of Mr. Coleridge out of sheer good nature' (Field, 1975, 62). His words here are not just the result of a tactical failure, moreover. One of his earliest prose pieces, the fragmentary 'Essay on Morals' of 1798, contains an even weightier condemnation of the theoretical habit of mind, in suggesting that 'lifeless words, & abstract propositions' are more likely to be the resort of those who have committed some crime than the vehicle of authentic moral sentiments (*PrW*, 1: 104). In a similar spirit, the preface to *The Borderers* describes the villain of the piece as one who 'nourishes a contempt for mankind the more dangerous because he has been led to it by reflexion' (*PrW*, 1: 77).

Wordsworth thus seems to have both an instinctive distaste for and a meditated objection to what we might think of as 'theoretical' speculation. Such statements as the above, taken together with his continual emphasis upon the need to speak to the elemental passions in human nature rather than to its more disputatious rational faculties, are almost enough to dissuade us from seeking any such 'theoretical' coherence in his works, poetic or prosaic. In the years around 1800, this preference of Wordsworth's amounts to a statement of political affiliation, for rational analysis and 'theory' had come to be associated with the Jacobins and the Painite radicals, who did indeed place a very high value on the adherence to method, and whose opponents naturally made them seem much more bloodlessly scientific than they actually were. Wordsworth's allusion to those of us who 'murder to dissect' (*LB*, 106), like that to the supremacy of love over 'fifty years of reason' (*LB*, 59), is by no means innocent of allusions to this debate about 'method' (which I cannot describe in detail here).

Furthermore, if Wordsworth overtly expresses a disapproval of the search for a 'theoretical' pattern, there can be little doubt that his own writings demonstrate an abundance of apparent contradictions. Some of these are perhaps the result of his long creative life, and of the changes in national events and their interpretations that he lived through. Others may be the result of apparent idiosyncrasy, or of unresolved tensions in his world-view that are differently emphasized at different times. The author of 'Goody Blake and Harry Gill', a poem about the effects of a guilty conscience on a man who has used the full force of the law to punish an impoverished old woman, is also the man who writes to Lord Lonsdale, in December, 1823, of his pleasure at Mr North's apprehension of 'a worthless Fellow who had robbed his Cornstack' (*LY*, 1: 235). Similarly, the outspoken opponent of the extension of the railway system to the English lakes had also, some twenty years earlier, expressed an interest in 'purchasing Shares in some promising Company or Companies' taking part in the railway boom centred in Birmingham (*LY*, 1: 299). Such apparent inconsistencies are not uncommon in Wordsworth's writings. Sometimes they can be resolved by attention to local details and specificities, sometimes not. Wordsworth did not, as a whole, disapprove of the railways, but he did oppose their presence on the shores of Windermere; and he never lost his sympathies for the poor, although he did become more sensitive to their potential for active radicalism.

This study does not aspire to adjudicate all such tensions or contradictions in Wordsworth's writings, though it does try to register and explore those that pertain to the particular poems that will be discussed. As such, I trust that it will contribute to complicate the popular myth of the 'two Wordsworths', early and later: the one an enthusiastic young radical and supporter of the French Revolution, the other an embittered Tory reactionary standing out against all democratic movements or arguments. Sometime between, the myth goes, there was a moment of apostasy, when the leader lost his way and grasped the handful of state silver. There is of course a limited truth to this idea, and there are significant changes of mind in the course of Wordsworth's career – on suffrage, and on the French Revolution, for example. But some of these changes are conscious and principled, and themselves at times quite complicated. Wordsworth turned, for example, against the French in the aftermath of revolution *before* he became a supporter of the British government that opposed them. Furthermore, changes in some aspects of Wordsworth's political personality did not entail changes in his 'total' outlook, if indeed there ever was such a thing. Although he learns to admire the wisdom of Burke's analysis of events in France, for example, he never accedes to his views on the treatment of the poor.

These remarks are enough to suggest, I hope, that the question of Wordsworth's political development demands an attention that is detailed and specific. In particular, as we have already seen with 'Gipsies', the ways in which these political ideas register themselves in poetry can be complicated and unresolved. Their ambivalence indeed is their very life and identity. In the model of social–psychological agrarianism that I am about to describe, we can trace one dominant moral and political preference that will help to explain some of the transitions in Wordsworth's career that might otherwise remain puzzling.

I have argued elsewhere that there is in Wordsworth's poetry and prose a precise though somewhat dispersed explanation of the human imagination as a faculty depending upon certain limiting environmental conditions for its ideal development, and particularly for its compatibility with the demands of a generous social sympathy and exchange (see Simpson, 1982a, especially 122–69). I shall not here repeat the detailed argument of this earlier study, wherein I intended to show (perhaps too obscurely) the particular problems in the nature of all figurative perception that Wordsworth was responding to. A few words of summary are in place, nevertheless, as a preface to the extension of the argument to be pursued here.

Wordsworth saw all creative human perception as basically figurative. The imagination, as it is described in 1815, is a faculty that works by conferring and abstracting, and thus by 'operations of the mind' upon whatever is given (*PrW*, 3:31). He does argue for these operations as proceeding according to 'certain fixed laws', whereby the nature of things (in themselves) sustains and legitimates these conferrings and abstractings, thus providing a basis for the agreement of others, a consensus (31, 37). At the same time, he was also well aware of the difficulty of making an absolute distinction between the imagination and the fancy in this respect. Fancy is the more whimsical and impermanent faculty, refiguring things in ways that do not threaten to reorder the world for others. Problems arise when the imagination becomes whimsical, preserving at the same time its authority and conviction.[1] On such occasions, it threatens to refigure the world in ways that may not be licensed by the visible nature of things in themselves, but only by the individual poet's preoccupations. Wordsworth certainly shared Adam's knowledge of how 'apt the mind or fancy is to rove/ Unchecked' (*PL*, 8:188–9), and he was very worried about figurations that might have the arbitrariness of fancy and the permanence or conviction of the imaginative, whose 'indestructible dominion' (36) over the received forms of nature might then reorder the consensus in tyrannical and self-projecting ways.

Moreover, there is much in his writings that questions the possibility of such a consensus being maintained in the first place. Not only the deviant poet, but also the larger social developments in the nation, are working to render it less and less likely that the reader of literature will be 'in a healthful state of association' (*PrW*, 1: 126). He may thus have a quite different notion of things in themselves, of the 'real'. Wordsworth is always aware that what Keats, with uncanny precision, called the 'egotistical sublime' (1958, 1: 387) is a dangerous experience for the self, both aesthetically and morally; he is also concerned about the incumbent national developments that render the authentic imagination unavailable to vast numbers of potential readers. As so often in other ways, he is in this caught in something of a double bind, half dreading in himself the onset of that which he knows to be his highest and noblest faculty, because of its capacity to transgress; and aware at the same time of the increasing improbability of even his properly imaginative poems being understood as such by others.

This series of insights led Wordsworth to place a positive emphasis upon a model environment providing the particular conditions in which the intrinsically and extrinsically problematic figurative faculty essential to imagination and to all perception might develop and be sustained. This environment had to be rural (indeed marginal), sparsely populated by both natural objects and other people, and governed by a subsistence rather than a surplus economy. A world in which there are few 'objective' elements for attention and distraction provides the necessary space and time for the 'second look' that provides the opportunity for the correction of improper figurations, and the modification of authentic ones; for Wordsworth often suggests that the perception of 'similitude in dissimilitude' (*PrW*, 1: 148) is the only permanence that the imagination should seek. In a rural, outdoor environment, natural objects (as figured) are most visibly modified by climate and season, always at once the same and changing. They are thus the less likely to become fixed or reified. In the town, not only are the natural modifications less visible, but the oversupply of visual and other sensory stimuli makes it more difficult for any one figured object to be retained in the memory and re-experienced in the 'second look'. The occupational element in Wordsworth's ideal agrarianism is perfectly fulfilled by shepherding, which is constantly responsive to natural cycles and in many ways the complete opposite of urban divided labour. It is also part of a culture of frugality, never providing either the excess income or the leisure to invite the temptations of luxury and idleness that Wordsworth felt to be almost inevitable when people had too much time and money – a temptation he experienced most anxiously within himself, as we have seen. Finally, the whole system is bound together by a society of owner-occupiers. The experience of working for oneself makes hardship palatable by a sense of independence, and it reconciles the otherwise schizophrenic energies of self-interest and corporate concern, labour and leisure. All those aspirations which are in the incumbent commercial and urban economy the sources of division and dissent are here rendered creative and socially bonding.

We have already seen enough to recognize at once the awkwardness of such an ideal, which seems to provide, for Wordsworth as for Goldsmith before him, no place either for a poet or for an audience for poetry. The above may stand as a summary of the major arguments of *Wordsworth and the Figurings of the Real*; this and the immediately following chapters will attempt a more careful and complete account of Wordsworth's agrarian idealism, and also of its complex and frequently thwarted relation to various kinds of 'facts'. For it is in the interplay between the ideal and the actual that much of the tension of Wordsworth's poetry is generated.

At the time of my earlier study, I was shamefully unaware of the contributions of earlier scholars toward closely related (though not identical) conclusions. In particular, Jane Worthington (1946), Z.S. Fink (1948) and Kenneth MacLean (1950) had prepared the way for a serious examination of Wordsworth's agrarian preoccupations, and thus of their place in his critique of urbanization. Worthington shows the importance of classical republican theory in the poet's education and intellectual orientation, and Fink demonstrates the added importance of the English republican thinkers of the seventeenth century. All of these writers were obsessed with the nature and possibility of civic virtue and its relation to power, and Wordsworth would have been aware of them both through his own culture and through his acquaintance with the Girondins, who were great admirers of Sidney, Harrington, Milton and their kind. Particularly important for Wordsworth is Fink's emphasis on the republican equation of civic virtue with some form of social constraint. Wordsworth seeks this principle not so much in laws (though he does not discredit laws) as in creative habits bred by experience and environment. This is where the agrarian element enters in. MacLean has described many of the writings and debates that were current both in the English tradition and among the French Physiocrats. Political philosophy had always of course had a soft spot for the country life as the true locus of virtue, and this conviction was especially strong for certain writers of the eighteenth century. In ways that were variously politically polemical, ideological and mythological, the rural alternative seems to have been an especially tempting prospect for those disposed or obliged to set themselves against what they saw as the incipient hegemony of a metropolitan and commercial culture. Between the extremes of pastoral retirement and Georgic honest labour, there are a whole range of positions, and Wordsworth's writing, as we might by now suspect, partakes of most of them. In its two extraordinarily rich chapters on the eighteenth century in England, Pocock's *The Machiavellian Mo-*

ment (1975) makes much of the connection between agrarianism and civic virtue in some among Wordsworth's predecessors.

I shall now explore in detail the nature of Wordsworth's contribution to and use of this tradition. His most original invention upon it consists in the closeness and complexity of the relations demonstrated between the social, the economic, the environmental and the psychological. Most important of all, perhaps, his agrarian idealism is more coherent when seen as a *negative* critique of urbanization, than it becomes when we try to imagine its implementation as a *positive* alternative. This has all kinds of consequences for the interpretation of his poetry.

In a famous passage in the 1800 preface, Wordsworth writes about his attempt to prove that the human mind may be excited without the application of 'gross and violent stimulants', an attempt all the more necessary in these times:

> For a multitude of causes unknown to former times are now acting with a combined force to blunt the discriminating powers of the mind, and unfitting it for all voluntary exertion to reduce it to a state of almost savage torpor. The most effective of these causes are the great national events which are daily taking place, and the encreasing accumulation of men in cities, where the uniformity of their occupations produces a craving for extraordinary incident which the rapid communication of intelligence hourly gratifies. To this tendency of life and manners the literature and theatrical exhibitions of the country have conformed themselves.
>
> (*PrW*, 1: 128)

The reference to the working conditions in the cities echoes a widespread concern among eighteenth-century political economists about the alienating effects of the division of labour. As the workmen's lives become regimented, mechanical and repetitive, they do indeed produce more; but the continual performance of the same limited task by the same worker renders him passive and alienated. His craving for relief then becomes all the greater, but because work discipline has made creative leisure impossible, this can only take the form of a superficial and passive consumption of whatever distractions are most readily available. Since the working day is dulling and soporific, leisure time must be filled with 'excitement', but an excitement that can be passively received. It is important to assume here, I think, that Wordsworth is not just suggesting that urbanization and divided labour has negative effects upon those who work in factories; they would presumably never have read much poetry, though they might have been more likely to spend time in the popular theatre, such as it was. He is suggesting, more comprehensively, that the world-view or ideology that emerges from and goes along with the manufacturing economy will corrupt many of those who live within it, and at all social levels. By 'great national events' he presumably intends a reference to the French war, the details of which would have been intrinsically melodramatic, and were rendered the more so by the rapid circulation of newspapers eager for more and more such events. As the factory worker is conditioned to receive such information passively by virtue of his 'almost savage torpor', so the polite reader, who may have never set foot in a factory, is reading the same newspapers, or others equally marked by various sorts of excess and hasty judgement, along with 'frantic novels, sickly and stupid German Tragedies, and deluges of idle and extravagant stories in verse' (128). If he goes to the theatre, he witnesses the dramatic analogue to the same superficial stuff. These tendencies, acting 'with a combined force', render the experience of authentic and creative imagination less and less available to *any* of the social classes. The masters are just as trapped within their commercial world-view as are the men who labour in the factories by their actual experiences of working within a system based on division of labour.

This passage from the 1800 preface is a powerful critique of the developing national economy, but we can also see here the seeds of Wordsworth's later fears about the possibility of universal suffrage and popular radicalism. He saw a future of incremental brutalization for urban workers, making them less and less able to use a vote even should they obtain it, and more and more open to exploitation by demagogues and opportunists. We do not of course have to agree with this analysis to recognize its coherence, and in merely empirical ways the prognosis was quite correct. The population of England was to *double* between 1801 and 1851 (Dorothy Marshall, 1982, 3), and a greater proportion than ever before would reside in the manufacturing towns and in London. These trends were noticeable even in marginal Westmoreland, and more so in neighbouring Cumberland. Between 1801 and 1821 the population of the first rose by 'a little over a quarter', and by 1811 some 29 per cent lived in Kendal and in three other towns. In Lancashire, another neighbouring county, the statistics are much more emphatic (Bouch and Jones, 1961, 215–18). Wordsworth was absolutely right about the 'encreasing accumulation of men in cities'.

The preface to *Lyrical Ballads* thus predicts a gloomy future for both urban readers (the greatest segment of the readership) and for the poets who try to placate or entertain them – at least, for the serious poets. The 'grand elementary principle of pleasure', in its connection with sympathy, will be refigured; and the 'infinite complexity of pain and pleasure' that is the psychosomatic, polite analogue of the shepherd's career will be deadened into a lifeless and passive experience of surfaces and substitutes to be assimilated without thought or effort (*PrW*, 1: 140). Thus the 'great and simple affections of our nature' (126) will either not be experienced at all, or not understood as such when they are communicated to others.

The place of pleasure in Wordsworth's analysis of the condition of

England cannot be overemphasized, not least because he here privileges a category of experience that has not, for reasons which may themselves confirm the accuracy of his negative prognostication, much preoccupied social theorists since. Lionel Trilling (1965) has provided us with the beginnings of an understanding of this important subject, in identifying the denigration of pleasure with the rise of a commercial–consumer economy whose hegemony has refigured the word into a frivolous or luxurious context. He notes, though does not closely analyse, the importance of pleasure in the argument of Wordsworth's preface. In our own times, it is only psychoanalysis that has preserved a serious function for the concept of pleasure, and here it is largely limited to individual–somatic significations. But in Wordsworth's argument we may discover the terms of a crucial transition between what he described as authentic pleasure and its shrunken, latterday counterpart. Authentic pleasure, for Wordsworth, is the primary bonding agent in any healthy society. It is not antithetical to pain and hardship, but continuous with them as it emerges along with them. It is constituted by strenuous effort, rather than by passive leisure, and thus belongs within a community governed by undivided labour in a pre-commercial phase. Its epistemological manifestation is the imagination, and its ethical energy is one that harmonizes love of self with love of others. Authentic pleasure of this sort is, in Wordsworth's argument, exactly what is reproduced and stimulated by the best poetry in its representation of the elementary human passions.

This analysis of Wordsworth's is thus much more than just a contingent complaint about polite standards and ignorant readers. Editors have quite rightly pointed out the derivations of various arguments in the preface from familiar eighteenth-century sources; but in accounting for the parts, they have mostly missed the integrity of the whole as an account of the 'revolutions not of literature alone but likewise of society itself' (120). In this sense the case against poetic diction, for example, is not just a coincidental polemic, but it is part of and is dependent upon the argument for the negative effects of urbanization and the debasing of 'popular' culture. The 'gaudiness and inane phraseology of many modern writers', their 'false refinement' and fondness for 'abstract ideas' (*PrW*, 1: 116, 124, 130), are thus not arbitrary; they are the precise literary manifestations of the negative changes in the condition of England.

In the appendix that further explains the phrase 'poetic diction' (*PrW*, 1: 160–5), Wordsworth accounts for the difference between authentic figurative language and the 'mechanical adoption' of the same that is affected by many modern writers. The first derives from 'passion excited by real events', the second from an alienated notion of decorum. The first remains in touch with 'the language of men', while the second is just 'a motley masquerade of tricks, quaintnesses, hieroglyphics and enigmas'.

The first thus contains or preserves a 'republican' element, in its plain and intelligible contract between poet and reader; the second is the analogue of social division and even tyranny, whereby the poet adopts 'the character of a man to be looked up to'. If the reader does not understand such poetry, he is merely intimidated, and if he does, his 'self-love' is all that is gratified.

Wordsworth's historical logic is somewhat scrambled in this appendix owing to his invocation of a long-lost primitive integrity in poetic language. Most of his negative examples of poetic diction are, however, from the eighteenth century, and anyone familiar with such writers as Smith, Kames, Millar, Ferguson and Rousseau will recognize that the analysis of the superfluity and superficiality of poetic diction is the literary analogue of what the political economists thought of under the general rubric of 'luxury' – an obsession with what Adam Smith called 'trinkets and baubles' (1976, 421).[2] It is divided labour that produces the wealth necessary to sustain an indulgence in luxury, so that poetic diction is the natural expression of a surplus economy. Writers such as Pope and Gray themselves opposed the same commercial culture that Wordsworth criticizes; but, in the terms of his account, their writings none the less reproduce the stylistic symptoms of the very forces that they deplore.

The political allusions and affiliations of Wordsworth's preface need, as always, very careful deciphering. Burke, in his *Letters on a Regicide Peace* (1796), had also spoken out against the 'gaudy and pompous entertainments' that he saw as coming to dominate the modern theatre (1906, 6: 299); but he related this tendency not to developments intrinsic to British social and economic life but to the excesses of republican France, somehow exported abroad. The French had, Burke contends, closed the churches and built up the playhouses, popularizing thereby a 'theatrical, bombastic, windy phraseology of heroic virtue' (399). In the same spirit with which he had turned the traditional 'country party' rhetoric against the financial reforms of the French republic and the new 'stockjobbing' personality (1976, 307f.), Burke is here diverting the traditional argument against luxury, dear to republican profession, against extreme republican practice. While Wordsworth's language has much in common with Burke's, his purposes are quite different. They are much closer in spirit to those of Rousseau's *Epistle to D'Alembert*, which mounts a famous case against the introduction of theatres into Geneva. Rousseau's ideal Swiss are an exact prototype of the owner-occupier paradigm that figures in Wordsworth's writings: 'each family finds its artizans in itself, who work for no body else' (1767, 3: 87). Rousseau draws explicitly upon the traditional relation between civic virtue and life in the open air. Thus the ancients were 'exposed to the sun and rain; and generally bare-headed' (145), and lived a life in which work and pleasure were not distinct (196).

It is this condition of undivided labour and open air sociability that the proposal to build a theatre is seen to threaten. Rousseau makes an explicit statement of a belief that is everywhere implicit in Wordsworth: that local environments, both social and geographical, can change people, making it implausible to speak of a single entity called 'mankind' (23). As laws and the force of opinions change human nature, so too do 'the allurements of pleasure' (31). The theatre removes us from authentic experience, making us 'exchange reality for appearance' (92). This is both a result of and a further incitement to the decline into luxury. As an artificial pleasure to which only those feeling the 'weight of indolence' will resort (22), the theatre is once again related to the urban division of labour. The poor man is driven to attend it partly by the force of example, but also by 'poverty itself, which, condemning him to incessant labour, renders some relaxation the more necessary for him to support it' (165). Rousseau's logic here is a precise and expanded prefiguring of the argument that appears in such a condensed form in Wordsworth's 1800 preface; so much so, that one might suggest Rousseau as a likely source. Wordsworth is not against theatres *per se*, so much as against the hegemony of trivial plays; but otherwise, his fears about the 'encreasing accumulation of men in cities' are very close to those of Rousseau.[3]

At the same time, Wordsworth's case is not totally remote from a concern that we find in Burke's *Reflections*. Here, Burke upbraids the way in which the city of Paris has come to dominate French social, political and economic life (1976, 314f.). The woes that he lists are principally financial, but behind them one may sense the awareness of a relation between the dense metropolitan population and the propensity for volatile political behaviour. Jacobinism itself was often held to be a result of this phenomenon, and Wordsworth makes this exact connection in his *Cintra* pamphlet (*PrW*, 1:332). This will be discussed shortly; but we must at least register here the potential, in the 1800 preface, for an argument that disapproves of urban life for political rather than aesthetic reasons. The case against men in cities contains the seeds of Wordsworth's later association of city life with unstable political radicalism. His most genuinely 'democratic' polemic, in which he deplores contemporary urban culture for its assault on the psychological and thus social well-being of those condemned by divided labour to monotonous occupations, also contains the seeds of his later fears about the likelihood of an irrational and therefore ungovernable revolution taking place within the great cities. The 1800 preface does not, however, emphasize this potential; it is still rooted in a positive commitment to the language of ordinary men in rural environments. At the end of Chapter 3 (see pp. 97–107), I shall discuss the nature and integrity of Wordsworth's proffered alternative to 'poetic diction', that is, 'the real language of men in a state of vivid sensation' (118). This discussion will make better sense after some of the tensions in

Wordsworth's ideal agrarianism have been explored. For now, we are still concerned with tracing continuities.

Leaving aside the poetry and the evidence of the letters (which is in fact significant and will figure in Chapter 3), the next public manifestation of Wordsworth's concern with the relation between urbanization and national virtue comes in the essay that goes by the abbreviated title of *The Convention of Cintra*, published in 1809. This was in fact Wordsworth's longest prose work. It is emphatic about putting the case for pursuing the war against France with the maximum effort, and as such has often been taken as evidence of a change of heart in Wordsworth's political identity. In fact, he is quite clear about the terms of his criticism in this respect, and still able to vindicate his earlier support for the Revolution, prior to the annexation of Switzerland and the rise of Napoleon (*PrW*, 1: 226, 308, 330). What is less often noticed is the degree to which this pamphlet mounts a challenge to the British political establishment, not just in its short-term conduct of the war, but to the underlying social decay that brings about such conduct.

Ever the man of caution, Wordsworth himself was very worried that he had gone too far in this challenge. His letters written between March and May 1809 speak forth an obsessive fear of bringing upon himself 'the old yell of Jacobinism' (*MY*, 1: 312), and of risking the fate of Wakefield and Flower when they had attacked Llandaff eleven years earlier (327, 329, 332, 350). Before we sneer at this apparent timidity, we should remember that there had been a long and recent history of prosecutions for libel, intimately connected to the political conveniences of various governments. Wordsworth was justified in having second thoughts, for his essay contains arguments that might well have been deemed 'unpatriotic'. It contrasts the 'universal military spirit' (*PrW*, 1: 234) pertaining among the Spaniards with the vacillating and opportunistic behaviour of the British generals, the betrayers of traditional British republicanism and her 'long train of deliverers and defenders, her Alfred, her Sidneys, and her Milton' (288). Spain has shown herself an exemplary civil society, displaying the 'spirit of moral justice' (294) and its military corollary (the two went together for a whole tradition of republican thought from Lycurgus to Machiavelli and beyond) in a popular campaign in which every man acts for himself and yet all are of the same accord. Britain, on the other hand, has been corrupted by a hereditary political aristocracy that has survived by short-term, cynical manipulation rather than by rational appeal to the true sources of national virtue (304–5). In Britain, the governors relate to the governed as does the writer using 'poetic diction' to his readership. They try to bluster and deceive, and to compensate in appearance for what they lack in substance. They project not a 'sense of equality' but 'a degree of superiority which can scarcely fail to be accompanied with more or less of pride' (304). Like the corrupted poet, such politicians appeal to and subsist through the 'selfish passions' of their fellows (305). Throughout the political class, 'lifeless and circumspect Decencies have banished the grateful negligence and unsuspicious dignity of Virtue' (325).

In view of the recent case made by James Chandler (1984, 42–4) for the importance of Burke to the argument of the *Cintra* essay, it is important to point out that Wordsworth is not making the same claims as Burke, nor asserting the same priorities. He *does* share with Burke a distrust of the French, and of the Jacobins in particular. Like Burke, he speaks against any policy of appeasement in the British parliament; and Burke also measures the decline in the 'national spirit' against the integrity of the 'ancient system of laws and manners' (1906, 6: 85, 130). But Burke is a much more conservative thinker here. He fears a republican Spain (379), whereas Wordsworth is applauding precisely the republican virtue of the popular struggle. As in the 1800 preface, he focuses here on the decline in national virtue since the days of the classic English republicans and explains it in socio-economic terms. The rise of the 'Mechanic Arts' (324) has been accomplished at the expense of the spiritual well-being of the populace. The ideal relation between poetry and science that the 1802 preface had thought possible (*PrW*, 1: 141) has been negatively redirected by the doctrines of utilitarianism and the experimental philosophy. The 'Peasant or Artisan' who is the supposed beneficiary of the progress in the mechanical arts – better tools and houses, more productive land – has instead been rendered little better than a 'slave in mind'.[4] Robbed of the experience of 'self-support and self-sufficing endeavors', the 'springs of emotion may be relaxed or destroyed within him', so that he has little active interest in past or future (326).

With this version of a traditional eighteenth-century diagnosis of the corruption of society from top to bottom, shared also by such writers as William Cowper and John Brown, Wordsworth exposes the disease at the heart of British political life, and thus the deep-lying causes of such events as the Convention of Cintra. He does not blame the 'Jacobins', as Burke does, but points instead to the atrophy of the very patrician class that had been the corner-stone of Burke's ideal of government. In British society, everything is upside down. Robbed of the 'feeling of being self-governed', the bulk of the community is dependent upon a corrupt ruling class that merely demeans it further; whereas where 'civil liberty' and 'national independence' truly prevail, 'the labouring man leans less upon others than any man in the community', and it is the 'wealthy' who are effectually dependent upon him (327). Spain, a different culture, has other opportunities, and it is these that Britain has betrayed. In particular, Wordsworth argues that

Spain has nothing to dread from Jacobinism. Manufactures and Commerce have there in far less degree than elsewhere – by unnaturally clustering the people together – enfeebled their bodies, inflamed their passions by intemperance, vitiated from childhood their moral affections, and destroyed their imaginations. Madrid is no enormous city, like Paris; overgrown, and disproportionate; sickening and bowing down, by its corrupt humours, the frame of the body politic. Nor has the pestilential philosophism of France made any progress in Spain.

(332)

As Madrid differs from Paris so, Wordsworth might have added, it differs also from London, whose analogous assault on human nature (qualified indeed by a certain appeal) had already been transcribed in the unpublished drafts of *The Prelude*. It is to the developing manufacturing centres that political power will tend to gravitate, and here too are to be found all the ingredients of national corruption. Wordsworth's voice is here in unison with those of a host of eighteenth-century ruralists, of the likes of Goldsmith, Cowper and Smollett. Burke partakes of the same antimetropolitan rhetoric, but never in the cause of the kind of popular republicanism that Wordsworth holds out as possible for Spain.

The preoccupation with the negative effects of urbanization continues to inform his prose writings. Shortly after finishing the *Cintra* essay he began work on the *Guide to the Lakes*, which went through various revisions between 1810 and the fifth edition of 1835. Here, as befits the subject, the critique of the role of urban life in the national economy and psychology takes the form of a celebration of the alternative: rural self-subsistence. Drawing upon Thomas West's *The Antiquities of Furness* (1774), and omitting those parts of West's account that are negative about the early economy of the Lakes (see, for example, *PrW*, 2:405), Wordsworth describes the 'unofficial' primitive republic that managed to establish itself within the confines of a basically feudal society. In the remoter areas, geographical obstacles led to 'baronial or signorial rights' being largely unenforced (196), and even in the lower elevations the customary tenants lived a life in which 'divisions were not properly distinguished; the land remained mixed; each tenant had a share through all the arable and meadow-land, and common pasture over all the waste' (197). Such enclosure as did occur was, especially in the remoter areas, small scale and socially non-divisive. Thus it is both ethically and aesthetically approved: 'the intricate intermixture of property has given to the fences a graceful irregularity, which, where large properties are prevalent, and large capitals employed in agriculture, is unknown' (199). One imagines a socialized landscape somewhat akin to that described by Goldsmith as typical of the Auburn of his youth.

Even though the old feudal population has largely disappeared, these essential elements of Wordsworth's ideal rural economy are described as having been in place 'till within these last sixty years'. Enough corn was grown 'to furnish bread for each family, and no more', and each family unit 'spun from its own flock the wool with which it was clothed' (200). No trinkets and baubles here. There is no spare cash to exchange for them, and they do not figure much in the experience of these remote communities. Not for nothing is Wordsworth's 'chosen vale' also a *veil*. Leaving aside the actual state of this landscape around 1800, which will be the subject of the next chapter, the world here described is very much that of 'Michael' and of *Home at Grasmere*, where the strong instincts of self-interest (family and property) are combined into a sympathetic community, a 'Unity entire' (*HG*, 48). This is the proper environment for fostering the traditional republican virtues that the *Cintra* essay had regarded as now almost absent from Britain. There is (or was) a minister, but he is not a patrician so much as a man speaking to men, one 'in no respect differing from themselves, except on the Sabbath-day' (200–1):

> this was the sole distinguished individual among them; every thing else, person and possession, exhibited a perfect equality, a community of shepherds and agriculturalists, proprietors, for the most part, of the lands which they occupied and cultivated.
>
> (201)

Wordsworth's most complete statement of this just-vanished paradise comes a few pages later:

> Towards the head of these Dales was found a perfect Republic of Shepherds and Agriculturalists, among whom the plough of each man was confined to the maintenance of his own family, or to the occasional accommodation of his neighbour. Two or three cows furnished each family with milk and cheese. The chapel was the only edifice that presided over these dwellings, the supreme head of this pure Commonwealth; the members of which existed in the midst of a powerful empire, like an ideal society or an organized community, whose constitution had been imposed and regulated by the mountains which protected it. Neither high-born nobleman, knight, nor esquire, was here; but many of these humble sons of the hills had a consciousness that the land, which they walked over and tilled, had for more than five hundred years been possessed by men of their name and blood.
>
> (207)

Wordsworth does admit that this 'almost visionary mountain republic' is technically dependent upon proprietors in the 'open parts of the Vales' (207), but he has already made the point that these rights are but loosely invoked if at all. The community is thus an effectual if not a legal republic. It is (or was) founded on hard work and frugality, in the true Spartan tradition. In an unpublished section of the manuscript, Wordsworth describes how shepherding is 'not languid & effeminate, but full of hardship, effort, & danger, & diversified by the fluctuations of hope & fear' (311). In the best of all possible worlds, this might be the ideal readership for Wordsworth's poetry; but this order of men probably never had much time for literature, and it is disappearing anyway. To recreate the same conditions among town dwellers would be almost impossible.

The political propriety in Lakeland society was the parent of an aesthetic propriety. Buildings tend to have been made from the stone that occurs naturally in the landscape, so that they 'appear to be received into the bosom of the living principle of things' (203). Such buildings might perhaps be the most enduring symbols of the otherwise vanishing rural manners and virtues. For the *Guide* is itself the product of an increasing interest in the region among tourists and retirees. Wordsworth's hymn of praise is itself enabled by the very trends that most threaten the continuance of its ideals. Thus it ends with a sober analysis of the disappearance of the 'perfect commonwealth'. Husbandry and the domestic spinning industry are on the decline, and the yeomen are 'no longer able to maintain themselves upon small farms'. The result is exactly analogous to the process described in *The Deserted Village*, as the land passes from the many to the one, and from productivity to imparkment:

> The lands of the *estatesmen* being mortgaged, and the owners constrained to part with them, they fall into the hands of wealthy purchasers, who in like manner unite and consolidate; and, if they wish to become residents, erect new mansions out of the ruins of the ancient cottages, whose little enclosures, with all the wild graces that grew out of them, disappear.
>
> (224)

Wordsworth never makes the point, but this tendency is very much at one with the general phenomenon of tourism that brings his own book into print. The money for such mansions tends to come from the wealthy manufacturing centres, so that the country becomes a place of retirement rather than of work. It also appeals to poets anxiously stranded somewhere between these two subcultures, preferring 'studious leisure' to a busy world, and compelled thereby to explore the tensions of the middle ground.

For the moment, however, we are making the case for continuities; the ambiguities will be aired later. The *Two Addresses to the Freeholders of Westmoreland* (1818) that Wordsworth wrote in support of the Lowther interest, and against the Whig cause in general and Henry Brougham in particular, are notorious as examples of the poet's change of heart in political matters. Here, all traces of the youthful 'radical' seem to have disappeared. This being so, it is all the more important to understand the continuities that do appear; in a Coleridgean spirit, we must try to understand Wordsworth's understanding before convicting him of moral errors or apostasy.

The *Two Addresses* are relatively devoid of explicit references to the rhetoric of republican virtue as we have seen it in earlier texts (and indeed as late as the 1835 edition of the *Guide*). One reason for this might well have been the ambiguity in the tradition itself, which allowed the same rhetoric to be invoked by both sides of the political fence, Whigs and Tories. Fink (1948, 117, 124–6) offers a good account of how this came about. Because the ideally balanced state was often felt to have come into being in the late seventeenth century, any subsequent party that found itself in opposition could accuse the other of betraying the terms of the settlement. Correspondingly, any party in power could claim to be upholding or refining it. In this way, an appeal to the 'ancient constitution' was always a rhetoric of convenience.

What did, however, divide the Whigs and the Tories in 1818 and thereafter was the question of parliamentary reform, and especially the prospect of enfranchising the urban (propertied) population. Many historians agree that the 1832 Reform Bill that finally emerged from this debate was a 'Whig' bill; that is, it was primarily a concession to the urban middle classes, and a shift in the balance of political power away from the country and toward the towns and cities. This was, as we have seen, that element in the body politic most feared by Wordsworth. The party that had 'originated' the rhetoric of civic virtue in the English tradition was itself coming to be, he thought, the tool of opportunistic commercial interests.

The urgency of the situation as he perceived it led Wordsworth, in the *Two Addresses*, into a more emphatic faith in the virtues of the great landowners than, perhaps, he was ever to affirm thereafter. Having recast the history of the Whig opposition to the French wars as that of a gang of deluded visionaries obsessed with abstract rights and unable to see the facts (even though admiration for Fox is expressed in much later drafts of what was to become *The Prelude*), Wordsworth borrows the language of Burke to offer Lord Lowther as an ideal patrician, a 'tried enemy to all innovations' and a 'condemner of fantastic theory', but one who remains (of course) a 'Lover of the People' (*PrW*, 3: 155). Instead of invoking the 'perfect commonwealth' (which he confessed had disappeared anyway), he now applauds the aristocratic faction among the landed interest:

> As far as it concerns the general well-being of the Kingdom, it would be easy to shew, that if the democratic activities of the great Towns and of the manufacturing Districts, were not counteracted by the sedentary powers of large estates, continued from generation to generation in particular families, it would be scarcely possible that the Laws and Constitution of the Country could sustain the shocks which they would be subject to.
>
> (160)

Wordsworth often intimated his fears of the relation between urbanization, political radicalism of the most unmeditated sort, and thus a potential social revolution that would be merely destructive. Like Godwin before him, he had never approved of any drastic social change that was not the result of a prior revolution in thought and habit, without which only anarchy could result. Even the Llandaff letter is clear about the ideally short-term chaos of revolutionary France, seen then as a prelude to stable and enduring changes (*PrW*, 1: 33–4, 38).

We will see in the following chapter that any projection of the Lowther family as paragons of benevolent aristocracy must have caused Wordsworth some (at least) unconscious discomfort. This is, however, the gesture to which his obsessive fear of urbanization and its political implications seems to have driven him. Despite the favours which Wordsworth had by now received from the Lowther family – most famously Lord Lonsdale's arranging for him to take over the Distributorship of Stamps in 1813 – it is not enough to see the *Two Addresses* as simply the product of excessive gratitude or toadyism. This element is certainly not absent: Wordsworth's relations with the 'great' were always complicated. But there is at the same time a definite doctrinal integrity to his case, one that is not simply a rhetoric of convenience, and one that we should at least understand, whether we approve of it or not.[5]

In these documents, it is thus now Lowther who is one of the last examples of the 'genuine English character' (*PrW*, 3: 163). He represents the very best dispenser of 'time-honoured forms of subordination' (170), the key figure in the preservation of what Wordsworth calls, in a telling phrase, 'mellowed feudality' (175). This is the other end of the system that had been connected to the perfect republic of the remote valleys. It is because the feudal rights and conventions are implemented so lightly that, Wordsworth argues, radical reform is unnecessary. Time is already 'carrying what is useless or injurious into the background' (173), and thus needs no help from radical Whigs. In this image of a 'naturally' self-adjusting political society, Wordsworth is at his most Burkean; and from Burke also he takes the emphasis on the particular case over the general principle. Regardless of the 'abstract' nature of aristocracy, Lowther's record is an enlightened one (176).

Wordsworth is tapping into a traditional argument here. Davenant had made a case for the political disinterestedness of the great landowners – they are so rich they can afford to be impartial – as an alternative to the unstable interest of the commercial faction (see Kramnick, 1968, 177–81, 240–1), and Burke too had emphasized the political stability of the landed interest (1906, 6: 303). But Wordsworth's immediate fear of urban radicalism drives him to a hyperbolic confirmation of the virtues of the lords and masters that is a sort of prose analogue to the rhetoric of 'Gipsies'. Thus we do not simply have a measured expression of support, but also an imperative, perhaps partly explained by the short-term polemical purpose of these texts, to a 'humble reliance on the wisdom of our Forefathers' (181). There are noticeable fractures in this mood of sublime confidence, as when we are asked to tolerate 'partial evil' for the sake of 'general good' (183). Thus:

> In spite of pride, hardness of heart, grasping avarice, and other selfish passions, the not unfrequent concomitants of affluence and worldly prosperity, the mass of the people are justly dealt with, and tenderly cherished.
>
> (186)

These qualifications are of course registered to make the primary argument the more convincing, but they are registered none the less. They suggest that not all landowners were as principled as the Lowthers – or as Wordsworth finds himself obliged to suggest that the Lowthers were. Despite such brief moments of retraction or qualification, it yet remains the case that we have in the *Two Addresses* an extreme statement of Wordsworth's alienation from his fellow beings, and thus of his own displacement. He was not always able to incorporate himself so comfortably within the aristocratic ideology; but he did maintain this dominating fear of the urban masses and of the populist politicians who competed to control them. Ever more prone to violent rather than rational social change (179–80), this increasingly large segment of the population had from the very first been analysed negatively by Wordsworth. This negativity became hyperbolic for a number of reasons, among them his discovery, in the likes of Beaumont and Lonsdale, of a positive after-image of the old relation between poets and patrons. But his own personal distance from those he feared, and his inability ever to be a man speaking to these particular men, is also a factor. So, once again, is the essential ambiguity of his own vocation as a poet, an oxymoronic apostle of labour-in-idleness and property-in-motion.

There are two other documents that require notice in this account of the continuity of Wordsworth's agrarianism – or, more accurately, his critique of urbanization. In 1835, he appended a postscript to *Yarrow Revisited and other Poems*. This contains an extended discussion of the Poor Laws (of which more later), and also an argument in favour of the founding of joint-stock companies to encourage manufacturing workers to develop a sense of 'property' (albeit portable), and thus to become more aware of the desirability of 'public tranquillity' (*PrW*, 3: 248). This is clearly a policy designed to avoid revolutionary confrontations between masters and men, wherein whatever these societies might generate of a 'democratic and republican spirit' would be offset by the power of the landed interest and by 'a Church extending itself so as to embrace an ever-growing and ever-shifting population of mechanics and artisans' (249). At the same time, it is not totally cynical, and Wordsworth approves the degree to which the societies might act to deter the masters from illegally keeping down the price of labour (248). The rhetoric of this text is much less hysterically alarmist than that of 1818, and much closer to what was becoming the standard mellowed Toryism of a number of nineteenth-century reformers who saw that a little change might preclude a great deal of trouble. This is of course a generally 'reactionary' policy, but it is not devoid of genuine concern for the well-being of the town workers. Here, the agrarian interest is defended by trying to stabilize the threat from the forces that might otherwise threaten it.

Finally, we turn to the two letters that Wordsworth wrote to the *Morning Post* in 1844, on the subject of the Kendal and Windermere railway. He was, as is well known, very much against it, and the reaction of many subsequent readers was summed up there and then by the Board of Trade as they approved the project, noting that certain individuals could not expect 'to retain to themselves the exclusive enjoyment of scenes which should be open alike to all' (*PrW*, 3: 334). This is in fact a rather crude rendering of Wordsworth's case, which once again rests upon the now familiar analysis of the urban psychology, first put forward in the 1800 preface. Indeed, his exposition of the problems of 'tourism' is one that continues to find echoes in the 'wilderness' debates of the late twentieth century.

Once again, Wordsworth feels able to speak on behalf of the much-invoked 'yeomanry' and their profound attachment to their 'small inheritances' (339). He then argues that the Lake District cannot be experienced with any authentic pleasure by those who live for fifty weeks a year in an urban environment. They inhabit a different world, and acquire a different notion of 'reality' as a result of the corruption of both work and leisure that is imposed upon them. Moreover, the landscape of the Lake District is sublime, and the sublime requires a cultivated rather than an innate response: 'it must be gradually developed both in nature and in individuals' (343). Without 'processes of culture or opportunities of observation in some degree habitual', the experience will be as good as useless. The argument is thus not against railways *per se*, but against the prospect of using them to convey large numbers of urban dwellers to the Lakes with the maximum speed and convenience. In Wordsworth's view this benefits nobody. The pleasures of habitual solitude are ruined for the permanent inhabitants of the region, while the satisfactions open to the tourists are superficial or even absent. They see only a spectacle, or 'scene', and are likely to be disappointed. There is of course more than a measure of condescension in this view, but it is one that is perfectly in line with Wordsworth's general theory of the urban and rural psychologies. The populations of town and country quite simply exist for him in two different worlds, with two different realities. If this is to change, it will not be as a result of townspeople having brief glimpses of the Lakes, but will require a complete realignment of the national economy. Meanwhile, if townsfolk are to acquire any feeling for nature, Wordsworth recommends 'little excursions with their wives and children among neighbouring fields', that they may be 'trained' to a 'profitable intercourse with nature' (344).

There is a serious argument here, whether we choose to accept it or not. Wordsworth's ideal rustics, after all, go through a strenuous experience in learning their place in the landscape. Similar questions recur every time the National Park Service thinks about paving a road or building a campsite. What is 'nature', and for whom? The nuances of Wordsworth's argument are quite challenging. He is aware, for example, of the strong potential for false consciousness among both masters and men:

> The rich man cannot benefit the poor, nor the superior the inferior, by anything that degrades him. Packing off men after this fashion, for holiday entertainment, is, in fact, treating them like children. They go at the will of their master, and must return at the same, or they will be dealt with as transgressors.
>
> (350)

This contention is not unheard of, to say the least, among British wage labourers to this day. Wordsworth's suggestion that the masters' acceptance of the Ten Hours' Bill without loss of wages would be a more positive contribution to the welfare of their workers is not easy to dispute.

The poet's opposition to the extension of the railways to the shores of Windermere is thus not merely a result of the frustration of his own, Goldsmith-like 'schemes of retirement' (*PrW*, 3:339). It carries the convictions that have consistently featured in his writings about the need to preserve an agrarian alternative to the incipient urbanization of British culture and the British economy. These convictions appear and disappear, and are always under stress in ways that we must soon begin to examine more closely. But they are always there, providing a coherence to Wordsworth's political positions that has not yet been properly appreciated. Various important letters express the same views, for example the letter to Charles James Fox of 14 January 1801 (*EY*, 312–15), and that to Francis Wrangham of 5 June 1808, which discusses the reading needs and abilities of the rural and the manufacturing poor (*MY*, 1: 246–51). Writing to Daniel Stuart on 7 April 1817, he notes the dissolution of the ties between the various social classes in terms that would have been immediately intelligible to the Tory 'radicals' opposing Walpole's administrations: 'Everything has been put up to market and sold for the highest price it would bring' (*MY*, 2: 375). But at the same time as he invokes various traditional political languages about civic virtue and agrarian life, Wordsworth also provides what may well be a uniquely sophisticated account (or representation) of how urban and rural environments can determine the perceptual faculties of the human mind.[6] So different are these worlds, that they produce two social systems, two cultures, and thus two literatures to sustain and delight them. The predicament of the 'rural' poet, for Wordsworth as for Goldsmith before him, is not only in crisis because his audience is increasingly smaller and less influential; it is also an audience that has little or no need for poetry. The poet is thus displaced from the very social units that he celebrates as a healthful paradigm of communal life. Being a man of two worlds, he is properly of neither.

This is one of the reasons why Wordsworth's views on civil society are much more coherent as an attack on urbanization than as a positive alternative in country life. Personal and objective perceptions or convictions both contribute to render the community of subsistence owner-occupiers a difficult ideal to envisage in practice. Wordsworth was never a radical agrarian, and was thus anxious to maintain his 'perfect republic' as in fact a subset of the feudal order. At times, as we have seen, he mounts a passionate defence of the landowning classes. Thomas Spence, for example, was also an advocate of the renewal of national virtue through the cultivation of economic independence and psychological wholeness. But for him this could only come about with the abolition of all private ownership of land, which he saw as responsible for 'every kind of lordship which overtops and choaks all the shrubs and flowers of the forest' (1797, 4). For Spence, even Thomas Paine was too cautious in being prepared to maintain existing property divisions: for all his 'boasted liberty and equality', he was still able to 'roll in his chariot on the labours of his tenants' (1793, 32). Wordsworth would never have gone this far, and the fact that others did might help to explain some of the tensions in his own image of the ideal rural economy. He agrees with such writers as William Ogilvie (1781, 37), that lack of land for independent cultivation must make a man 'mean spirited and servile', but he does not go as far as Ogilvie in asking for the practical redistribution of land, to a degree that is compatible with the general preservation of the social order. Godwin too had made practical suggestions, however implausible they might now seem to us, in appealing to education combined with an appeal to the 'love of distinction' in order to persuade the great and wealthy to give up land to the dispossessed and propertyless (1976, 736). Other writers made a similar argument for quite different reasons, to do with political expediency rather than moral conviction. Thus Arthur Young wants every man to have enough land to keep a cow and a pig, because 'such a man is always a faithful servant, has a stake in the country, and never prompt to riot in times of sedition' (1801, 139). *The Anti-Jacobin Review*, 3 (1799), 458–9, notes of a similar scheme that it 'tends to connect more firmly the links of the social chain; and to encrease that attachment to *home*, which is the source of much individual comfort and of infinite public good'. If Wordsworth did not make the argument for radical redistribution, no more did he make this explicitly 'repressive' case. To acknowledge the presence of such contemporary analogues to Wordsworth's agrarian ideas is to become the more curious about the particular emphasis that he gives to them. That they are almost always presented as the features of an ideal but tragically *vanishing* past makes us aware both of the problems in his available social models, and of his own vision as refracted through the consciousness of a poet of displacement. To the first of these reservations we may now address ourselves.

3
Another guide to the lakes

The real state of sublunary nature

It is with some trepidation that I enter upon a discussion of the 'real state of affairs' in Wordsworth's Lake District. Such a discussion is properly the domain of professional historians, who would rightly expect that any credible judgement be based upon a detailed and critical immersion in the available primary materials: parish records, figures for agricultural output, enclosure bills, precise conditions of tenancy, and so forth. This task is well beyond what I am able to attempt here, and I must therefore rely heavily upon available summaries and the researches of others.

Moreover, anyone familiar with the writings of the historians of the period 1750–1850 will already be aware that it is perhaps the most contested period in British economic and social history. The debate about the effects of industrialization and the capitalization of agriculture upon the standard of living and the yet more evasive 'quality of life' has sharply divided the professional scholars. Even where the 'facts' are relatively firm they have been interpreted in quite different ways, according to whether individual arguments have tended toward the legitimation or the negative criticism of the 'modern' society that was coming into being during the period. The fact that the population doubled between 1801 and 1851 tells us just that; it does not tell us that the social–economic revolution should be judged positive or successful *because* it enabled an unprecedented increase in population. The improvements in sanitation, medicine and nutrition brought about a dramatic decrease in mortality, especially infant mortality: there can be no doubt that in this sense people were better off than ever before. But any judgements about the comparative 'quality of life' must take into account many other factors, such as working conditions, crime rates and so on. Such judgements are rendered particularly unstable because, in asking the kinds of questions that Wordsworth himself was asking, we are making assumptions about the potential gaps between conscious and unconscious well-being. There is no doubt that the real wages of a Manchester factory operative were higher than those of a Westmoreland smallholder, but this does not prove anything about their relative happiness. Jeremy Bentham was indeed convinced that money provides the only *measurable* standard for estimating satisfaction in a social, intersubjective way: 'It is from his money that a man derives the main part of his pleasures; the only part that lies open to estimation' (1952, 3:438). Wordsworth would have contested both parts of this assertion, since the kind of satisfaction he envisages is antithetically related to the money supply and to a surplus economy. The Manchester worker may have more money to spend, but the options and temptations open to him in spending it may have powerful negative effects on his wholeness of mind and spirit. And, because his entire notion of 'reality' may have been effectively refigured, he will not be aware of the value of what he is missing.

We may note here two examples, one recent and one of longer standing, of the divisions among the historians about the period of early industrialization. The long-standing case has grown up around the writings of J.L. and Barbara Hammond, first published between 1911 and 1919, and subsequently reprinted. G.E. Mingay, in his introduction to the Hammonds' *The Village Labourer* (1978a, xxiv–xxv), accuses them of being 'unhistorical' in applying modern standards to eighteenth-century circumstances, and, in a strange appeal to some standard of 'fair play', of being 'unrealistic in expecting too much of the landed interest'. John Lovell, in his introduction to *The Town Labourer* (1978b, xxiv), wields a set of statistics: there were only 192,000 adult workers in the textile mills in 1833, whereas there remained 210,000 cotton hand-loom weavers, so why stress the disappearance of the latter? These and other related questions will continue to be asked and should be asked. But they do not 'refute' those aspects of the Hammonds' case that they purport to refute; they merely open up the whole question of the relations between facts, trends, and discourses – the structures of ideas that give 'facts' their contemporary import and urgency. Level-headed historians have taken some exception to the declamatory tones that open *The Skilled Labourer*

(1979, 1), which claim that the 'history of England at the time discussed in these pages reads like a history of civil war'. But the rights and wrongs of such a claim can only, I suspect, be adjudicated by assiduous research into limited and specific cases. Particularly, no totalized estimation of the 'quality of life' is likely to prove convincing or defensible. How can we measure, or propose, exact degrees of alienation or false consciousness when such terms are themselves argumentative and contested?

My second example is more recent: the argument between Michel Foucault and Lawrence Stone about the 'effects' of the Enlightenment. Stone (1982) attacked Foucault's image of the Enlightenment as an 'age of confinement' by stressing the humanitarianism apparent in both the declared motives and the results of many eighteenth-century scientists and reformers. He is right to expose the limitations of such totalizing schemas of psycho-historical change, tending as they do to propose a unitary 'Enlightenment' which, once established, will tend to accommodate subsequent inquiry and make it less open and sceptical than it should be. Fanned by the winds of fashion, we will start to see confinement everywhere. Stone is right to demand the careful and minimally opinionated scrutiny of empirical data as a prelude to grand interpretative gestures (a scrutiny that Foucault himself has often applied). But Foucault is right to dwell upon the degree to which facts themselves come into being within discursive frameworks that help to constitute which of them are found meaningful. He is also right to recognize the place of the unconscious: to mean well is not to do well, on many occasions. As so often in such debates, both parties are defending different varieties of truth, and the task for others must be the understanding of the place of each perspective in the examination of particular cases.

These are only two examples of the kinds of issues that divide the historians of the period of Wordsworth's life. The 'facts' *are* facts, but seldom *simply* facts, and some may not be facts at all. Only close and precise attention can resolve these questions. For, despite all these and other related difficulties, history is emphatically neither 'bunk' nor a nightmare from which we had better awaken. It can inform us from the position of difference, even as we must weigh its evidence very carefully. Certain kinds of information about the identity of literature can only come from a historical inquiry, as I hope that this study will demonstrate. The continuities and discontinuities between the arguments of Wordsworth's poems (and prose) and the recoverable details of life in the Lake District are not always open to conclusive proof, but they are occasionally so, and always pertinent to any explanation of the poetry of displacement.

I have argued in Chapter 2 that much of Wordsworth's aesthetic and social commentary can be coherently understood as a negative criticism of the process of urbanization. In the broadest sense, there can be little doubt that he had definite empirical grounds for being concerned about the process itself, leaving aside its arguable consequences. As the population of Britain approximately doubled between the publication of *Lyrical Ballads* and the death of their (major) author, that of London grew at a still greater rate, from 957,000 to 2,360,000. Even more dramatic was the population increase in the northern industrial towns nearer to Wordsworth's home. In the same period, Preston grew from 12,000 to 70,000, Salford from 14,000 to 63,000, and Manchester from 70,000 to 303,000 (Dorothy Marshall, 1982, 20). Thus, even though only about half of the 1851 population could be described as truly urban, we must note the rapid *rate* of change that would vindicate Wordsworth's perception of 'the encreasing accumulation of men in cities' (*PrW*, 1: 128) as a perfectly convincing one. It also seems to have been the case that, despite the general improvements in sanitation and so forth, very few of these towns were able to cope with their burgeoning population explosions without the creation of slum conditions for many of their poorer residents. Other evidence suggests that the sobering details of Engels's *The Condition of the Working Class in England in 1844* were not at all imagined (see Dorothy Marshall, 1982, 28–55 *passim*). Thus the figures for life expectancy, if they can be relied upon, seem to confirm a strong empirical base for the traditional distinction between city and country life that Wordsworth refines upon in his own writings. Edwin Chadwick's 1842 *Report on the Sanitary Condition of the Labouring Population of Great Britain* notes that for the agricultural county of Rutland, professional and gentlefolk had a life expectancy of 52; tradesmen, farmers and shopkeepers 41; and mechanics and labourers 38. The corresponding figures for Manchester were 38, 20 and 17; for Liverpool, 35, 22 and 15 (Dorothy Marshall, 1982, 39). Even if these figures should prove to have been exaggerated, it is hard to think away completely such a dramatic difference.

The statistics for and against a trend toward rural depopulation need to be set against the likelihood that population was increasing almost everywhere. J.D. Marshall's (1961) study of rural Lancashire has found that the remoter areas tended to lose population – mostly young, single people (like Luke in 'Michael') – while agricultural areas close to developing urban centres tended to show an increase (93, 114). Even if massive rural depopulation did not occur, the effects of this sort of redistribution would surely have appeared in the remoter areas as among the effects of urbanization. Moreover, Wordsworth is reacting less to a general phenomenon than to the disappearance of a particular class of people, the so-called 'statesmen'. Bouch and Jones's evidence does indicate a significant increase in the population of the two Lakeland counties in the period 1801–21, with Cumberland growing faster and urbanizing more dramatically than Westmoreland (1961, 215–18). But they also suggest that these growth

rates were much smaller than those of the neighbouring northern counties, Lancashire in particular. Even by 1830, Carlisle and Whitehaven
held only 20,000 and 17,000 people, respectively (317). Nothing in this
evidence conflicts with Wordsworth's analysis. Even if growth was slower
in Westmoreland, as it was, the perception of an incipient threat could
only have been enhanced by an awareness of what was happening in
Lancashire. At the same time, the fact that Westmoreland was relatively
more agrarian must have made it at least partly convincing as an alternative.

In Britain at large, the percentage of the labour force that was in
agriculture seems to have dropped substantially between 1700 and 1800.
Between 1760 and 1860 the proportion of the national investment
accounted for by agriculture dropped from 33 per cent to 12 per cent
(Floud and McCloskey, 1981, 90, 132). Various qualifying details need to
be remembered: there were more handloom weavers than we might think,
and many people still lived the traditional village life. But it remains clear
enough that both the actual stability and the imagined integrity of country
life were changing in most parts of Britain. Wordsworth's sense of the
increasing rate of urbanization, whether or not we agree with his sense of
its implications, seems to have been well founded in fact. And on the
matter of implications, even a set of statistics about the relative pleasures
of country life and town life, culled from a number of people who had
lived both, would not prove or disprove his arguments. Wordsworth's
conviction of the importance of thinking about this question, moreover,
could only have been sharpened by the popularity of utilitarian approaches
to social analysis in which all such non-quantifiable terms of analysis were
being eschewed. By insisting that the best potential of human nature is
inseparably tied to the kind of pleasure principle that *cannot* be measured
in scientific or mathematical terms, Wordsworth is standing out against
the major trends in contemporary political economy.

We cannot, then, hope to decide upon the justice or injustice of Wordsworth's pleasure thermometer as applied to various groups of town
dwellers and country dwellers. He admits implicitly, as Rousseau had
admitted explicitly, a high level of false consciousness at work in this
disjunction. Like many later social theorists, Wordsworth argues that
people are unlikely to know their own best interests, most of all when they
have had no authentic experience of the alternatives. Indeed, the disabling
condition of urban life is that the townsfolk *cannot* know what is best for
them; the culture of divided labour and crowded lives has corrupted the
interaction of work and leisure to such a degree that proper judgements
can no longer be made. We might choose to see something uncomfortably
condescending in this analysis of Wordsworth's, depending as it does on
the totalized dismissal of accurate self-consciousness in the city dweller;

and one of the major historians of the period, none other than E.P. Thompson, has argued in *The Making of the English Working Class* and elsewhere that the working man knew exactly what was best for him, and how to get it. He was defeated, when he was defeated, not by his own analytical confusions but by superior power. I suspect that for the most part this question can, once again, only be decided in the particular, and that different particulars would produce different answers. Wordsworth's image of the psychology of the city dweller is certainly hyperbolic and reductive; but the fact that it registers as a symptom of his own displacement does not entail that it can contain no measure of objective credibility. In the case of the relations between city and country, Raymond Williams (1975) among others has shown the degree to which the whole subject is from the first embedded in mythologies both dead and living.

Great care is thus required in trying to build up a picture of the life that some of Wordsworth's unpoetical neighbours might have been leading in the remoter parts of the Lake District. We have seen that his analysis certainly reifies the city workers, with whom he had little actual contact, even as we have recognized a polemical purpose to this reification, as well as a degree of intrinsic credibility. But what of the 'statesman' class to which he turns for his alternative image of civic virtue? Were they paragons of Spartan frugality, immune to the temptations of luxury and idleness? Did they stand secure upon their inherited lands, in happy harmony with the local aristocracy? Wordsworth, of course, never puts things as simply as this; but by asking such questions we can come to an understanding of the terms of his more complex presentation of the facts of life in rural Westmoreland.

There are a number of contemporary accounts of the 'statesmen'. Bailey and Culley's *General View of the Agriculture of the County of Cumberland*, first published in 1794 – significant parts of which were reprinted in William Marshall's *Review and Abstracts of the County Reports* (1818, 1: 156–203) – notes the relatively high incidence of small, owner-occupied properties in the county. But only about one third of the land was freehold, the rest being held

> by that species of vasselage called *customary tenure*; subject to the payment of fines and heriots, on alienation, death of the lord, or death of tenant, and the payment of certain annual rents, and performance of various services.
>
> (1794, 11)

The authors are eloquent about the hardships involved in such customary tenure, and very much aware of the degree to which it inhibits improvement in farming and management techniques:

One great obstacle to improvement, seems to arise from a laudable anxiety in the customary tenants to have their little patrimony descend to their children. These small properties (loaded with fines, heriots, and boon days, joined to the necessary expense of bringing up and educating a numerous family), can only be handed down, from father to son, by the utmost thrift, hard labour, and penurious living.

(44)[1]

The fact that 'every little saving' is hoarded up for the payment of the *'eventual fine'* leaves nothing over for the modernization of farming or the acquisition of knowledge through travel. Marshall also refers to the fines and heriots as 'a train of evils ... which must necessarily gall and fetter every man who holds under so base a tenure' (1818, 1: 174). But he goes on to quote a passage that first appeared in the 1797 Newcastle edition of Bailey and Culley's work (181), in which the very psycho-social attributes of Wordsworth's ideal personality are ascribed to the statesmen, i.e. those who *do* appear to hold their land in true freehold:

These 'statesmen' seem to inherit with the estates of their ancestors, their notions of cultivating them, and are almost as much attached to the one as the other: they are rarely aspiring, and seem content with their situation, nor is luxury in any shape an object of their desires; their little estates, which they cultivate with their own hands, produce almost every necessary article of food; and clothing, they in part manufacture themselves; and have a high character for sincerity and honesty, and probably few people enjoy more ease and humble happiness.

(1818, 1: 182)[2]

These men are happy in themselves, in other words, even if in the eyes of others, and according to national standards of productivity, they are somewhat backward.

Bailey and Culley thus seem to make an important distinction between the true freeholders and those who hold the land under the conditions of customary tenure. Andrew Pringle, the author of the companion volume for Westmoreland (1794), makes the same distinction, and adds to it a strikingly Wordsworthian elegy on the decline of the true statesmen:

It might be useful to know what proportion of the lands in the county is possessed by that numerous and respectable yeomanry already men-tioned as occupying small estates of their own, from 10 l. or 20 l. to 50 l. a year. These men, in contradistinction to farmers, or those who hire the land they occupy, are usually denominated *statesmen*. They live poorly, and labour hard; and some of them, particularly in the vicinity of Kendall, in the intervals of labour from agricultural avocations, busy themselves in weaving stuffs for the manufacturers of that town. The consciousness of their independence renders them impatient of oppression or insult, but they are gentle and obliging when treated by their superiors with kindness and respect. This class of men is daily decreasing. The turnpike-roads have brought the manners of the capital to this extremity of the kingdom. The simplicity of ancient times is gone. Finer clothes, better dwellings, and more expensive viands, are now sought after by all. This change of manners, combined with other circumstances which have taken place within the last forty years, has compelled many a *statesman* to sell his property, and reduced him to the necessity of working as a labourer in those fields, which perhaps, he and his ancestors had for many generations cultivated as their own. It is difficult to contemplate this change without regret; but considering the matter on the scale of national utility, it may be questioned whether the agriculture of the county may not be improved as the landed property of it becomes less divided.

(40–1)

There is a great deal in this passage that is precisely akin to some of Wordsworth's views. He could never have written the last sentence, since he regarded such 'improvement' as merely a means of stimulating the further expansion of the towns and cities. He is also reluctant, as we shall see, to attribute the decline in the well-being of the statesmen to any internal corruption, any receptivity to finer clothes and more expensive viands. Furthermore, Wordsworth is often rather vague about the distinction between true freeholders and customary tenants. This distinction is important to both Bailey and Culley and to Pringle, as it had been to William Hutchinson, whose *Excursion to the Lakes* (1774, 292–4), had also been emphatic about the 'badges of servility' that affect the copyholders, those subject to customary tenure (see MacLean, 1950, 102).

It seems important, therefore, to try to establish a rough sense of the particular landholding patterns of Westmoreland and Cumberland, since the early commentators often make firm distinctions between freeholders and customary tenants, while Wordsworth tends to blur them, or to suggest (as we have seen him doing) that the latter were effectively as well off as the former.[3] According to an article in *The Gentleman's Magazine for 1766*, cited by Bouch and Jones (1961, 229), about one quarter of Cumberland belonged to some 30 lords and gentlemen, but there were also 10,000 small landholders with estates of £10 to £100 a year. Various writers found these small proprietors either abjectly deprived or sturdily independent, or something in between the two. Bouch and Jones (230) use the term 'statesmen' in a sense that includes the customary tenants, while many of the early sources and all of the *Oxford English Dictionary* definitions are clear that it properly applies only to the freeholders in possession of the fee simple. They also note that the 1829 *Directory* uses the term 'yeoman' to include both these classes (334).[4] This makes it hard to be sure of the exact proportions of each type of yeoman in the 1829 figures, which indicate that in the various wards of Westmoreland between 21 per cent and 41 per cent of the land was held by that class as a whole, with the lowest figure applying to the Lonsdale ward. Bouch and Jones do however maintain that there were 899 true 'statesmen', i.e. freeholders, remaining in 1829, and 439 as late as 1885 (237). They were obviously in decline, but they had not disappeared; we will find ourselves wondering why Wordsworth seems to have been more emphatic about their disappearance than he need have been.

The most detailed account of local landholders is to be found in the regrettably unpublished doctoral dissertation of Wallace Douglas (1946, 73–100). He explores the tendency to identify the freeholders with the customary tenants, but concludes from a close examination of a number of sources that the legal distinctions were always carefully maintained. He confirms the views of the contemporary commentators in suggesting that the customary tenants, in view of the encumbrances and insecurities of their holdings, would have been unlikely to fulfil the ideals of Wordsworth's 'perfect republic'. Not only were the fines and heriots a burden when they could be paid; their implementation was also a way for the owners to bring their land back into demesne, converting the tenants into labourers. Douglas further suggests, following his sources, that the customary tenants were more numerous than the freeholders, making up perhaps two thirds of the Cumberland 'yeomen'.

Douglas argues that the real character of the remote parts of the Lake counties was primitive and backward, so that the old ways of life were disappearing more from their own inner contradictions than from outside pressures (130–7). In particular, the decline of the yeomen was at least in a large part the result of the engrossing tendencies of the local county families. After a study of one detailed case history, that of the Flemings of Rydal (Wordsworth's neighbours), he suggests that the local yeomen were vanishing not only because of large economic trends and the impact of industrialism, 'but also because of the profit-seeking of a family from the Tory gentry' (154). When we look again at such poems as 'Michael' and 'The Brothers', we must bear in mind the evidence he puts forward.

So much, for the moment, about the real state of sublunary property among Wordsworth's yeoman neighbours. On the national level, it has been suggested that the decline in the numbers of owner-occupiers was checked by about 1750, and was followed by a period in which this class consolidated and perhaps expanded, until its fortunes faded once again in the years after Waterloo (Chambers and Mingay, 1982, 131–3). Wordsworth was not alone in seeing the demise of the owner-occupiers as a matter of national concern. He shares with Cobbett, for example, a sense of the virtues of smallholdings. As late as 17 March 1821, Cobbett writes in the *Political Register* arguing for 'a return to *small farms* to be *absolutely necessary* to a restoration of anything like an English community', and for an end to the process of pauperization that has become a national trend (cited in Hammond, 1978a, 153). In 1822 he published *Cottage Economy* to instil a measure of self-sufficiency in vegetable growing, bread making, and the brewing of beer, advocating also an abstention from tea drinking (a form of luxury) and a commitment to native provisions and sheer hard work. Wordsworth might well have winced at the prospect of any alliance with Cobbett; but on the matter of the psychological and social benefits of a frugal, owner-occupier existence (as on the corresponding dangers of urban life) they are in significant agreement. The difference is, of course, that Wordsworth does not seem ever to have been engaged in urging the return to small farms as an active policy for the present; his affiliation to the ideal takes instead the form of lamenting a vanished past.

Setting what we can recover of the 'facts' against Wordsworth's own reports, we may suggest the following conclusions: the so-called 'statesmen' were not so much a thing of the past as Wordsworth seems to suggest, though they were in decline; fewer of the customary tenants than he suggests probably lived effectually free from crippling 'feudal' obligations; and the doings of the local landlords might have been less unambiguously benevolent than he finds himself, especially in 1818, deciding. While many of the 'yeomen' who figure in the poetry are shepherds, J.D. Marshall's analysis of the period before 1749 suggests that to the average dalesman cattle were more important than sheep, so that it was more common for them to have cattle without sheep than the other way around (1973, 192, 197, 199). Thus, unless things changed drastically before 1800, we may suspect Wordsworth of playing up the 'pastoral' motif, though of course it might have been true that the very poorest land in the remotest vales was indeed more suitable for sheep.[5]

The Lakeland economy was not, however, based entirely on pasturage or agriculture. As well as the textile industry, the landscape would have registered the signs of slate quarrying, and of the mining of coal and iron ore – the last especially important here, relative to the rest of England (Bouch and Jones, 1961, 246ff.). It is surely the case that the trend from an agrarian to an industrial base was proceeding more slowly here than in many places. These mining and quarrying concerns were well established before the 'industrial revolution'; although the mechanization of the textile industry seems to have been a more recent phenomenon, it probably never kept up with the pace of things in Lancashire and Yorkshire. The second (1797) edition of Pringle's *General View* includes a more detailed account of manufacturing than had appeared in the first edition, but his conclusion is still that the 'commerce of Westmoreland is not yet so extensive as to have any sensible effect upon its agriculture', and that the 'manufactures ... are not of much greater importance than its commerce' (1797, 299). Douglas (1946, 137–41, 333–4) makes a rather stronger case. And we should note the now-common assumption that Britain 'experienced a commercial revolution before an industrial revolution' (Floud and McCloskey, 1981, 102). In other words, whatever exact degree of industrialization had or had not taken place in particular places, the nation as a whole had, from the 1690s onwards, been experiencing psychological and structural changes of the sort that would make an industrial revolution possible. This earlier 'revolution' has been linked to the foundation of the national debt (Dickson, 1967) and to the growth of the consumer economy (McKendrick *et al.*, 1983). From Defoe and Mandeville onwards, we can trace a constant curiosity about the relations between luxury and surplus and the national virtue (see also Pocock, 1975, 1985; Sekora, 1977). The socio-economic elements of Wordsworth's writings are thus not *simply* to be judged against the precise empirical conditions of the Westmoreland economy, but must be understood within a discursive–factual complex of a century-old tradition of speculation. At the same time, the empirical conditions cannot be ignored, and it is often in the play between the two kinds of information that the tensions of some of Wordsworth's poems can be contextualized and understood.

There are three other major topics that we need to consider in this attempt to construct another guide to the lakes: the local status of the enclosure movement, the actual record of the Lowthers as landowners and employers, and the general state of the rural manners that these and other conditions supported. Exact conclusions are, as ever, hard to come to, but much may be learned nevertheless.

In the generally combative field of social history, the specific subject of enclosure may well be the most contested topic of all. Broadly speaking, historians tend to emphasize the gains and the losses according to whether they attend to increased productivity as a way of supporting population growth, war, and industrialization, or to the loss of common rights and the passing away of a pre-capitalized agrarian life.[6] Although enclosures had been going on since the Middle Ages, they were especially common in the period of the agricultural revolution. In the period 1750–1850 there were some 4000 private parliamentary acts of enclosure, three quarters of these falling in the years 1760–80 and 1793–1815 (Hobsbawm and Rudé, 1973, 6; Chambers and Mingay, 1982, 77). The matter of enclosure was able to focus and relate a large range of urgent debates – common rights, productivity, the game laws, pasturage and tillage and, connected to all of these, the aesthetics of landscape (see Barrell, 1973). Given the high level of sensitivity that most contemporaries showed about enclosure, Wordsworth seems surprisingly unconcerned with the subject. Some of the reasons for this are surely personal; he was not a 'peasant' poet, and did not see the land in the same way that John Clare, for example, did. But it is also the case that enclosure was less important in the north of England than in the arable lands of the southern counties. What was the local profile of the enclosure movement?

Bouch and Jones (1961, 233) conclude that about half of Westmoreland was enclosed by about 1830, following particularly heavy activity during the Napoleonic wars. The precise details and implications of this are hard to gauge. On the lower, more fertile lands, it is likely that enclosure involved the conversion of pasture to tillage. But on the higher pastures, where little if any agriculture of any sort could be carried out, enclosure would probably have brought about some redistribution of land, along with an improvement in the breeding performance of sheep as a result of keeping apart the healthy and unhealthy animals. It seems that exact records of Westmoreland enclosures are hard to come by (Douglas, 1946, 142), though one imagines that the engrossing activities of such families as the Flemings would have been accompanied by the practice of enclosure. Wordsworth's references in, for example, the *Guide to the Lakes*, are not negative and suggest, if anything, a small-scale process set going by the tenants or freeholders themselves rather than by the larger landowners (*PrW*, 2: 167, 189, 198–9). Wordsworth does not mention the enclosure of common land, energetically proposed by some and bitterly resented by many among the poor.

If the Flemings and others were rapidly enclosing the landscape, we may suspect that Wordsworth's relative silence on the subject has to do with a reluctance to acknowledge the less than benevolent doings of the local gentlemen; but we should note that his position was certainly very different from the vigorous advocacy of enclosure voiced by many observers. Arthur Young, for example, organized much of his prolific output around the conviction that 'a waste acre of land is a publick nusance' (1767, 167). He argued against all further emigration, and against the development of all but the most essential manufactures, until no such acre might remain (191f.). Travelling between Penrith and Keswick, he is 'melancholy' at finding so much land still uncultivated, and his heart leaps up when he beholds a few enclosed fields around the shores of Windermere and Derwent Water (1770, 3: 134). Wordsworth's early political antagonist, Richard Watson, Bishop of Llandaff, wrote a preface to Pringle's *General View* (1794) in which he described the 'improvement' of Westmoreland as a matter of 'national concern' (7). And Sir Frederic Eden, in *The State of the Poor* (1797), noted the sufferings consequent upon enclosure as 'an evil to be lamented' (1: xiii), but not one weighty enough to balance the advantages. For

> the advantages which cottagers and poor people derive from commons and wastes, are rather apparent than real; instead of sticking regularly to any such labour, as might enable them to purchase good fuel, they waste their time, either like the old woman in Otway's Orphan, in picking up a few dry sticks, or in grubbing up, on some bleak moor, a little furze, or heath.

> (1: xxviii–ix)

He neglects to ponder the condition of the Goody Blakes of this world, unable to find regular labour, and now deprived of their few dry sticks.

We have seen that when his defence of the agrarian ideal seems to have been under greater than usual stress, in 1818, Wordsworth put forward a vision of rural Westmoreland in which the peasants and yeomen were in a harmonious and co-operative relation with the local gentry.[7] This alone would have inhibited him from developing, had he wished to, any critique of the capitalization of agriculture. Wordsworth's resonant description of 'mellowed feudality' (*PrW*, 3: 175) depends upon a remarkably extravagant faith in the virtues of the ruling class. Here is another specimen of the Burkean rhetoric that we have already noted in the *Two Addresses*:

> Opulence, rank, station, privilege, distinction, intellectual culture – the notions naturally following upon these in a Country like England, are, protection, succour, guidance, example, dissemination of knowledge, introduction of improvements, and all the benefits and blessings that among Freemen are diffused, where authority like the parental, from a sense of community of interest and the natural goodness of Mankind, is softened into brotherly concern.

> (186)

This passage is remarkable for its total avoidance of the possibility of self-interest entering into the behaviour of the great families, and also for its artful containment of the fraternal relation (one of the leading rhetorical initiatives of republican France) by the parental. Wordsworth goes on to assert that this is 'no Utopian picture' of the condition of England. To what degree did the Lowthers live up to this image?

Wordsworth's personal experiences alone ought to have taught him the limits of any recourse to the general good nature of the aristocracy, since he had suffered from one Lord Lonsdale the sins of omission that were rectified by the next, on the matter of the money that had been owed to his father. Perhaps, like many an Englishman, he was the more grateful for a gesture of redress from the high and mighty than he would have been from one of his own peers. For he is never closely critical of the local gentry, a class he described in 1844 as a 'blessing to these vales' (*PrW*, 3: 352). Whatever potential for misused authority that the patrician role might contain, Wordsworth gives no sense that it was so exercised in his own neighbourhood. We have already noted Douglas's account of the Flemings of Rydal (1946, 150–5), whom he presents as putting real pressure on the customary tenants. His account of the Lowthers describes their manipulation of the electoral divisions of the county (100–6), and their reliance upon coal mining in the increase of the family fortunes (106–18) suggests that they might have been far from the ideal agrarians intimated in the *Two Addresses*. Bouch and Jones (1961, 258–9) note that the Lowthers became more rather than less involved in coal mining through the eighteenth century; and if the Hammonds' account of the working conditions of the Tyne and Wear miners (1979, 10–37; 1978b, 120–3) is at all typical, then it is unlikely that labour relations in the Cumberland coalfields would have been especially enlightened. The Cumberland mines were deeper than those in Northumberland, and even more difficult to work.

The wealth that the Lowthers derived from mining was mostly put into land, so that by the end of the eighteenth century they were not simply affluent patricians, but one of the greatest families in England. Douglas's account of the self-interested politicking of various individuals does not give a clear sense of the minute particulars relating to treatment of tenants; but it does suggest that the policy of aristocratic disinterest that Wordsworth describes in 1818 was not at all their dominant motive for entering politics. At the wider national level, we may assume that the ideal of benevolent paternalism was sometimes fulfilled and sometimes not. J.D. Marshall (1961, 117) does refer to the ready charity of the Lancashire gentry as a 'stabilising factor' during the hard times of 1820, and Cobbett applauds the foresight of Lords Winchelsea and Stanhope in allowing each of their labourers 'a piece of ground sufficient for the keeping of a cow' (1979, 107). But such charity was often political rather than heartfelt, and instances of sheer indifference could certainly be adduced on the other side.

Without conclusive details about the Lowther record on the treatment of tenants and freeholder neighbours, we can still suspect that, in a world where good and ill were so frequently mixed, Wordsworth's hyperbolic panegyric partakes of more than a measure of the improbable. Once again, his argument probably takes its energy more from a negative perception of the alternatives, than from a positive case for the Lowthers of this world. He almost says as much in a letter to Lord Lonsdale of 21 January 1818:

> What else but the stability and weight of a large Estate with proportionate influence in the House of Commons can counterbalance the demo-

cratic activity of the wealthy commercial and manufacturing Districts? It appears to a superficial Observer, warm from contemplating the theory of the Constitution, that the political power of the great Landholders ought by every true lover of his Country to be strenuously resisted; but I would ask a well-intentioned native of Westmoreland or Cumberland who had fallen into the mistake if he could point out any arrangement by which Jacobinism can be frustrated, except by the existence of large Estates continued from generation to generation in particular families, with parliamentary power in proportion.

(*MY*, 2: 413)

If his major concern is to resist what he sees as the threat of Jacobinism in the urban centres, then Wordsworth can perhaps not afford to question too closely whether the Lowthers' control of six out of ten of the local parliamentary seats (Bouch and Jones, 1961, 326) is really 'in proportion'.

Having at least questioned the credibility of Wordsworth's image of the ruling class, we must now consider the 'real state' of public manners in rural Westmoreland in the same period. Much of the contemporary assessment of this situation tells us more about the priorities of the observer than about 'things as they were'. Wordsworth himself never pretended to be a man 'of the people', nor to be writing *for* them, with any direct address. And his writings contain many more qualifications of the ideal of rural virtue than has often been acknowledged by detractors anxious to convict him of some fundamental blindness. We do not need the peregrinations of a Rawnsley, or the affected 'realism' of Harriet Martineau's exposure of the 'drunkenness, quarrelling and extreme licentiousness with women' in the town of Ambleside (cited in Chambers and Mingay, 1982, 194), to realize that such things must have been going on in Westmoreland as in many other places. Douglas, as ever, is admirably precise – about the poor nutrition, the high density of alehouses, and the consequent instances of alcoholism (1946, 118–37). Wordsworth was less blind to this than has often been supposed, and his theory of civic virtue is moreover not based on any appeal to innate good nature, but on the disciplinary effects of poverty and hard work. It is thus open to him to relate the woes of local life to an incumbent present, and to locate his ideal in a vanished past. He was not alone in the polemical direction of his remarks. Sir Frederic Eden spoke of the northern peasant as living 'as long, and as healthy, and, probably, far more contented and happy, than the South-country labourer, who is forever receiving, and forever wanting, assistance and charity' (1797, 1: viii). J.D. Marshall (1961, 91; 1973, 200) offers evidence that the empirical prototypes of Wordsworth's Michael were indeed committed, as much by necessity as by choice (and Wordsworth's point is that the one becomes the other), to a life of undivided labour, and a good deal of it. And such figures must surely have lived a frugal and unluxurious life. Eden notes that while southern labourers tended to buy their clothes, those of the north made their own, 'shoes and hats excepted' (1: 554–5). In this respect, life in Kendal, because of its manufacturing industries, was an exception to that in 'other parts of the county' (3: 752–3).

Clearly, a great deal more primary research would be necessary in order to present anything approaching a complete picture of the actual life of rural Westmoreland around 1800: the work of Wallace Douglas (1946) would be the proper point of departure. We can suggest, meanwhile, that Wordsworth is not engaged in a complete falsification of the evidence, but that he is prone to heighten certain aspects of the situation to enhance the polemical force of his arguments, and perhaps to avoid facing some of the more uncomfortable implications of his position. In particular, the ambiguities of the behaviour of the great families, and the blurring of the distinction between freeholders and customary tenants, perhaps explains why the 'perfect republic' that he speaks of is located in the *past* (though it does appear in the present in the – unpublished – *Home at Grasmere*). After reading Wordsworth's published writings, we might assume that the statesmen had disappeared completely, whereas they clearly had not. It is tempting to compare Wordsworth, in this respect, with those writers in nineteenth-century America who lamented the 'inevitable' extinction of the Native American, in a way that appeared sympathetic but was also a way of avoiding facing the question of what to do about those who had *not* disappeared. If the Flemings were at all typical in their treatment of the customary tenants, we can see why Wordsworth would have found it more credible to locate his image of benevolent feudalism in past generations.

This does not of course rob it of all integrity or conviction. We may say, rather, that Wordsworth's case is best understood as a negative vision of urbanization rather than as a credible representation of life in the country at the time of writing. The present, I suggest, could not bear the weight of the alternative argument that Wordsworth was anxious to propose. Having said this, it must be noted that his own writings do include a good deal of evidence against the present viability of the rural ideal. Sometimes such evidence is left to stand for itself, and sometimes it is awkwardly disavowed. For example, it is in the *un*published parts of the manuscript of the *Guide to the Lakes* that we find an extended description of the slate quarries, things that oblige the author to bring himself 'back to the appearances of an ordinary day' (*PrW*, 2: 314). There is a half-successful attempt to incorporate these images into a sort of 'industrial sublime', but details of the miserable working conditions of the quarrymen do come through in their tendency to breed 'savage tempers and dispositions somewhat infernal' (316). Later in the same unpublished text, there are details about the preponderance of gambling among the yeomen of Borrowdale

(346–8). This is partly excused as a 'natural' way of preventing 'tranquillity from settling into stagnation'; then, in a moment of inspired synthesis,
Wordsworth blames the lead (i.e. plumbago) mines. So valuable has this
substance become, that local youths were tempted to start stealing it from
the mines. They thus acquired habits of dangerous excitement and the
expectation of ready profit: 'extravagant expectations & comparatively
inordinate longings with a train of novel & reprehensible indulgences
could not [but] be the consequences of these irregular incitements' (348).
The heady market for black lead is thus the begetter of the card tables of
Borrowdale! Rural manners are not perfect, but their failings are related to
the 'gross and violent stimulants' (*PrW*, 1: 128) of urban commercial
society.

There is a convenient neatness to the fact that these parts of the manuscript remained unpublished, as if Wordsworth did not want to contamin-
ate the *Guide* with such forthright details of rural life. The ambulatory
gentlefolk who would have been its likely readers might not have appreciated such information. It is however very typical of Wordsworth that he
wrote these passages, instead of ignoring the subject altogether, as a more
efficiently repressive consciousness might have done. His letters contain a
good deal of evidence that he knew perfectly well that the state of rural
manners was less than exemplary. This evidence is apparent in both early
and late letters. The miserable state of the Racedown poor is the subject of
a letter to William Mathews in October 1795 (*EY*, 154); the letter to Fox
of January 1801, blames the 'spreading of manufactures' for breaking up
the 'bonds of domestic feeling among the poor' (*EY*, 313); and in June
1825, he writes to Lord Lonsdale, opining that 'this whole neighbourhood
is in sad disorder from the habit of excessive drinking, becoming more and
more prevalent' (*LY*, 1: 370). Even in 1825, however, Wordsworth does
not blame rustic human nature for such phenomena, as a George Crabbe
might have done; he blames high wages, the indifference of the local
clergy, and the fact that the 'Resident Gentry' neither exist nor behave as
true proprietors. In very similar terms, he had written to Daniel Stuart
some years earlier (April 1817) about the dissolution of the 'moral cement'
resulting from the hegemony of a utilitarian economy:

> The connexion between the trading and landed interests of country
> towns undergoes no modification whatsoever from personal feeling,
> whereas within my memory it was almost wholly governed by it.
>
> (*MY*, 2: 375–6)

The image of how things had been 'till within the last sixty years' (*PrW*,
2: 206) or, elsewhere, until 'within these 30 years' (*MY*, 2: 375), thus
exists in part as a polemical alternative to a present that Wordsworth saw
as open to an inevitable corruption.

Knowing what we now know about the 'real' state of affairs in Wordsworth's Westmoreland, and imprecise as much of this account has had to be, we can begin to understand some of the tensions and confusions, as well as the evasions, that appear or fail to appear in Wordsworth's poetry. These tensions are there from the first, and are not simply the result of later revisions in political priorities. Wordsworth's ideal 'moral cement' depends upon the image of benign co-operation between the very highest and the next-to-lowest in the social order, the great landowners and the smallest landowners, those on the verge of disappearing altogether. As such, his social model is very like that of a later conservative, W.B. Yeats, whose facsimile of an Ireland consisting of peasants and hard-riding country gentlemen similarly writes out the middle class, the inhabitants of that contested space to which Wordsworth himself belonged, and which he saw as the origin of all that was negative in the incumbent urban economy and culture. Given the historical inevitability of such changes in the condition of England, it is not surprising that the desire for the *locus amoenus*, the 'spot of holy ground' (*DS*, 38) with which the poet is constantly obsessed, should be so often threatened by the overt or implicit perception of discordant details. Even in *Home at Grasmere*, where he is seeking to become the 'owner' of an 'unappropriated bliss' (42), he notes that he is

sometimes forced to cast a painful look
Upon unwelcome things, which unawares
Reveal themselves

(82)

The 1794 drafts for *An Evening Walk* contain details of an industrial accident that do not appear in either of the published texts of 1793 and 1836 (*EW*, 140). The images of labour and industry that do remain in the published poem do not interfere with a 'peace unbroke' (80); the 'thunders' of the blasted quarry are only 'heard remote'. Wordsworth is already at work on the evasive reference that typifies, for example, the 'Tintern Abbey' poem.[8] But it remains reference, even when in the form of repression. The peculiar integrity of much of Wordsworth's poetry is that it records so much of the evidence that counts against its own arguments. At times this is most apparent in the processes of revision, at times in the published texts themselves, when we can learn to read them. As representations of a personality both individual and historically typical, these poems then become records of displacement and conflict. The assertions of unity and integration that Wordsworth's writings contain are then best understood not as achieved conclusions and stable dogma, but as symptoms of an aspiration.

The real language of men

Much of the personal–historical insecurity that we have traced in Wordsworth's poetry may be related to the tension we have now seen to be apparent between things as they probably were and things as Wordsworth wished them to be, as set forth in his polemical ideals about the social imagination. His arguments are more convincing, we have seen, when they explain what is wrong with the condition of England, than when they propose to set it right. Hence, indeed, the tragically retrospective mood that pervades much of Wordsworth's social criticism.

The aspiration toward organic wholeness and harmony is not just a part of this social criticism; it appears in various other vocabularies in Wordsworth's writings, which cannot be analysed in any detail here. For example, as the editor of his own poems, Wordsworth was constantly trying to arrange them into some natural or easeful order that might constitute a 'legitimate whole' (*PrW*, 3: 28).[9] The *Poems* of 1807 were introduced with an apology for their status as short, occasional items rather than as the 'work of length and labour' that Wordsworth had hoped to have finished (*1807*, 527). And, had he ever faltered in his image of himself as the ideally whole author of a whole body of poetry, he had Coleridge to urge him on by prescribing impossibly perfect preconditions for the composition of the great philosophic poem (*HG*, 4–7), itself only to be produced by a poet who could 'assume the station of a man in mental repose, one whose principles were made up' (*HG*, 3). Wordsworth was never such, nor did he ever write a poem that could have proved him thus. So little so, indeed, that we might wonder whether his famous image of *The Recluse* as a 'gothic Church' (*PrW*, 3: 5–6) might have meant to leave some space for the sort of 'careless exuberance' that Thomas Warton identified as the 'Gothic' essence of Spenser's *Faerie Queene* (1762, 15). Wordsworth never did quite see his way to producing what he described in an unpublished fragment as the prototype of all great art:

A function kindred to organic power,
The vital spirit of a perfect form.
(*Prelude*, 1959, lvi)

In the context of the argument of this study, there is one aspect of Wordsworth's organic aspiration that must be examined in some detail. In Chapter 2 we discussed the close connections between his important critique of the fashionable 'poetic diction' and his analysis of the corrupting influence of the urban psychology. It is now appropriate to look at the positive arguments for an alternative language also proposed in 1800 and 1802. They too are best understood when we have digested the evidence for how things were in the English rural economy. The preface to *Lyrical Ballads* was probably written in the Lake District, and the ideals that it puts forward are significantly formed by the poet's sense of the effects of a marginal subsistence culture. We have seen that poetic diction is the literary corollary of a surplus, luxury economy; what would be the literary equivalent of the frugal life led by the ideal (and vanishing) statesmen?

An understanding of this subject has been hampered by its intrinsically confusing prospectus – of which more in a moment – and by the eagerness of Coleridge and others since to convict Wordsworth of proposing for poetry a simple facsimile of 'the language of *real* life' (Coleridge, 1983, 2: 8). Having interpreted Wordsworth's intentions as such, it is very easy to make fun of them. Coleridge's main account of the language question (1983, 2: 42–57) is complex and up to a point quite just. He is especially right to point out that Wordsworth's ideals pertain not to 'low and rustic life in and for itself', but to 'a particular mode of pastoral life, under forms of property, that permit and beget manners truly republican' (45). Such a qualification is entirely and perceptively consistent with Wordsworth's major premises, and the author's own failure to point this out may be attributed either to blindness, to haste, or to a tendency to locate the argument a bit too loosely within the vocabulary of an inherited primitivism. Coleridge is right to observe that the essential human passions, and thus their linguistic expressions, do not appear in all country people in the same way.

As Coleridge continues his account, however, it becomes clear that his deepest objection is based on an alternative model of the social order from that upheld by Wordsworth in 1800 and 1802. For him, the best parts of language come not from objects, but from 'reflection on the acts of the mind itself' (54). He interprets the word 'objects' in the familiar modern sense, meaning things outside the self; but it is possible that Wordsworth intended a less exclusive usage, namely 'that to which action, thought or feeling is directed' (*Oxford English Dictionary*, 1586–1845), or 'something which on being seen excites a particular emotion' (*Oxford English Dictionary*, 1588–1878). His reference to 'objects from which the best part of language is originally derived' (*PrW*, 1: 124) may then refer not to inert matter, but to things already acted upon by the mind. Be that as it may, Wordsworth's vocabulary is less than transparent, and Coleridge takes it in the way that is most convenient for him in setting forth his ulterior conviction, that the best part of language is to be found in the speech of *educated* people. They are the true initiators, and from them the norms descend *down* through the scale of society:

> If the history of the phrases in hourly currency among our peasants were traced, a person not previously aware of the fact would be surprized at

finding so large a number, which three or four centuries ago were the exclusive properties of the universities and the schools; and at the commencement of the Reformation had been transferred from the school to the pulpit, and thus gradually passed into common life.

(1983, 2: 54)

Whatever the precise logical connections that hold together Wordsworth's account of language, it clearly depends in the most general sense on the notion of education from 'below'. Vague as he might be on the question of ultimate origins, he means to contend that in the *present* it is precisely the educated orders that have been corrupted. Just as the critics of luxury saw the disease to be spreading from the top to the bottom of the social hierarchy, so 'poetic diction' begins among the fashionable classes and taints the rest of the language by example. His argument is thus aimed at educating the learned class *out of* their predilection for gaudiness and superficial excitement. By 1817, when he published his account, Coleridge was clearer than ever that what was essential to the health of the body politic was an ideally disciplined clerisy whose dogma would percolate downwards and outwards (and indeed 'upwards' to an inert aristocracy) through the medium of the established church. A passage in *The Friend* makes it clear where Coleridge's priorities lie. He is seeking to argue for organic coherence as the best part of speech, and he finds it in the language of the educated man:

It is the unpremeditated and evidently habitual *arrangement* of his words, grounded on the habit of foreseeing, in each integral part, or (more plainly) in every sentence, the whole that he then intends to communicate. However desultory and irregular his talk, there is *method* in the fragments.

(1969, 1: 449)

Coleridge is not simply defending a class system, so much as making a case for the more coherent speech of the educated man. But the system is there nevertheless. Coleridge makes syntax the yardstick of integrity, whereas Wordsworth is more concerned to privilege the relation between particular words and phrases and the perceptions and emotions that call them forth. Coleridge's rearrangement of Wordsworth's argument is convenient for his own polemical priority, which depends upon the organization of parts into wholes, and is implicitly political while explicitly linguistic. The one who controls the grammar of the language and masters its complex rules of subordination is also the one who should be entrusted with the governing of society at large.

What exactly are the proposed features of Wordsworth's alternative? Many commentators have failed to find any startling sense in his ideas about language; it is indeed a confusing prospectus, and if the relation to political economy is not perceived, then it can easily seem an insignificant one.[10] Editors have rightly pointed out that it is a highly eclectic assimilation of common eighteenth-century notions about the integrity of primitive speech (see *PrW*, 1: 167–89). This indeed is the case, and further confusion arises from Wordsworth's three successive descriptions of the kind of language he intends to draw upon for poetry. In the 1798 advertisement he specifies his source as 'the language of conversation in the middle and lower classes of society', and then immediately worries that he might have 'descended too low' (*PrW*, 1: 116). In 1800, this language is deemed to include an element of passion or excitement: it is 'the real language of men in a state of vivid sensation'. But it is also a 'selection', and one that has been fitted to metre (118). In 1802 the selection has only been made 'as far as was possible', and it has been further modified by 'a certain colouring of imagination' (123) which we must deduce to be the poet's own.

Despite these confusions, no version of the argument ever suggests that Wordsworth intends a *simple* transcription of 'ordinary language'. He always notes the superaddition of metre, and the purification of the source-diction from 'what appear to be its real defects, from all lasting and rational causes of dislike or disgust' (124). No recourse to what is 'really the case' about ordinary language will either prove or disprove the point; what Wordsworth maintains is that the best parts of language are likely to be used by speakers who have remained uncontaminated by the vanities and superficialities of 'polite' culture. Moreover, he does not mean us to focus upon words as things in themselves, but to perceive the relative integrity of their relation to, that is their publication of, authentic passions and feelings. The appeal of simple and unpretentious language is exactly its minimal potential for distracting; it does not substitute surface complexity for a signification of what is behind it and has brought it into being.

Thus, in one of the most satisfying accounts of Wordsworth's language theory that I have seen, Stephen Land (1973) emphasizes the poet's 'profound mistrust of words' (163). He argues conclusively that Wordsworth has no tolerance for organicist models according to which a word might be regarded as essentially rather than arbitrarily connected with a state of mind or passion. Words are by nature devious, so that the poet's task is one of limiting their potentially distorting effects by keeping his language as simple as possible. Extending this case, we may see that the models for such simplicity are indeed those who have been least corrupted by urban life. It is not education that is corrupting, in principle (and Wordsworth's yeomen are not conceived as illiterate), but the manners of the commercial economy and their literary analogues.

Wordsworth thus gives four associated explanations for his choice of 'low and rustic life' in demonstrating the 'primary laws of our nature' (*PrW*, 1:122–4). First, the 'essential passions' can develop better here, being less 'under restraint'; second, in this state of 'greater simplicity', they may be more accurately contemplated and communicated; third, the 'manners' that develop from the elementary feelings are more 'durable' and are integrated into rural 'occupations'; and lastly, because the 'passions of men' are here 'incorporated with the beautiful and permanent forms of nature'.

In the context of the psycho-social model of mind whose details were explained in Chapter 2, these statements make sense. The first and second are clear enough: the best that is potential in human nature develops most fully in the lower and middle ranks of rural society, and is also best expressed there because the people are less under the influence of 'social vanity' (124). Theirs is a 'subsistence' rather than a 'surplus' language, devoted to plainness and propriety. Wordsworth's third claim makes the point that there is less in the working lives of country people, involving as it does a higher than normal degree of undivided and owner-occupier labour, that works to corrupt the modest, expressive speech habits and the culture ('manners') that supports it and which it represents. It is the fourth claim that needs the most careful interpretation. The 'beautiful and permanent forms of nature' are 'the best objects from which the best part of language is originally derived' (124). We have seen what Coleridge made of this; alternatively, it can be read as a very shorthand summary of that prominent Wordsworthian idea that objects in conjunction with acts of mind create the feelings and passions that produce the best parts of language. Speaking of 'The Brothers', Wordsworth analogously describes a 'moral attachment' that is 'early associated with the great and beautiful objects of nature' (126); that is, associations with other people are also bonded into these objects, as they are in the 'Poems on the Naming of Places'. These objects are the more impressive in a visually uncluttered landscape, and thus more efficient for registering both continuity and change, i.e. the measure of each in the other that Wordsworth saw as essential in preventing both fetishization and formlessness (see Simpson, 1982a, 1982b). Whatever hints Wordsworth's account might contain of the popular Tookean materialism, according to which the maximum possible number of words would be explained as deriving directly from sensory experiences or things in themselves, are more than offset by the implicit logic of the argument, and by the later description of mind and world as 'acting and re-acting upon each other, so as to produce an infinite complexity of pain and pleasure' (140). It is the action and reaction that produces the best part of language – the language of the essential passions.

Wordsworth's claims for the positive nature of rustic language do then make sense as part of his criticism of urban, so-called 'polite' culture. This language is not a thing in itself, but an expression and embodiment of an entire way of life; of the available literary languages, it is the one most innocent of corruption. Of course it must be used selectively, modified by metre, and in obvious ways reorganized. Of course Wordsworth does not claim that all country dwellers speak like Michael, but his argument is not implausible in the ways that Coleridge and others have suggested, and it accords with that famous passage in the third of the 'Essays upon Epitaphs' where he insists that if words be simply a 'clothing' instead of an 'incarnation' of thoughts, then terrible damage will be done to their user, whom they can 'alienate from his right mind' (*PrW*, 2: 84–5). Clothes can be taken off and changed at will, and in their finer varieties were traditionally an image of the luxury economy; countless eighteenth-century moralists comment on their tendency to encourage both disguise and fetishization. Wordsworth's alternative to 'poetic diction' is a republican alternative, akin to an appeal to the 'naked truth' with which Godwin sought to present virtue. Vice, thereby, 'deprived of that varnish with which she delighted to gloss her actions, of that gaudy exhibition which may be made alike by every pretender, will speedily sink into unheeded contempt' (Godwin, 1976, 478).

Having said this much, it remains striking that Wordsworth does not present any elaborate examples of the speech of the lower and middle orders of rural society, except those which find their way, selected and modified, into the poetry. Most strikingly, he refrains from any incursion into dialect, of the sort that had marked the poetry of his beloved Burns. It is interesting to reflect upon this decision. Rawnsley (1889) takes great delight in trying to reproduce the Westmoreland dialect, and Wordsworth himself probably spoke with a modified north-country intonation. But, unlike Burns, Clare, Lawrence, Tennyson, Hardy and various other British poets, he makes no attempt to reproduce this in his poetry.

The first point to make is that such an attempt would have been embarrassing to his argument. For dialect is in itself an indicator of social difference, and would not thus have much assisted a poet who was consciously seeking to encourage his readers to meditate upon the essential similarities between man and man. There are thus very few instances in literature where the representation of dialect has not tended to consign its speakers into the realm of the comic or the unintelligible. In *Tom Jones*, for example, Squire Western's dialect is a fitting expression of his crude manners and archaic politics; it cannot be shared by his daughter, who is a 'heroine'. Shakespeare's rustics always know their place, or always end up there, however appealing a pastoral alternative they occasionally present. Clare's localisms kept his poetry from the audience that needed most to learn from it, and continues to do so to this day. And Burns, for whom Lallans was more than a mere dialect, seems to have become popular in spite of rather than because of his commitment to the representation of his language. Matthew Bramble, in Smollett's *Humphry Clinker*, finds that Lismahago's Scots intonations give 'a clownish air even to sentiments of the greatest dignity and decorum' (1983, 215); and Henry Mackenzie, reviewing Burns in 1786, remarked that the pleasure of reading him involved 'such a constant reference to a glossary, as nearly to destroy that pleasure' (Low, 1974, 69).

It is perhaps a mark of Burns's own schizophrenia that the poem published as 'The Twa Dogs' was originally titled 'Stanzas to the Memory of a Quadruped Friend'; even in the same poem, Scots and 'polite' English often sit side by side. At times this may be ironic, but the evidence is also there for the kind of anxious uncertainty that has been felt by many a speaker of English as he or she moves between regional and received pronunciation. Despite Wordsworth's consistent admiration for Burns, most eloquently expressed in the 'Letter to a Friend of Robert Burns' (1816), there is no mention of the dialect question. Wordsworth's silence is surprising, given how marked a feature of Burns's poems this is. The poems collected as 'Memorials of a Tour in Scotland, 1803' (*PW*, 3: 64–96) are full of conscious references to Burns, including such Scots locutions as *braes* and *gowans*. But they are never prevalent enough to strain easy intelligibility, so that they appear more decorative than substantial. In January 1807 Wordsworth wrote to Scott requesting a Gaelic phrase for the poem that would become 'The Blind Highland Boy' (*MY*, 1: 123); he takes the trouble to seek an authentic image of the alternative language, but again does not allow it to take over the diction of the poem. Dorothy's journal account of the tour often registers Scots idioms in italics or speech marks, for example '*varra halesome*' and '*wee* lad' (1952, 1: 209–10); and, of course, many of the people they met were Gaelic speakers, with only a few words of English if any. Thus, in such poems as 'To a Highland Girl' and 'The Solitary Reaper', the otherness of the subject's language is the essential drama of the poem. In 'Stepping Westward' we see one of the very few occasions on which the actual speech of a country person does in fact stimulate and demonstrate the poet's convictions about the medium. Dorothy describes meeting two 'neatly dressed women, without hats', one of whom speaks the line 'What! you are stepping westward?' (1952, 1: 367). The coincidence of this expression with a fine Sabbath sunset is a perfect example of a diction that is in expressive but quiet harmony with the great and permanent forms of nature. The fusion of the literary, pagan and Christian traditions, with the soul's journey and the simple act of walking forth each intimated in the other, are perfectly expressed in this unsolicited phrase heard in a remote place. But of course this is not dialect; it is the plain, biblical English that most of Wordsworth's admired protagonists employ.

   This is the clue, I think, to the language that Wordsworth most admired: it is one devoid of dialect features. Such features could only have complicated his presentation of his own relation to his subjects, awkward enough at the best of times, given his common status as a man between all factions or classes and participating wholly in none. And they would also, in all likelihood, have divided his readership, or at the very least distracted them from his real priorities. The poetry does include a few local words, but they are usually glossed, and are never allowed to threaten the dominance of a plain, general English. Words like *pike, sugh, intake, gill, clipping, potter,* and *tarn* (*DS*, 74, 80; *EW*, 36; *LB*, 164, 231; *PW*, 2: 339; *1807*, 7) are glossed in footnotes, while *merry night* (*BW*, 69) is explained as a local custom. In the first editions of the 1807 *Poems*, Wordsworth used the dialect form *poll*, but altered it to *pole* in 1815 (*1807*, 233).
   This is not to be read as evidence of some distance from or disrespect for 'the people', although the distance was indeed there and comes out in other ways. On the contrary, the absence of dialect words and of the phonetic transcription of local accents is an inclusive rather than a divisive strategy. What Wordsworth reproduces is a plain and unmarked simple English that can be *read* by speakers of any dialect convention, regardless of how the imagined original speakers might have pronounced their words. The commitment to a basic 'national' English without the markers of the polite classes means that there is little or nothing in the diction that cannot be read by all, however they might be in the habit of *sounding* the words. Wordsworth agrees, implicitly, with Cobbett, who maintained that as long as the words of the language remained nationally standard, how they might be pronounced makes little difference (1906, 16).
   Wordsworth's case against poetic diction, and his proposed alternative language for poetry, thus makes perfect sense as a prospectus for widening the readership and reforming the language of poetry along basically 're-publican' lines. But it is the language *of poetry* that is at stake. He never did pretend, except in such instances as that of 'Stepping Westward', to be transcribing the language that 'the people' as a whole were actually speaking. (On the other hand, we should not forget that some among them surely were speaking it.) For he knew well that there was no such entity as 'the people', except as composed of an increasingly divided collection of subgroups. And, of course, his was never a poetry *for* the people, even though it did not preclude their attentions. In 1808 he wrote to Wrangham opining that there was among the rural labourers neither much 'disposition' nor 'occasion' to read at all, let alone read poetry (*MY*, 1: 247). Along with the Bible, Wordsworth finds only a few 'halfpenny' ballads and histories in local circulation, and continues rather plaintively:

I have many a time wished that I had talents to produce songs, poems, and little histories, that might circulate among other good things in this way, supplanting partly the bad; flowers and useful herbs to take place of weeds. Indeed some of the Poems I have published were composed not without a hope that at some time or other they might answer this purpose.

(248)

And yet rural life, Wordsworth admits, can manage without him, and people like him. Not only are his ideal communities very busy ones; but in small societies where all are known to all, reading and writing are relatively less necessary for basic communication and recollection (hence the unmarked graves in 'The Brothers'). The Lakeland yeomen are not (or were not) living in the kinds of dispersed societies in which print was needed to compensate for the certitude of immediate exchange.

Wordsworth does not carry this case to the point of disclaiming the positive functions of basic literacy, which would be a gesture of romantic proletarianization. But his emphasis on the oral as against the written tradition does contain a slight element of condescension. James Chandler (1984, 140–83) makes a very good case for the reactionary implications of this emphasis by showing the degree to which radical politics were associated with the spread of the print culture; he sees a Burkean traditionalism in Wordsworth's converse privileging of things handed down by word of mouth. This is an important aspect of Wordsworth's record on this question, but it needs to be set against at least two others. First, the written word tended to be identified with a dispersed and impersonal community; writing is unnecessary as long as immediate, public verification is possible. (Wordsworth does not however explore the opposite interpretation, whereby lack of written records encourages demagoguery.) Second, Wordsworth's self-inscription into the oral culture is almost always ambiguous. As the poet of 'Michael' he writes down what has hitherto been an oral tale. If he takes his authority from the spoken tradition, he also signals his departure from it, and his own displaced position as a translator or mediator between two worlds. Luke only needs to write letters after he has left home.

There is, then, no great audience for poetry among those whose lives are the ideal models that Wordsworth's poetry recommends. In this, Wordsworth's position is very like Goldsmith's in *The Deserted Village*. Like Goldsmith again, Wordsworth has even fewer hopes of the urban or ruling classes. The case of the manufacturing workers is especially urgent, since the monotony of their occupations makes 'some sort of stimulus, intellectual or bodily, absolutely necessary for them' (*MY*, 1:248). They have more leisure (though little enough), and more money (though little enough); thus it is all the more to be desired that their lives be filled with something wholesome.

But we have already seen ample evidence of Wordsworth's lack of conviction about being able to appeal to an urban readership at any level of the social hierarchy. As he declares in this same letter:

> Heaven and Hell are scarcely more different from each other than Sheffield and Manchester, etc. differ from the plains and Vallies of Surrey, Essex, Cumberland, or Westmoreland ... What form of discipline, what Books or doctrines, I will not say would equally suit all these; but which, if happily fitted for one, would not perhaps be an absolute nuisance in another?
>
> (250)

It must always have been unlikely that exhausted factory hands whose education had been cut short, if it had ever commenced, were going to read, if they had an inclination to read at all, the best that had been thought or expressed. Dickens wrote to Charles Knight that the English are

> the hardest worked people on whom the sun shines. Be content if in their wretched intervals of leisure they read for amusement and do no worse. They are born at the oar, and they live and die at it. Good God, what would we have of them!
>
> (Webb, 1955, 31)

If Wordsworth did at times, in an excess of fastidious condescension, appear to blame such workers for their lack of interest in authentic leisure, we should remember that he too understood how they were being tragically 'remade' by their environments and by the demands of the captains of industry. For him, even the country is not a single social entity, and the particular virtues of the Lake District (themselves open to questioning, as we have seen), are related to the 'fact' that 'our land is far more than elsewhere tilled by Men who are the Owners of it' (*MY*, 1:250). Even here, he is, as a poet, separated by vocation and education from those who afford him his inspiration. And he is even more alienated from those whose manners he is attempting to correct. Hence, perhaps, the frequent Wordsworthian recourse to the respect and understanding of a 'few natural hearts' (*LB*, 227), fit audience though few. Wordsworth's version of an authentic language for poetry stands forth with a great deal of moral and logical integrity. In its plain and simple correspondence with the most straightforward parts of the King James Bible and of *Pilgrim's Progress*, it really does function as a prospective new standard diction for a poetry of civic virtue. But with the inexorable decline of the potential readership at both extremes of the social scale (as he saw it), it had to remain a part of his organic aspiration. His own 'later' poetry departed more and more (though seldom entirely) from this ideal diction, but few poets in the language have ever thought harder about how to bring it into being, or thought out its implications more clearly. If his ambitions for the reformation of poetic language be deemed to have failed, then the failure is not to be attributed to intrinsic contradictions so much as to the larger forces of history. Wordsworth still finds readers who are so taken aback by his simplicity that they cannot understand him. Coleridge, his most assiduous contemporary reader, understood him very well, to the extent that he committed himself, in *Biographia Literaria*, to heading off the challenge to his own priorities that Wordsworth's poetics represented. No more was the linguistic premise of that poetics understood by Wordsworth's 'democratic' successors, Keats, Shelley and Byron. Only his enemies, in their enduring campaign on behalf of decorum, seem to have glimpsed the truly radical potential in the poet's faith in the real language of men in a state of vivid sensation.

4

'In single or in social eminence'? The political economy of *The Prelude* and *Home at Grasmere*

Forced hopes and proud rebellion

The syndrome of displacement that was demonstrated in 'Gipsies' has now, I hope, been placed within the context of Wordsworth's variably coherent analysis of the major trends in British social and political life. The *Poems* of 1807 seems to me to be a volume in which this syndrome is powerfully apparent, but it is not the only place where we may trace its features. The first version of the expanded poem that would become *The Prelude* was completed in 1805; and by 1806 Wordsworth had put together (from drafts that may have been substantially coherent as early as 1800) that prospective part of *The Recluse* now known as *Home at Grasmere* (*HG*, 16–19). These poems offer rich reworkings of the languages of displacement. They are the poems in which Wordsworth offers his most detailed representations of himself as, respectively, a mobile subject and a person in habitual contact with others in a dear perpetual place. Not for nothing, I shall suggest, did *Home at Grasmere* remain unfinished or unpublished. As 'Gipsies' speaks forth the hyperbole of excessive self-esteem, and thereby undermines itself, so the rhetoric of belonging, of being in place, is pursued in *Home at Grasmere* with an intensity that similarly calls itself into question. On this second occasion, moreover, Wordsworth was trying for something more than the communication of a mood of his own mind.

I shall argue that the self that is presented in both of these poems is always conceived of as a social or intersubjective entity; none the less, the topic of *The Prelude* announces itself as singular and individual, while *Home at Grasmere* attempts to place that self within a community. Having discussed these two cases, the remainder of this study will focus on important examples of Wordsworth's representation of others, and on the species of 'self' that is interactive therein.

Once again I begin at a tangent, with the published poem that most closely forecasts the dramas of *The Prelude*: the 'Lines' written near Tintern Abbey that conclude the first (1798) edition of *Lyrical Ballads*. The social–historical evidence for understanding this much-anthologized poem as an example of displacement rather than of the Wordsworthian affirmation of nature and imaginative memory has already been brought to light.[1] We know that Wordsworth images himself as writing on the eve of Bastille Day, and that 'five summers' (*LB*, 113) thus looks back to a period of youthful optimism about the cause of the French Revolution in particular, and of democratic reform in general. We also know that the ruined Tintern Abbey was a famous sheltering place for vagrants and displaced people, the very classes whose presence in the poem would most threaten its apparent effort at readjustment and reconciliation. The poet's locating himself 'a few miles above' the Abbey may thus be an explicit act of avoidance, but it is one to which our attention is deliberately drawn by the very precision of the title, which tells us what we are missing, just as the date signals the French connection. Even above the Abbey, however, the actual landscape would have been likely to have included barges trafficking in coal and iron ore, the major industries of the Wye Valley. Wordsworth's footnote, telling us that the river is at this point unaffected by 'tides' (113), may also function as a wishful allusion to the tides of men and nations.

With all this in mind, the speaker's reluctance to specify what is invoked by the 'still, sad music of humanity' (116) can seem to stand as part of a desire to tame or deflect social and political realities. For it is the personal vision, forcefully set off against these realities by the poem's rhetoric, that seems to be given priority. But it is entirely Wordsworthian that what is 'excluded' or displaced is also covertly admitted and signified, both by the location and date specified in the title, and in the language of surmise ('as might seem/ Of vagrant dwellers in the houseless woods') that enters into the description of the scene. Similarly, the language of affirmation and restitution that expounds Wordsworth's alternative response is also flawed and qualified from within, in a way that looks forward to the expanded debates of *The Prelude*.

This poem is remarkably devoid of the language of presence. As many of its confirmations are in fact to be deduced from negations – 'nor less, I trust ... Nor, perchance ...' and so forth – so the speaker's voice seems to define itself in the here and now largely by reference to past recollections and predictions of the future. Memories of this place have brought about 'tranquil restoration', and have *perhaps* encouraged the growth of a moral dimension in the poet's character. They *may*, furthermore, have created the 'serene and blessed mood' in which he has been able to transcend the limits of time and place to achieve a visionary insight (114). Even if this be but a 'vain belief', the argument goes, the 'sylvan Wye' has certainly served as a spiritual resource in times of trouble. And, if the spontaneous energies of early manhood have been lost, 'other gifts' have followed.

All these conditionals and back-up explanations inscribe into the poem an impression of tentative or partial conviction. But even if we accept, as many readers do, that the speaker is at this point at peace with the relation between mind and nature here adduced, the end of the poem must yet present a challenge. Instead of ending at line 112, with the expressed faith in nature and the 'language of the sense' as the guardians of heart, soul and moral being, the poem moves into another back-up explanation of why Wordsworth might preserve good spirits:

> Nor, perchance,
> If I were not thus taught, should I the more
> Suffer my genial spirits to decay:
> For thou art with me

(116)

The address – one that will be repeated at various points in *The Prelude* and *Home at Grasmere* – is to Dorothy, the largely (*pace* line 117) silent partner of his meditations. The complex affirmation by negation, telling us that he *has* been 'thus taught' tends to make us wonder whether he really has. In contrast to 'Gipsies', where the companionable presence of Beaumont's gardener is written out of the poem to enhance the narrator's Satanic–divine independence, this poem does acknowledge access to a community, in the shape of the poet's sister. But it is a self-reflecting community, for what he sees in Dorothy is an image of his former self. This in turn gives way to a prayer that *she* might be blessed by the beneficent forces of nature, as if again to call into question whether *he* has. And, should William cease to be, or to be with her, Dorothy at least may recall this landscape as a place of both intrinsic vision and personal consecration, 'dear' both in itself and because of the personal faith here plighted.

This concluding passage, following as it does the strong closure suggested by lines 103–12 ('Therefore am I still . . .'), seems disjunctive. Even if we choose not to unsettle the credibility of the visionary faith that the poem has thus far proposed, the final lines make us aware that it has been a hitherto private experience that the speaker now seems to want to share. The expressed possibility that life might not hold happy prospects for Dorothy, and for William, works to heighten the urgency of the personal bond between them, and also to call it into question. The relation between the two proposed forms of renovation, one deriving from nature and the other from human contact, is not pushed to the point of mutual exclusivity; on the contrary, the poet hopes that each may lead to the other, much as love of nature leads to love of man in book 8 of the 1805 *Prelude*. But the abruptness of the turn to Dorothy, and its habit of defining positive prospects in negative language, does suggest that natural and human resources may be in a state of tension. This possibility is further reinforced if we specify Wordsworth's 'language of the sense' (line 109) as a Lockean formulation. In his great *Essay* (Bk 4, ch. 11, sect. 9) Locke had argued that ideas conveyed through the senses offer an efficiently absolute certainty of the existence of objects giving rise to those ideas; but the certainty expires as soon as the object is not being perceived (1979, 635). Memory, and a presumption based on habitual experience, then become the tools that create a continuing sense of the world. Wordsworth's problem is almost the opposite: his memories and presumptions are so strong as to make the experienced present seem insubstantial or mysterious. What 'nature' might then be, and what might emerge as an authenticating 'language of the sense', are thus called into question, or at least left to reside at the level of mysteries unexplained.

Dorothy, thanks to her near relation to and deep sympathy with the poet, and owing to her apparently similar experiences, *may*, if all goes well, be a sharer in the reconstituted personality that the poem seems to propose. This personality will be proof against the negatively envisaged social environment made up of 'evil tongues', 'rash judgments', and the 'dreary intercourse of daily life'. But it is an ideal personality, threatened not only by its reliance upon an inconstant nature – inconstant in itself, in its relation to culture, and in its recollection by the mind – but also by its necessary career in the public world, a world whose defining terms Wordsworth, as we have seen, felt to be decidedly unnatural. As so often, it is inexpedient to try to discuss the epistemological language of the poem without attending to the social–historical, or the private without the public. The transcribed difficulty of experiencing 'presence' does belong to a personalized, philosophical discourse, but it must also be set within a history which itself has various operative dimensions. Thus we have noted the importance of this particular landscape, with its vagrants, its industries, and its 'revolutionary' associations. But we must also position the poem's rhetoric within what may be a larger-scale determination stemming from the financial revolution that is now widely recognized as a major energy acting upon the eighteenth-century sense of self. It is surely more than mere coincidence that the summary here offered by J.G.A. Pocock of the perceived threats of a credit economy is so closely analogous to the indeterminate tensing of Wordsworth's poem:

> Property – the material foundation of both personality and government – has ceased to be real and has become not merely mobile but imaginary. Specialised, acquisitive and post-civic man has ceased to be virtuous, not only in the formal sense that he has become the creature of his own hopes and fears; he does not even live in the present, except as constituted by his fantasies concerning a future.
>
> (1985, 112)

This is not just a magisterial generalization of the sort that we are trained to resist: it can be seen to apply to the tiny details of Wordsworth's financial predicament, which itself included a large measure of the imaginary. Throughout his early career, at least, he never thought he had enough. The language of 'was' and 'shall be' belongs explicitly to the philosophical and psychological dimension of Wordsworth's poem, and to *The Prelude* which it so aptly forecasts; but it must also be positioned within the discourse of what Pocock calls 'speculative fantasy' (112). Again, as we have seen in the case of 'Gipsies', the aspiration for presence has economic as well as other constituents.

We can now see how fully the two redemptive prospects intimated at the end of the 'Tintern Abbey' poem, the one a recourse to nature and the language of the sense, the other to a close human consensus, are implicated one with another, and not just by the degree to which that 'language' is an entity both private and public. Both are fragile and tentative, explicitly so for the relatively privileged William and Dorothy, and thus even more definitely for a readership with little or no experience of nature. How can others hope to achieve what is even for the 'chosen' such a difficult access to restorative powers? Success must be unlikely, given Wordsworth's sense of the psychological redeterminations resulting from urban life. Thus, if the 'language of the sense' be interpreted as that vital agency deriving from the conjunction of the great objects in nature with the most elemental human passions – that ideal language whose genesis and features I have explained in Chapter 3 – then we have to wonder whether that language is still functioning for a poet who has been living in the city for so long. And nature itself, in this particular place, has already been refigured by those troublesome phenomena described above, and mentioned by the poet only in terms of negation or surmise. The end of this poem, and of the 1798 *Lyrical Ballads*, images a brother and sister standing on the banks of a river, far from home, and seeking in each other the terms of an understanding that is both private and 'public'. But the community of experience may be possible only between themselves, if it is possible at all; and even individual experience is qualified by the constant displacement of presence that the poem's language performs.

Read in this way, the 'Tintern Abbey' poem does not then stand as the record of a highly affirmative moment in Wordsworth's life.[2] It seems indeed to offer some experience, variously human and natural, as an alternative to the general music of humanity, but it remains a poem of aspiration rather than achievement. The conviction of particular passages is unsettled by their contiguity to other passages, and by the general rhetoric of hypothesis. We see here neither the successful displacement of the social by the natural, nor the convincing subsumption of the natural within the social. On the contrary, the poem transcribes the speaker's sense of the reciprocal instability of both social and natural environments. The displacement from man to nature, in the sense for which McGann argues (1983, 81–92), is indeed proposed, but also countermanded, both by the qualifications about the efficiency of nature and by the final turn toward the desperately limited version of the social world represented by Dorothy. The true displacement is thus to be traced in the poet's own alienated language, and in the subjectivity for which it speaks.

In this respect, I suggest that the 'Tintern Abbey' poem is a prophetic anticipation of the 1805 *Prelude*, in which a wide spectrum of relations between self, nature and society is presented and discussed. The shorter poem is free of the rhetoric of work and effort, since it chronicles a moment of self-constitution that must be prior to any contribution to the public sphere. And *The Prelude* too offers itself as a propaedeutic poem, its entire argument merely preparatory to the 'other tasks' (13:370) that should have followed it – most obviously the completion of *The Recluse*, which Wordsworth thought of as a possible 'work that should endure' (13:278). At the same time, *The Prelude* is constantly defining *itself* within the vocabulary of labour, fulfilled and unfulfilled. So indeed it is, as the longest and most worked upon of all Wordsworth's poems. It is both ironic and typically Wordsworthian that in so being it should become an object of constant anxiety and conflict, and remain unpublished until after the poet's death.

The first, expanded version of the poem was, as has been said, completed in 1805. Thus, when Wordsworth strode off to Nottingham with the gardener and passed by the band of gypsies, he might have been recollecting not only the immediate self-esteem of his career as a landscape architect, and the medium-term satisfaction of being well along with the manuscript that would appear as the two volume *Poems* of 1807, but also the more enduring and disturbing state of the autobiographical poem, complete and yet incomplete in terms of the greater project of which it was but a part. We have seen that the 1807 volumes were introduced by an apology for the author's failure to produce a single, major work. Similarly, the narrative of the search for a 'determined aim' that might result in some 'glorious work' (1: 124, 158) takes up much of the first book of *The Prelude*, which develops its argument largely through a continual scrambling of the language of honest labour with that of indolence and inertia. The knight of arts and industry and his foes in the Castle of Indolence that are represented as antithetical in Thomson's poem are both housed within Wordsworth's mind and heart, and in constant struggle. The famous opening reference to the expulsion of Adam and Eve from paradise (1: 15) is deployed by Wordsworth to describe his declared joy at being released from city life. As such, it forecasts the oxymoronic character of the entire poem, whereby loss and gain, value and waste, effort and idleness, are each continually undercutting the other. Adam's entry into the world is emphatically regretful, however fortunate we may seek to render his fall. If it is for him a place of possible restoration, then there will be much grief and frustration along the way, as Michael's vision of the future has made clear. Odd, then, that Wordsworth should allude to this moment in describing what he claims as a positive release from bondage. One could argue that he is here subverting or rewriting Milton in a gesture of high Romantic self-confidence. But there is much evidence that a darker purpose may be at work, casting doubt upon this instant of apparent reorigination by troubling intimations of impropriety.

There are, in support of such a reading, at least two other references to the fall that are similarly disjunctive. One occurs where Wordsworth is describing his coming to terms with London, at first a negatively overwhelming environment but then accepted as a place where the traces of the 'unity of man' (8: 827) may yet be found. The speaker's being able to see the good in spite of the bad is compared to Adam, 'yet in paradise/ Though fallen from bliss' (8: 818–9) seeing the *bad* or the ominous superseding the good, as he is about to be banished – darkness at noon, and the morning light brightest in the west. Again, it could be argued that Wordsworth is on his way *back* to paradise, a paradise on earth, making this reversal appropriate enough. He turns *from* the 'rueful prospect' (line 811) into the inner world of imagination, which provides the positive alternative, and appears all the brighter because of the contrast. But the poem does not support such an interpretation, and does not assert or propose a paradise regained, so that this particular affirmation is again tainted by a covert negation.

Again, later in the poem, as Wordsworth celebrates his return to nature, so long delayed while he played out his youthful commitments to political and philosophical idealisms, the regaining of the true path is imaged in a way that flagrantly undercuts its credibility, by being metaphorically proposed as the moment *after* the fall. Wordsworth has just announced that he will direct his narrative away from 'man's unhappiness and guilt'

(11:1) and back to beneficent nature. But the appeal to that nature is phrased in the following conflicted way:

> And you, ye groves, whose ministry it is
> To interpose the covert of your shades,
> Even as a sleep, betwixt the heart of man
> And the uneasy world – 'twixt man himself,
> Not seldom, and his own unquiet heart –
> Oh, that I had a music and a voice
> Harmonious as your own, that I might tell
> What ye have done for me.
>
> (11: 15–22)

Not only does the poet lament his lack of voice; but he images his return to nature in terms of Adam's hiding from the face of God by entering the woods (*PL*, 9:1084f.). Nor is it just a matter of hiding the self from the world; Wordsworth trumps Adam by claiming the need for one part of the self to hide from another, man from his own unquiet heart. And once again, Wordsworth's moment of restoration is troubled by the rhetoric of defeat, impropriety and alienation.

We can of course try to accommodate these retractions, and others like them, by emphasizing the degree to which *The Prelude* is a largely corrective narration, written to put to rest an unproductive or misguided past. But this ignores the moments of enlightenment that the poem does claim, such as the example just given, where what enters the narrative as a positive redirection is negatively contextualized. This syndrome occurs throughout the poem, and to take it seriously is to question the tradition that reads *The Prelude* as an epic of the self conceived as something separate from society, and therefore productive of a triumphant outcome. To adopt a standard phenomenological perspective, within which the successful constitution of an exemplary self is deemed the major point of the poem, is to miss the evidence transcribed of a tension between individual and social development, a tension that indeed calls into doubt the very possibility of a separate self. The rest of this chapter will seek to describe the importance of the social dimension of *The Prelude*.[3]

Looking again at the first book of the poem, I think that we must take seriously the degree to which the celebration of freedom, 'enfranchised and at large' (1:9), also brings about the postlapsarian anxiety about choice, and choosing properly. Indeed, when Wordsworth says that he is *not* 'scared' at his own 'liberty' (line 16), we may be excused for assuming the opposite. The prospects for 'ease and undisturbed delight' (line 28) soon give way to more stringent concerns about effort and productivity. Wordsworth first remembers himself, in the recent present, as a sort of poetical hunter and gatherer:

If not a settler on the soil, at least
To drink wild water, and to pluck green herbs,
And gather fruits fresh from their native bough.
                                        (1: 36–8)

If this passage portrays the poet affording himself access to an innocent insouciance that is so often suspicious in the Wordsworthian psyche, then our willingness to suspend disbelief must be further tested by the first 'incident' of the poem – a somnolent reverie lasting from around two in the afternoon to sunset (1: 68f.). Confessionally or sacramentally interpreted, this event may be made positive – a mystical reacquaintance with the natural world from which he has been too long excluded (see Hartman, 1977, 51–4). This reading can be defended, and is even perhaps intended. But it is also qualified from within. In a gesture of *willed* lassitude, 'slackening my thoughts by choice' (line 72), the poet ponders some future 'work/ Of glory' (lines 86–7). But we soon learn that these expectations were not fulfilled (line 105). The first of the many turns to nature in this poem in fact produces a series of false starts, a list of possible subjects that will *not* enter into the eventual constitution of *The Prelude*. Its immediate outcome is also phrased in a string of images that seem to unsettle one another, as he sets out 'like a peasant' on a 'pleasant, loitering journey' towards his 'hermitage' (lines 110–15). The poet as loiterer suggests a satisfaction with the world, albeit one tending toward improper indolence; but in presenting his goal as a 'hermitage' he implies a retreat from that world. And if he is a peasant, then he is not a working peasant, but an idle one, who has dreamed away much of the day. Peasants, moreover, do not live in hermitages, or in disengagement from the world at large.[4]

And so on. The rest of the first book continues to juxtapose the language of 'rigorous inquisition', 'steady choice', and 'honourable toil' (lines 159, 171, 653) with the preference to 'stray about/ Voluptuously through fields and rural walks' in a mood of 'deliberate holiday' (lines 252–6). Pondering all the yet-unwritten themes for a public poem or historical epic (many of them deriving from figures of exile or opposition), he casts himself as a 'false steward', one who has 'much received/ And renders nothing back' (lines 270–1). It is thus in a *lament*, in an expression of embarrassed failure – 'Was it for this' – that Wordsworth initiates his true subject, and the matter of the rest of the poem: his own life. To regard this as a clever irony is to read it too affirmatively, and to miss one of the major dramas of *The Prelude*. For the way in which this initiation is founded in a reluctant negation of the public dimension of writing is an important prefiguring of one of the poem's primary tensions. He *has* found his subject. The 'road lies plain' before him, and the 'labour', both of birth and of effort in the world, has begun. But it will not prove to be a theme 'Single and of determined bounds' (lines 668–74). In fact, the 'ampler or more varied argument' that he thinks he is laying aside will constantly impinge upon his writing, in ways that make clear that the history of a self must also be the history of a society, or at least of the tension between inner and outer forms of determination. The dismissal of the public dimension is as much of a false start as is the opening desire to write a historical epic.

Wordsworth may not have known it as such, however. It may well be that had he been more convinced of his typicality, of the degree to which his own singleness was truly representative of a general condition, then he would have been less anxious than he was about the apparently excessive egotism of an autobiographical poem. His conviction of his particularity is itself the result of his displaced predicament, the condition of whose articulation is that it condemns the individual to the sense of solitude. Thus he is enduringly anxious about designating *The Prelude* as any kind of worthwhile *task*, something that might make amends for a fallen condition rather than being itself just one more outgrowth of it. The uncertainty that is spectacularly apparent when he revises the line 'With an exhausted mind worn out by toil' (4: 381) to the specification, in 1850, of a day 'Spent in a round of strenuous idleness' (4: 377) is evident also in much of the rest of the poem. If Shakespeare and Milton were 'labourers divine' (5: 165), then Wordsworth was seldom comfortable suggesting the same of himself. Cambridge gave him 'no settled plan' (6: 29), and here again 'idleness and joy' are in uneasy tension with 'forced labour' and 'forced hopes' (3: 236, 213). His 'proud rebellion' against the demands of prudence and the expectations of his family is only imperfectly heroic–Satanic. It is partly inspired by a dignified 'over-love/ Of freedom', indeed, but also by an

> indolence, by force of which I turned
> From regulations even of my own
> As from restraints and bonds.
>   (6: 41–8)

Wordsworth thus casts himself again as the *prince* of poetical *idlers*, to recall Hazlitt's great epiphet. He has his demonic, lordly side, but it is directed to nothing more momentous than idleness. As this form of self-undermining characterizes the narrative of the events of the poet's early life, so it also enters into the meditations upon the process of composition in the present that interrupt that narrative. The same indecisions that are written *about* are recapitulated *in* the writing; thus both 'outward hindrance' and 'voluntary holiday' are responsible for the poem's lack of progress (7: 19–20). In his summary of the shepherd's life, Wordsworth is able to justify a measure of idleness, as an earned ingredient of a life otherwise marked by great efforts and by the sturdy conviction of self-dependent powers:

> He feels himself
> In those vast regions where his service is
> A freeman, wedded to his life of hope
> And hazard, and hard labour interchanged
> With that majestic indolence so dear
> To native man.
>
> (8: 385–90)

But poets are not shepherds, hard as they may try and much as they may wish it so. *The Prelude* seldom pushes aside for long the language of anxiety, and ends with promises of what is yet to come. It is in the final book that Calvert's legacy is remembered as the means whereby Wordsworth could 'pause for choice, and walk/ At large and unrestrained' (13: 358–9), a freedom that once again obliges him to call frequently and hyperbolically upon the vocabulary of labour (e.g. lines 362, 369, 370, 399, 409, 439). In thus taking over part of a 'patrimony' (line 356), Wordsworth is a Luke to Calvert's Michael (cf. *LB*, 233); and if he has not yet given himself over completely to dissolute habits, the signs are ominous and the anxieties strong. The language in which he describes, to Coleridge, the vision of the whole poem is again allusive in familiar complex ways:

> Anon I rose
> As if on wings, and saw beneath me stretched
> Vast prospect of the world which I had been,
> And was; and hence this song.
>
> (13: 377–80)

The passage echoes the temptation of Christ in the wilderness, when he is led by Satan up 'an high mountain' and shown 'all the kingdoms of the world in a moment of time', which he may possess if only he will consent to worship the devil (*Luke* 4: 5). Wordsworth, explicitly, *does* have power over what he sees, the history of his own life. Has he then given way to a pact with Satan, to an improper temptation? The image of ascending on wings plays an important part in the moral narrative of *Paradise Lost*. Wordsworth's language most closely echoes that of Eve as she recounts the details of her Satanically inspired, proleptic dream:

> Forthwith up to the clouds
> With him I flew, and underneath beheld
> The earth outstretched immense, a prospect wide

And various: wondering at my flight and change
To this high exaltation.

(5: 86–90)

Milton too feels himself led by Urania into the 'empyreal air', but begs to return to earth, his 'native element', lest he fall from this 'flying steed unreined' (7: 14–17). Milton thus articulates a modesty and propriety specifically not invoked by Wordsworth, whose own rhetoric then becomes either blasphemous or spoken from what is already a sinful condition. And, later in Milton's poem, it is indeed Sin who feels 'Wings growing, and dominion given me large/ Beyond this deep' (10: 244–5), the same Sin who claims 'Nor can I miss the way, so strongly drawn/ By this new felt attraction and instinct' (10: 262–3), prefiguring almost exactly the 'I cannot miss my way' that opens *The Prelude* (1: 19).

The echoes and associations of impropriety and blasphemy thus flood in upon Wordsworth's gesture of ascent in a fashion much too complex to be explained by reference to some authentic self-confidence, or search for the same. Adam's rather modest hope for 'proportional ascent' (9: 936) as a result of eating the forbidden fruit is answered by an ecstatic experience of delusion: they 'fancy that they feel/ Divinity within them breeding wings/ Wherewith to scorn the earth' (lines 1009–11). Wordsworth's language is inevitably and perhaps even consciously positioned within this Miltonic dimension. But there is a further Miltonic dimension that offers to invert the attribution of blasphemy. For Wordsworth's passage also remembers (as Milton's passages forecast) Michael's leading Adam up a high hill (11: 366f.) in order to elicit a gesture of submission to 'the hand of heaven' (line 372). Milton here recounts the education of Adam into the facts of fallen life, a prelude to his being cast out of paradise, the event recalled at the start of Wordsworth's poem. If much of this is a tale of woe, it also has a hopeful tendency, leading to eventual redemption. Michael teaches Adam, among other things, the dangers of 'man's effeminate slackness' (line 633). It seems significant that Wordsworth's ascent 'As if on wings' comes near the end of his poem, at roughly the same point as Adam's ascent in Milton's poem, while it most precisely recalls the details of Eve's dream. Once again, the allusion is at least a double one. But the two moments are not completely antithetical. Eve's prefiguring of the fall is not cancelled out by Adam's stoical hope of future restoration. As Wordsworth seems to try to pass off his ascent as a description of *achievement*, we may then sense that much is yet to be done. The true cancellation of all these visions of improper ascent will only come with the second Adam, with Christ's refusal of temptation, as recounted in *Paradise Regained* (3: 251f.).[5] It is thus hard not to conclude that the 'progress' of Wordsworth's poem has been in some coherent sense illusory. Either it has almost come back to its own beginning, with the world still all before the poet; or it has left him with the imperative to a further beginning in *The Recluse*. Origin and tendency are uncomfortably correlative.

|Wordsworth's 'vast prospect' seen 'As if on wings' is then a pseudo-angelic ascent. As such it again invites our familiar uncertainty about what kind of an angel, demonic or divine, Wordsworth might be. Is he a Daedalus or an Icarus? The consummation of this metaphorical complex occurs perhaps in the 'prospectus' to *The Recluse* (as it came to be), where Wordsworth contends that to speak of 'nothing more than what we are' is already to supersede all the machinery of the Christian as well as the classical epic (*HG*, 104). But here the gesture is uncertain. Satanic assumptions exist throughout *The Prelude*, as elsewhere in Wordsworth's poetry, as at once appealing and deeply troubling. For the prospectively positive redirection of the Luciferic energies that a paradise on earth might seem to promise does not sit convincingly with the constraints and doubts that Wordsworth voices about the possibility of such a return to innocence ever coming about. Even if it did, he would not be sure of his own place therein. If we choose to hear in Wordsworth's 'hence this song' another echo, that of the *hinc illae lacrimae* of Horace's epistle to Maecenas (*Epistles*, 1:19:41), then the instabilities become even more bewildering. For Horace's poem is another famous exercise in self-justification, by way of an appeal for a delay in the final judgement of his public.

The end of *The Prelude* is thus very much an exercise in prospects, and a strenuous one at that. It is also a moment of high anxiety. Whether Wordsworth has done anything

> Sufficient to excuse me in men's sight
> For having given this record of myself

is a seriously urgent question, 'all uncertain' (13:388–90), and not just part of the rhetoric of false modesty. The fact that his judges will be men, rather than God, might seem to afford him some relief. But the avoidance of a potential theological anxiety is certainly made up for by the poet's anxious need to justify himself to a public, and to produce something than can be approved of as visible labour. *The Prelude* remains forcefully indecisive in this respect, a fact that its reputation as one among the 'greatest' poems of all time can tend to make us forget.

Thus far I have written about the narrative self of the poem very much *as* a self, though it is worth repeating that such simple distinctions between the individual and the social are finally untenable in *The Prelude*. Accepting the logic of singleness in this qualified, heuristic manner, however, I have tried to show how completely the rhetoric of affirmation is coloured by the language of retraction. The degree to which this second language is evocative of the Christian–Miltonic tradition already serves to place the Wordsworthian self in a public sphere, and presents it as the medium of crises that are discursively general, part of the culture to which the poet belongs. But the public dimension of the poem is far more clearly apparent in other ways: in its references to a world made up of natural objects, and of other human beings who are not Wordsworth.

The world of all of us

Almost all of the features of the ideal political economy that are laid out incompletely and propositionally in the preface to *Lyrical Ballads* and in other prose sources, and which I have expounded propositionally and all too completely in Chapter 2, are to be found versified in one way or another in *The Prelude*. Here, Wordsworth expands upon the terse sentences of the 1800 preface that describe how nature works upon the human mind to produce the closest possible experience of the essential passions, and therefore the best language. For Wordsworth himself, nature exercised a parental role, either generous or disciplinary according to the needs of the moment. After stealing boats and woodcocks, it was from nature that the boy poet received apt admonishment – or thought he did, since nature here functioned as a companionable form for the projections of his own guilty mind (1:428f.). The sparse and majestic landscape of the Lake District both left him space and time for the exercise of his own figurative faculties, and remained resistant enough to his refigurations to correct them when they threatened to get out of hand, becoming 'rebellious' and 'acting in a devious mood' (2:383). Nature is here to Wordsworth as parent to child, and as Messiah to Satan.

Being grand and various enough to allow for the objectification of all human passions and thoughts without themselves being damaged, these natural objects gradually became 'allied to the affections' (1:640) in a process of re-envisioning through time which I have described elsewhere, and which is frequently referred to in *The Prelude* as leading to

A balance, an ennobling interchange
Of action from within and from without.
(12:376–7)[6]

Nature creates within an ideally responsive individual the psychological equivalent of undivided labour. When the eye, the 'most despotic of our senses', threatens to achieve an 'absolute dominion', and to make us slaves to an exclusively materialist perception of the outer world, it is nature that intervenes

to thwart
This tyranny, summon all the senses each

To counteract the other and themselves,
And makes them all, and the objects with which all
Are conversant, subservient in their turn
To the great ends of liberty and power.

$$(11:178-83)^7$$

This idea of nature is no mere sentimental identification with trees, lakes and mountains, but a precise and pointed alternative to the mental disposition formed by the increasing accumulation of men in cities, and by the monotony of their occupations therein.

Cambridge and London both threatened to swamp in the poet himself precisely this creative and interactive relationship with nature. Cambridge introduced him to an alienated world of superficial pastimes and unsubstantial social distinctions, all the 'surfaces of artificial life' (3:590) that the surplus economy could support. Participating in his own undoing, his life became 'rotted as by a charm' (3:339), and his subsequent return to the rural environment was appropriately compromised. Thus he experienced an 'inner falling off' (4:270), a cultural schizophrenia resulting from the baffled attempt to assimilate two different worlds with different and antithetical values, habits and pleasures:

Strange rendezvous my mind was at that time,
A party-coloured shew of grave and gay,
Solid and light, short-sighted and profound,
Of inconsiderable habits and sedate,
Consorting in one mansion unreproved.

$$(4:346-50)$$

London, though much more of a shock to the senses, was less so to Wordsworth himself by virtue of his early Cantabrigian training in the ways of the world. He was able to survive the deconstruction of the authentic self that was threatened by the metropolis, which is the socially objectified analogue of poetic diction – all glitter, false excitement and deceit. But to those who do not have the poet's special experiences of nature and of Cambridge, London is a fiercely negative environment, a 'blank confusion' creating

The slaves unrespited of low pursuits,
Living amid the same perpetual flow
Of trivial objects, melted and reduced
To one identity by differences
That have no law, no meaning, and no end –
Oppression under which even highest minds
Must labour, whence the strongest are not free.

$$(7:701-7)$$

Wordsworth here recognizes the power of the metropolis in rearranging the mental dispositions of those who come to reside within it; those who are born there have even less chance of experiencing or understanding an alternative. When the 'highest minds' are threatened by such an environment, then the average man has little hope of surviving uncontaminated. In a country experiencing urbanization at the rate Britain was in the early nineteenth century, what prospect could there be of Wordsworth's ideal rural microsociety becoming a credible alternative to life in the towns and cities?

The answer, as we have seen in Chapters 2 and 3, is that there was very little chance of a return to that rural economy, and the complex retractions that Wordsworth inscribes into his own personal history are themselves symptoms of its general implausibility as a wider social ideal. When the culturally privileged poet is always liable to deviate into error, requiring nature's severer interventions to correct him, then not much hope can be held out for those who have not shared the special circumstances of his upbringing. For Wordsworth, it was love of nature that led to love of man, as it also prepared him to be able to distinguish what is true from what is false in the world of literature (5: 610–19). Early experiences of nature left him with a due sense of proportion about man's follies and limitations, as it also mediated human nature to him in the exemplary shapes of others who lived with that same nature (8: 450f.). The inference is, then, that those who have not lived thus among the lakes and mountains will develop an even more imperfect love of man than the poet himself has. Wordsworth defers, at times, to a capacity in human nature to overcome even the most extreme forms of negative environmental determination, as he speaks of

How the immortal soul with godlike power
Informs, creates, and thaws the deepest sleep
That time can lay upon her, how on earth
Man if he do but live within the light
Of high endeavours, daily spreads abroad
His being with a strength that cannot fail.
(4: 156–61)

But when this works only intermittently for the poet himself, it can hardly compensate for the harmful changes at work in society at large.

There is much in *The Prelude* that argues against the possibility of closing the gap between the solitary and the social forms of restitution that Wordsworth investigates. To do so would clearly alleviate the more anxious symptoms of the poet's displacement. It would create an audience, a public validation of the author's labours; and it would afford Wordsworth a reciprocally reconstituted self. There are two prospective forms of renewed consensus that *The Prelude* explores as alternatives to the incumbent culture of alienation. One gives way to the other, and neither achieves conviction, either historically or rhetorically. The first is the philosophical idealism that was for the poet associated with the early days of the French Revolution; the second, brought in as a second line of defence, is dependent upon the owner-occupier society of rural Westmoreland and Cumberland. This ideal persists up to a point, but in a somewhat confused and ambivalent way. It is involved with nature, but it is nature alone that finally emerges as the poet's best hope. These are the movements in the poem's argument that we must now examine, for they are the terms in which Wordsworth, at various moments in his life, tries to find a *social* vocabulary for being in

> the very world which is the world
> Of all of us, the place in which, in the end,
> We find our happiness, or not at all.
>   (10: 724–7)

Wordsworth images his reactions to the French Revolution as aspects of a misguided youth; perhaps because of this, his account is able to admit to both good and bad in the evolution of events in France. He supported the early phase of the revolution, seeing prospects of a new consensus on egalitarian principles, a 'whole' people 'Fresh as the morning star' (9: 391). He joyously predicted the abolition of poverty, inequality, and of the outmoded forms of the inherited luxury economy (9: 520ff.). He was able to accept the September Massacres as an inevitable evil, although he was concerned, for reasons that must by now be very clear, about the increasing centralization of political power in the metropolis of Paris (9: 106f.). He did *not* reject the revolution at the first sign of violence, seeing in such violence only the residue of former cultures, 'a reservoir of guilt/ And ignorance, filled up from age to age' (10: 436–7). No more did he support the British reaction, the declaration of war against the young republic (10: 645f.). Even 'ten shameful years' (10: 178) have not, he tells us, dimmed his faith in the moderate republicanism that the Girondins advocated, a 'just government' founded in the 'ancient lawgivers' (lines 185, 188).[8]

This positive, early phase of the revolution promised the restitution of an earthly paradise, not just in 'favored spots' but in the 'whole earth' (10: 701), which could then seem to be a 'home'. Had this worked, Wordsworth would have found the perfect way of holding together his desire to wander and his longing for a perpetual place; when all the earth is home, then wandering entails no absence or displacement. But it did not work. Like the Solitary in *The Excursion*, the poet had to cope with disappointment, not only at his own nation's reactionary responses, but also at the developments for which those responses were in part responsible (10: 306f.), the victory of the Jacobins and the tyranny of Robespierre, itself giving way eventually to Napoleon. Wordsworth thus turned back to his roots, to the ideal society of man in nature whose features we have described in Chapter 2.

This was indeed the vision of authentic community that upheld him before he went to France, and whose 'Manners erect, and frank simplicity' (9: 220) first made him susceptible to democratic principles in general. To this ideal he now returns:

> Man free, man working for himself, with choice
> Of time, and place, and object; by his wants
> His comforts, native occupations, cares,
> Conducted on to individual ends
> Or social, and still followed by a train,
> Unwooed, unthought-of even: simplicity,
> And beauty, and inevitable grace.
>
> (8: 152–8)

This is a harsh life, 'unluxuriant' and 'Intent on little but substantial needs' (lines 208–9). But among the remote hills and lakes, no one received 'attention or respect' from 'claims of wealth or blood' (9: 225–6). Knowing thus what was 'strong and pure in household love/ Benevolent in small societies' (10: 668–9), Wordsworth had been more than willing to believe in the extension of such a prototype to the national level. However, the course of events in France did not fulfil this hope, so that he had to turn back to the microsocial incarnation of this ideal, paralleled by the movement away from general theories of social reform that is intimated in the composition of *Lyrical Ballads*, with its emphasis on the 'familiar face of life' (12: 67).

The Prelude's account of this return to origins versifies and expands upon the 1800 preface in significant ways. The disappointment with France is explained in terms of the sad fate of moderate republicanism (still quite radical for Britain in the 1790s, it must be said), but also as the result of the poet's unreasonable faith in philosophically or methodologically motivated historical change. It is now accepted as a matter of faith that the 'glorious creature' that man is capable of becoming is to be found 'One only in ten thousand' (12: 90–1). And it is not to the towns and cities but to the 'pathways' and 'lonely roads' (line 124) that Wordsworth turns in hopes of finding this creature, or of becoming one himself. Thus solitary wandering is now, paradoxically, the poet's best image of a community:

> wandering on from day to day
> Where I could meditate in peace, and find

The knowledge which I love, and teach the sound
Of poet's music to strange fields and groves,
Converse with men, where if we meet a face
We almost meet a friend, on naked moors
With long, long ways before, by cottage bench,
Or well-spring where the weary traveller rests.
                                        (12: 137–44)

This world is inhabited largely by fields and trees, and only occasionally by people. That they are 'almost friends' is another telling ambivalence: people are scarce enough that even strangers can be intimates, but they are also *not* friends, not able quite to put aside the reserve and distance that so often obtains between human beings in Wordsworth's reports of his encounters. This passage in *The Prelude* can in fact be read as explaining the *Lyrical Ballads* as the result of Wordsworth's displacement. The 'public road' that he so much loves is 'like a guide into eternity' (lines 145, 151), a passage out of this world and into some other. It is the 'wanderers of the earth' with whom the poet now empathizes, the 'strolling bedlamites' and 'uncouth vagrants' (lines 157–9) whom he meets upon his walks. This was indeed perceived as the most radical aspect of these poems (and also of *The Excursion* of 1814): that such characters could be presented as having an essential humanity that could in turn figure in a public poetry. The crime against decorum was seen as a challenge to polite taste, and intended as such, as Wordsworth

There saw into the depths of human souls –
Souls that appear to have no depth at all
To vulgar eyes.
                                        (12: 166–8)

But in representing himself as speaking for or about the wanderers of the earth, Wordsworth was himself, as we have seen and will see again, at a distance from them, in a no man's land between the bourgeois commitment to place and property and the vagrant ease imaged in the gypsies' tents. No more could he, an insecure poet, be at one with the rural owner-occupiers who were economically and spiritually 'their own upholders, to themselves/ Encouragement, and energy, and will' (lines 262–3).

As Wordsworth is unsure of his own place in this ideal economy, so too is his portrayal of it as an objective entity also unstable and inscribed with conflict. At one crucial point in *The Prelude*, at least, the celebration of rural independence is framed within a language that seems to belong to a quite different political system – that of feudalism and patriarchy. Having described the perceptual and psychological assault that Bartholomew Fair presented (7: 649ff.), Wordsworth relates how his own upbringing among the grand objects of nature enabled him to maintain an integrated vision, seeing the parts 'As parts, but with a feeling of the whole' (line 713). This is the vision that counters the society of the city, where the parts persist without an interplay between part and whole, the products of divided labour and deadened minds. Living with nature, Wordsworth had both the 'steady forms' of the mountains to provide stability, and the 'changeful language of their countenances' (lines 723, 728) to prevent their reification in the mind's eye.

So far so good; but it is when he describes, as he goes on to do, how this environment functions for *others* that questions begin to arise. The account of Helvellyn Fair that opens book 8 presents the ideal Wordsworthian political economy: a small band of rustics meeting once a year to exchange (and only occasionally sell) their produce, and to enjoy themselves without the gross and outrageous stimulants of booths and spectacles (8: 1–61). The hawkers who do show up are regulars rather than strangers, and the surplus economy has made only minimal inroads into this favoured place.[9] The mountains here function as a protective barrier, keeping out the negative influences of the urban life; but in making possible an egalitarian society for these few human beings, the landscape itself is imaged in a language deriving from a feudal tradition. Helvellyn is figured as a lordly presence in the 'silence of his rest' and in his occasionally 'unshrouded head' visible for all to see (lines 13, 15). He looks down upon a 'little family of men' which he and his 'tributary vales' protect from the incursions of the wider world (lines 7, 12), just as the patriarch might protect, or claim to protect, his tenants, also traditionally represented as a family. This family is emphatically not a 'crowd' (line 6), though it seems so to the mountain. For it was the *crowd* of Bartholomew Fair that most threatened Wordsworth, apparently in its capacity for ungoverned, mob behaviour:

> What say you then
> To times when half the city shall break out
> Full of one passion – vengeance, rage, or fear –
> To executions, to a street on fire,
> Mobs, riots, or rejoicings?
>
> (7: 645–9)

The crowd is imaged as 'anarchy and din/ Barbarian and infernal' (lines 660–1). Wordsworth must here have had in mind not only the London mob, but also the Parisian, that had appeared to play such a large part in the political life of revolutionary France. His fear of the potential power of an ungovernable urban populace in part explains why his alternative democracy in the Lake District subsists within a landscape whose presence is feudal. The mountain is authoritative and potentially disciplinary, as it is also beyond the reach of the people it looks down on:

How little they, they and their doings, seem,
Their herds and flocks about them, they themselves,
And all which they can further or obstruct –
Through utter weakness pitiably dear,
As tender infants are – and yet how great,
For all things serve them.

$$(8:50-5)$$

Two antithetical perspectives are here superimposed one upon the other. All things are said to serve this community, but they are looked down upon, by a great mountain that is figured as a sort of geophysical Lord Lonsdale, 'from high' (line 57). It is this conflation of two normally opposed political relations that allows Wordsworth to look upon his fellow men in terms of a fraternal contract, 'a brother of this world' (line 79). This whole scene is very much a poetical version of the society that Wordsworth would describe in *A Guide to the Lakes* and elsewhere: one that is effectively democratic and free because the restraining functions of feudality are not enforced. But they are always there, in case things get out of hand. The revolutionary ethic of fraternity is here preserved, but only as contained within a limiting framework of paternal–feudal forms. The whole passage is, as so often, teasingly ambivalent. On the one hand, we can choose to read it as a perfect compromise, in which only natural forms (and *not* human institutions) are allowed to occupy a hegemonic position; on the other hand, we might suspect the occluded presence of a great lord for whom old Helvellyn is here doing symbolic guard-duty. This second option is made the more convincing when we know something of the actual conditions of tenancy in the Lake District, as described in Chapter 3.

My own preference is to read this scene as ambiguous, rather than as a clear allegory of social hierarchy. Wordsworth did wish to preserve the 'pure Commonwealth' of shepherds and rustics (*PrW*, 2:206), although he was to describe it as *disappearing*. In effect, if the feudal conventions and obligations were not imposed, a 'perfect Republic' could arise, in which only Helvellyn and other mountains exercised any governing powers. But we have seen that many contemporary commentators felt that such feudal obligations were all too evident, making Wordsworth's ideal somewhat unstable, and perhaps accounting for his decision to locate it in a vanished past. At the same time, in the passage that we have in *The Prelude*, the signs of or allusions to a feudal order existing in the present do impinge upon the description of an egalitarian ideal in a striking way. The passage is perhaps thus best read as the expression of a Wordsworthian confusion, rather than as evidence of a clear decision about how man should relate to other men.

In fact, Wordsworth often seems to seek to create a mediated equality for his ideal society. He wants to see 'One brotherhood of all the human race' (11: 88), but to bring it about by appealing to the 'mysteries of passion' (line 84) rather than to any version of radical reason or theory. He thus places himself in a sort of middle ground between Paine and Burke. Paine sought equality through reason, Burke sought to shore up authority by appealing to passion. If Wordsworth here rejects reason, with its radical and Jacobinical associations, as the basis for any enduring equality among men, so he also distances himself from the devious exploitation of traditionary feeling that Burke had relied upon to uphold monarchy and aristocracy. Wordsworth did resort to a Burkean rhetoric, as we have seen, in the 1818 political pamphlets and elsewhere; and he does confess to a sympathy for the chivalrous past, which he had had to discipline in order to maintain his 'Hatred of absolute rule' (9: 504) and his early faith in the revolution. But he does not put forth a Burkean defence of traditions for their own sakes, even though his image of an egalitarian community is more than tinted with faith in timeless social conventions. The 1800 preface and its versified analogues in *The Prelude* seek to articulate a precise rather than a mystified role for the passions in the prospectus for a new form of social bonding. The role of the Wordsworthian poet is certainly complicated by covert insinuations of authority; but it remains, emphatically in its intentions and largely in its arguments, a democratic one.

We have seen, then, that Wordsworth's hopes of bringing together single and social energies were not fulfilled in the course of the French Revolution, and that when they are posited for others in the ideal owner-occupier economy under Helvellyn, they are unsettled by an apparent rivalry of political rhetorics. Wordsworth often seems to complicate his statement of the rural ideal, whether by lamenting its disappearance, by questioning it from within (as at Helvellyn Fair), or by presenting it as a world in which the poet himself seems to have no place. The most memorialized passages of *The Prelude* have been those in which some vaguely visionary intensity is reported or aspired to – the stolen boat, the low breathings, the drowned man, the blind beggar, the discharged soldier, the spots of time, the crossing of the Alps and the ascent of Snowdon. What *connects* these luminous memories has been less attended to. On close inspection, we find that the kinds of community that the poet tries to return to are all in one way or another ineffective or unstable. To recognize this provides us with a different vocabulary for reading the arguments of the great 'moments' of the poem, which are themselves far from being simply reaffirming. They do not take place beyond space and time, and they always demand a return to space and time: we might recall again Geoffrey Hartman's serious insight that 'Apocalypse is not habitable' (1977, xvi). As they are contextually informed by what happens before and after, so they are intrinsically complex in their forms of self-affirmation, if any. I cannot here analyse all of these famous passages in the proper detail. This chapter will conclude with some remarks about the discharged soldier (see pp. 137–9). For now, I should like to look again at the account of the ascent of Snowdon that plays such an important part in the final book, and therefore seems to stand as something of a conclusion to *The Prelude*.

Wordsworth seems to intend this event to assume an exemplary status, since he presents it out of chronological order.[10] The poem's narration has brought us up to the composition of *Lyrical Ballads*, but the Snowdon climb took place some years before, in 1791, *before* the negative turn of events in France and the onset of anxious middle age in the poet himself. On the climb up the mountain, Wordsworth once again writes himself into a state of separation from the others in the party – he is the 'foremost of the band' (13:35) – and into a magisterial posture, with the sea of mist 'meek and silent' (line 44) at his feet. This posture may be partly (though I think only partly) ironized by the lunatic presence of the moon, 'Immense above my head' (line 42) and 'in single glory' (line 53), looking down at 'this show' (line 52). Once again, as in 'Gipsies', Wordsworth places himself somewhere between the moon and the spectacle it looks upon, though here there is less of a sense that he identifies himself with the heavenly presence. He is part of the 'show', but he is also outside it, sharing the lunatic perspective at a lower altitude.

The whole passage, familiar enough not to need extensive citation, is a parable of displacement. The view downwards is cut off by the sea of mist, and the origin of a 'voice' that is itself 'homeless' (line 63) now seems to be beneath, welling up through a Delphic 'deep and gloomy breathing-place' (line 57). The spectacle of the sea of mist as a 'still ocean' through which 'A hundred hills their dusky backs upheaved' (lines 45–6) recalls not only Milton's account of the creation (*PL*, 7:285–7), with Wordsworth in the position of creator, his vision 'meek and silent' at his feet (line 44), but also the prefiguring of the end of the flood that Michael reveals to Adam, wherein 'the tops of hills as rocks appear' (line 852). Wordsworth's allusions are once again hyperbolically magisterial. But the verbal play within this passage seems itself to be a sign of uneasiness, whether of event or recollection, as origins and tendencies turn round upon themselves. The place that has been left behind, or remains below, now presents itself (in the hole) as the 'soul' (sole) and the 'imagination of the whole' (line 65). Typically, it is *after* the scene has passed away that Wordsworth claims to have had the 'meditation' (line 66) that begins to find a meaning in this experience. He casts it as the 'perfect image of a mighty mind' (line 69). That mind must impress even the 'grossest' among other minds to see, hear and feel what it puts forth (lines 83–4). Readers have often seen in this after-recollection one of the poem's crucial moments of redemptive and reconstitutive insight. But there are two or three things to say about this. First, the whole comparison of the vision with the workings of a mighty mind is a supposition or surmise: 'it appeared to me' (line 68). Second, Wordsworth finds in the scene a 'perfect image'. If this phrase is not an outright oxymoron, it is at least odd in its specification of perfection for a form of *representation*, i.e. a gesture presupposing some gap or distance between signifier and signified. Wordsworth unscrambles this somewhat in the 1850 by using the words 'type' and 'emblem' (14: 66, 70), at the same time as the notion of perfect signification is weakened. Third, and most important, Wordsworth's own mind is a long way removed from this 'mighty mind'. This mind is itself only the 'express/ Resemblance ... genuine counterpart/ And brother' of the very highest *human* minds (lines 86–9), those that are 'truly from the Deity' (line 106). The relation is again unclear: counterparts and resemblances suggest something rather weaker than the Coleridgean symbolic in which the part belongs integrally to the whole of which it is a part. None the less, these highest human minds do enjoy an unusually positive attitude to life on this earth:

Hence sovereignty within and peace at will,
Emotion which best foresight need not fear,
Most worthy then of trust when most intense;
Hence chearfulness in every act of life;
Hence truth in moral judgements; and delight
That fails not, in the external universe.
                    (13: 114–19)

And now, the most important point of all that can be made concerning this climactic event: Wordsworth does *not* cast himself as one of these highest human minds. If these minds are already slightly displaced from any clear identity with the great mind of God-in-nature, then Wordsworth's own is at one further remove:

Oh, who is he that hath his whole life long
Preserved, enlarged, this freedom in himself –
For this alone is genuine liberty.
Witness, ye solitudes, where I received
My earliest visitations (careless then
Of what was given me), and where now I roam,
A meditative, oft a suffering man,
And yet I trust with undiminished powers;
                    (13: 120–7)[11]

The narration continues in the apologetic mode, as Wordsworth goes on to disclaim any improper intentions in what he has done. This is not at all the rhetoric of achievement or reconstitution; if the vision on the mountain invokes any sort of triumph, then it can for the poet only be one that has yet to come, and in despite of failures and limits hitherto experienced. The ideal synthesis of love and imagination that the final book goes on to describe (lines 149ff.) *may* be the poet's; this is not clear. He claims at least 'imagination' as the 'moving soul' of his narrative (line 171), so we can assume that he sees himself as part way there. Even if we grant him the conviction of participation in imagination and in the 'intellectual love' that ideally goes with it (line 186) – and such a concession is definitely in tension with what has been said before – then we still have to register the social displacement that such participation brings about:

> Here must thou be, O man,
> Strength to thyself – no helper hast thou here –
> Here keepest thou thy individual state:
> No other can divide with thee this work,
> No secondary hand can intervene
> To fashion this ability. 'Tis thine,
> The prime and vital principle is thine
> In the recesses of thy nature, far
> From any reach of outward fellowship,
> Else 'tis not thine at all.
>
> (13: 188–97)

The account continues in the third person ('But joy to him') and in the future conditional tense. Once again we must query Wordsworth's relation to this condition, both rhetorically and substantially. If *The Prelude* were a paean to Protestant individualism, then this would be a confirming moment. It is only partly such a poem, so that the gains to be acquired by such self-cultivation, in strict isolation, have to be set against the losses. Indeed, Wordsworth goes on to say that such a 'prime and vital principle' is but the radical beginning of a personality, which must be completed in love and friendship. Any renunciation of outward fellowship has to be, for Wordsworth, fraught with anxieties. These are in the broadest sense 'political', suggesting as they do a total retreat from the democratic aspirations that have so preoccupied the young poet, and also private, in that they seem to suspend his chances of a relationship to a reading public, and also to his nearest and dearest. In putting forward the case for the central importance of love and friendship, he again turns to his sister Dorothy, who has softened his own tendency to 'over-sternness' (line 227), and to Coleridge, who has provided timely reminders of the public dimension of the intersubjective life in 'man and his concerns' (line 258). The rest of the poem recounts what has not yet been mentioned – and it is typical of Wordsworth's displaced identity that the mention of Calvert's bequest appears here almost as an afterthought, in the fully Freudian sense – and gives itself over to promises of what may yet be to come. The poet is left with Coleridge, and perhaps his sister, as 'joint labourers' (line 439). As an image of community, this is a sad contraction of the earlier hope that joy of one might be joy of tens of millions (6: 360). Wordsworth is not quite in *single* 'eminence' (10: 389), but his society is small, and somewhat beleaguered by a generation that threatens to return to 'servitude' and 'old idolatry' (lines 432–3). There is hope, indeed, that 'what we have loved/ Others will love, and we may teach them how' (lines 444–5). But the notion of a 'redemption, surely yet to come' (line 441) is, as ever, hesitant and insecure because of all that has come before it. Since the end of the 'Tintern Abbey' poem, the poet's community has been rhetorically augmented by one, in the person of Coleridge. But by the middle of 1805, Coleridge had left for Malta, and John Wordsworth had drowned at sea. The end of the poem is composed in the teeth of a profound 'private grief' (line 416) that also shatters the integrity of the already fragile community. The absence, from this final social gesture, of Wordsworth's wife of three years' standing, is also peculiar. There is not even a pretence to the standard domestic scene that the poetry of retirement conventionally invites.

I shall return to *The Prelude* at the end of this chapter (see pp. 137–9). The time has now come for a glance (all too brief) at MS. B of *Home at Grasmere*, completed in 1806 and perhaps substantially composed well before. This poem certainly confirms any scepticism one might have about the conviction of the affirmative rhetoric of *The Prelude*. In the intensity of its hyperbole, though not in its object, it is one of the few poems in the canon that matches 'Gipsies'. It is the later version of the poem that most fully works up the Satanic dimension, in the third person: 'Alone and devious, from afar he came' (*HG*, 39). But the earlier manuscript projects the now familiar vacillation between the desire for indolent repose, 'entertained as in a placid sleep', and the more urgent awareness that 'something must be done' (*HG*, 62, 94). Similarly, the poet is again caught between the urge to wander and the desire to stay still. He tries to solve the dilemma by imaging himself not in a fixed place but in a limited *space*: the 'huge Concave' of the Vale of Grasmere, within which he may preserve the sense of wandering, without ever being too far from home. The whole earth can no longer offer itself as a 'home', as it did for that brief period in the early course of the French Revolution (*Prelude*, 10: 731). But in the vale, the poet can still 'flit from field to rock, from rock to field', and from 'open place to covert' (a choice of paradisal and postlapsarian environments, as we have seen), without leaving the nurturing and protective space that cuts him off from the world at large (*HG*, 40). This might seem to be a perfect compromise for the Wordsworthian schizophrenia; but even this does not satisfy him entirely. Thus, he looks at the waterfowl and comments as follows:

Happier of happy though I be, like them
I cannot take possession of the sky,
Mount with a thoughtless impulse, and wheel there
One of a mighty multitude whose sway
And motion is a harmony and dance
Magnificent.

(54)

Once again Wordsworth seems to be at his old Luciferic–angelic ambitions. Watching the birds circle 'Orb after orb' in 'wanton repetition', he
projects not only an ideal reconciliation of the single and the social, seeing
a 'mighty multitude' behaving 'As if one spirit was in all' (56), but also a
celestial relocation of the self. We have discussed this gesture in the final
book of *The Prelude*, where the poet sees a 'Vast prospect' from a
perspective 'As if on wings' (13: 378–9), in terms of its allusions to Eve's
dream and to Christ's temptation in the wilderness. Here too the birds are
busy with an exhilarating vainglory, as imaged by the earthbound poet:

They tempt the sun to sport among their plumes;
They tempt the water and the gleaming ice
To show them a fair image.

(*HG*, 56)

It is surely a disjunctive moment in this narrative of a chosen place to see
the poet thus envying those natural creatures that behave 'As if they
scorned both resting-place and rest'. Our suspicions of a highly unstable
psyche are further encouraged when we encounter an alternative hyperbole
applied to the possession of the world below. For Wordsworth figures
himself as the 'owner' and 'Lord' of an 'unappropriated bliss' (42), and
one which not only matches but actually *surpasses* that allotted to the first
couple:

The boon is absolute; surpassing grace
To me hath been vouchsafed; among the bowers
Of blissful Eden this was neither given
Nor could be given – possession of the good
Which had been sighed for, ancient thought fulfilled,
And dear Imaginations realized
Up to their highest measure, yea, and more.

(44)

The bliss that is described is literally an internal one but, as with the
account of Helvellyn Fair, it is hard not to sense the alternative sphere that
the images that Wordsworth chooses habitually occupy in the sphere of
public language: here, those of earthly authority and possession of the
and. Since Wordsworth did *not* own the vale, such a projection must

remain at the level of the imaginary. Indeed, it had best remain so, since it is in clear conflict with the cohesive and egalitarian society that the poem postulates for the locality: a 'small abiding-place of many men' that is

> A Whole without dependence or defect,
> Made for itself and happy in itself,
> Perfect Contentment, Unity entire.
>
> (48)

The versions of community that *Home at Grasmere* projects are variously emphasized, but none of them involve lords or squires! There is a 'paternal sway', but it is exercised only by God, over 'high and low', who form 'One family and one mansion' (90). It is not a perfect place, since 'selfishness and envy and revenge' exist here as they do elsewhere; but it yet comes as close as perhaps any place could to the Wordsworthian ideal. Labour is 'free and unenslaved' and poverty is not so extensive as to be beyond the capacity of the immediate community to relieve it (66). Thanks to the high proportion of owner-occupiers,

> In this enclosure many of the old
> Substantial virtues have a firmer tone
> Than in the base and ordinary world.
>
> (68)

This cannot, however, be a means for readjusting the social contract at large. The word 'enclosure' tells all (and again seems to beg reference to some of the harsher practices of the local gentry).[12] Despite the poet's desire that what is experienced by him might be extended to 'all the Vales of earth and all mankind' (52), he is well aware that this chosen vale is a 'termination and a last retreat', a place 'divided from the world/ As if it were a cave' (48, 90). His rhetoric tends toward the Utopian, as well as toward the near-hysterical possessiveness that we have already noted: with the mention of the 'happy Valley' (60), it is hard to avoid recollecting the drama of *Rasselas*. When not inviting us to regard himself and his sister as members of an ideal society, he is casting them as a 'solitary pair' (58). Again, the omission of any mention of wife and children is striking; the affirmative image of domesticity is refused. Trying to dismiss his doubts about whether the other inmates of the vale are worthy of their places, Wordsworth launches into another affirmation by negation that precisely parallels the disturbing final section of the 'Tintern Abbey' poem:

> And if this
> Were not, we have enough within ourselves,
> Enough to fill the present day with joy
> And overspread the future years with hope
>
> (92)

Home at Grasmere has indeed admitted enough qualifications of the sort that will reappear in *The Excursion* – the adulterous husband, for example (68–70) – to make it clear that there are imperfections to be noted. This is not in itself too troubling; on the contrary, it functions as the measure of retraction that makes the ideal all the more convincing. What *is* striking about Wordsworth's accounts of his neighbours, however, is that they never come in the form of encounters, conversations, or shared occasions. Nor are there any reports of daily intercourse at the common-place level. In fact, the most intimate communication that the poet and his sister have with the other dwellers in the vale is by means of objective corollaries. As they look upon natural objects, so they are conscious that others have done so, and have endowed them with their own meanings, whether private or sociable (78–80). The vale may indeed 'swarm with sensation', but it is all indirect, mediated through rocks and stones and trees. The language that the Wordsworths share with their neighbours is thus a silent one; direct discourse is avoided or displaced.

The ethic of sociability and the desire for (or experience of) solitude are thus uneasily yoked together in this poem, continuing to appear the heterogeneous ideas that they are. Cowper's poem 'Retirement' had argued that a profitable and healthy retreat from public life could only occur if the retiree devoted himself to God and good works, and had the sustaining presence of a small circle of close friends:

> Such friends prevent what else wou'd soon succeed,
> A temper rustic as the life we lead,
> And keep the polish of the manners clean
> As theirs who bustle in the busiest scene.
> For solitude, however some may rave,
> Seeming a sanctuary, proves a grave,
> A sepulchre in which the living lie,
> Where all good qualities grow sick and die.
> (1787, 1: 295)

In Wordsworth's poem, it is as if the single self can convince itself that it is social, without ever being put to the test. And yet the conviction is only partial, questioned as soon as asserted. It would be a mistake to see Wordsworth as a 'natural' solitary who expressed a commitment to an intersubjective world only out of some sense of guilt or obligation. The single and the social are both living parts of his divided personality. Thus, if *Home at Grasmere* presents a poetic self that is more than ever private, then this is not so much a resolution as a heightening of the tension that this study has been arguing for throughout. The gap between the public and the private does here seem especially acute. Wordsworth will try again to represent and redress it in the dramatic form of *The Excursion*.

The Excursion is a poem built around encounters, though they are mostly (excepting those involving the Solitary) between people who are at some remove from what they are describing. The absence of such encounters is, as has been said, one of the factors that troubles the communal aspirations of *Home at Grasmere*. Nor is *The Prelude* much richer in reports of meetings or conversations between Wordsworth and others. John Fleming and Michel Beaupuy are singled out for honourable mention, and Coleridge is rhetorically produced at various points in the poem. But there are remarkably few social interactions that seem in any sense crucial. The drowned man of Esthwaite and the blind beggar of London are seen, but they do not respond; and the man with the sickly child does not know that he is being watched, let alone memorized for future versification (8: 844f.). The one major encounter in the poem, that with the discharged soldier, is one of its oddest and least 'resolved' events.

The student Wordsworth is home for his first summer vacation, walking at night along a road, in that 'listless' state that so often precedes a moment of error or correction in his poetry, and claiming an 'exhausted mind worn out by toil' (4: 379, 381).[13] The mood of the landscape is one of 'peace and solitude', into which there intrudes the 'uncouth shape' of the discharged soldier (lines 389, 402). This man is uncommonly tall, thin and 'ghastly' – a word used three times in this account (lines 411, 468, 493). Wordsworth watches awhile, in awe, but overcomes his 'specious cowardice' (line 435) and reveals himself, offering to lead the man to a neighbouring cottage where he may receive shelter for the night. In his reported air of detachment from both man and nature, pushed indeed to the point of almost complete insensibility (lines 444, 472, 474f.), the soldier recalls two other solitaries in Wordsworth's poetry, the old man travelling and the Cumberland beggar. As they reach the cottage, the speaker seems to express his own discomfort in voicing a mild 'reproof' (line 492), bidding the man resort to charity or to the parish as a way of relieving his condition:

> I entreated that henceforth
> He would not linger in the public ways,
> But ask for timely furtherance, and help
> Such as his state required.
>   (4: 489–92)

This somewhat complacent faith in society's ability to alleviate such situations is entirely convincing in a young man struggling with conflicting feelings of his own. As if sensing those feelings, the soldier's reply comes in the form of a denial or a challenge:

> He said, 'My trust is in the God of Heaven,
> And in the eye of him that passes me'.
>   (lines 494–5)

He refuses, in other words, the passing on of responsibility that the speaker's advice seeks to bring about. Wordsworth leaves the scene feeling that he *has* done his duty, and goes home 'with quiet heart' (line 504). But he has also sought to avoid ever being faced with such an encounter again, by trying to force the old soldier into a clear, public signification of his needy condition. The man's refusal to beg or apply for relief makes many points at once, some in conflict with one another; as such, this account prefigures many of the problems we will encounter in the rest of this study when we try to plot the political implications of Wordsworth's interactions with the poor and dispossessed.

On the one hand, the soldier's response establishes the dignity and independent self-respect of this vagrant man, who is far from being the exploitative, conniving n'er-do-well that a significant proportion of the poet's 'polite' readers would have been likely to assume him to be. In thus making clear the pride and dignity of a member of the vagrant class, Wordsworth gestures against those who would have sought to discredit *all* forms of charity or relief on the grounds of the unworthiness of their objects. On the other hand, this encounter also questions the need for or advisability of such charity or relief by showing a man who does not want it, and who should perhaps not be encouraged to want it, lest these positive qualities of independence and self-respect be eroded. Wordsworth does not quite reproduce the terms of one argument dear to the hearts of the taxpayers, and voiced by Burke among others: that charity be encouraged at the expense of parish relief or formal welfare. Had he sheltered the man himself, or dipped into his own pocket, this interpretation might have been invited. But he does not do so. Nor does the soldier ask for anything. He is minding his own business until the poet happens along in the role of potential good Samaritan. The focus of the exchange is more on the poet's feelings than on the soldier's. Those feelings are not marked by any convincingly pious self-esteem, such as the charitable gesture might be thought to bring about. On the contrary, he attempts to duck the challenge that this man represents by advising him to announce his identity and condition in a socially unambiguous way. Wordsworth was very much against the 'methodical' versions of poor relief that he associated with the utilitarian philanthropists, as we shall see; he thought them corrupting for both giver and receiver. The speaker's attempt to avoid the need for an *individual* response is here held up for critical inspection. But what exactly is the alternative? Wordsworth never publicly or consciously discredited the need for a system of public relief; indeed, at various times he explicitly defends it, against Burkean social doctrines of *laissez-faire*. Nor does he sentimentalize the practice of charity, allowing himself any glow of self-esteem following the act of giving. In fact, he seems *not* to resolve precisely the 'political' implications of the meeting with the discharged soldier, so that what the scene finally reproduces is a confusion in the speaker's relation to him and to his kind. There is a clear challenge to the assumptions of a polite readership, who might see only something dishonest, inhuman or grotesque in this distracted old man. But the poet does *not* place himself in a convincing posture of identity or sympathy. The residually Gothic details of the soldier's appearance may indeed stem from his standing for an admonitory, paternal presence in the Wordsworthian psyche (Onorato, 1971, 248–53), but they also speak for a social and personal distance between the poet and the pauper. Once again, Wordsworth occupies an ambiguous middle ground between two worlds and is simply representative of neither.

Kenneth Johnston (1984, 5–6) has argued that Wordsworth intended this and two other 'encounter' scenes for the opening section of *The Recluse*. It is both instructive and puzzling to imagine this prospectively major public poem beginning with three such unstable rehearsals of the relation between poet and society. Wordsworth is so constantly amazed, arrested, confused and rebuked by the otherness of others that these meetings often have the air of providential interruptions of an otherwise obsessive solipsism, as if he were being 'admonished from another world' (*Prelude*, 7:623). Finding such significance in the wanderers and strolling bedlamites is indeed a breach of 'decorum' and was clearly a challenge to readerly expectations. But it also clothes them with an air of melodrama and hyperbolic eventfulness that speaks for the poet's own previous detachment and isolation. As we will see in the following chapters, Wordsworth's reported encounters are richly inscribed with the symptoms of his own displacement.

5
'By conflicting passions pressed': 'Michael' and 'Simon Lee'

The starting point of this study, Wordsworth's 'Gipsies', revealed a sophisticated anxiety about the related topics of poetry, property and labour; the speaker judges the gypsies harshly, but covertly envies them, and he cannot inscribe a convincing integrity to his own position. Poetic hyperbole reveals upon analysis a whole range of conflicting undercurrents that are at once, though to different degrees, idiosyncratic and intersubjective, personal and generically historical. In Chapters 2 and 3 I have explained Wordsworth's negative criticism of the symptoms of urbanization, which is much more coherently imaged in his writings than any simply available alternative in the rural life. When he speaks of life in the towns and cities, he speaks from a distance that is certainly falsifiable or questionable, and that is in itself a sign of his displacement; but the same distance allows him at least a discursive objectivity and the privilege of coherent argument, however remote his argument might be from someone else's sense of the facts. In writing about the rural life, however, Wordsworth is more frequently able to draw upon his own habitual experiences and observations, and thus more prone to write about what is 'present'; though he does not always do so.

As we might predict from the example of 'Gipsies', and from the conflicts evident in *The Prelude* and in the prose writings, that present is defined by contradictions and discomforting ambiguities. If the mark of alienation in Wordsworth's view of the cities consists in an over-zealous objectivity, then we may find the same alienation inscribed in the poems of rural life in the form of a tortured or unstable subjectivity. It is not always the same; we cannot read one poem and assume that the schema it suggests can be simply transferred to another, because the nature of the conjunction between personal and general energies varies with the particular circumstances. Thus, in the remaining chapters, I find myself writing in great detail upon a few poems. Only by so doing, I think, can the finer tones of that conjunction be appreciated. At the same time, some general tendencies do emerge from these close readings, and taken together I hope that they will provide a new perspective on the 'great years' before 1815, and in particular one that makes fresh sense of the relation between some of these poems and *The Excursion*.

The poetry of property

While 'Gipsies' has remained largely unread and certainly unanalysed, 'Michael' is understandably recognized as one of the great achievements of English poetry. Here, in some of the finest blank verse in the language, and in a diction that perhaps comes as close as poetry can come to the language of ordinary men, is Wordsworth's most detailed exposition of the virtues of the rural statesman's life, and of the tragedy of its disappearance. Knowing what we now do about the conditions of land holding in the Lake District, we can appreciate the degree to which the tragedy is enhanced by the hard work that Michael had to put in to free his land from inherited debts or obligations:

> These fields were burthen'd when they came to me;
> 'Till I was forty years of age, not more
> Than half of my inheritance was mine.
>
> (*LB*, 237)

We are not told precisely *how* they were burdened. Perhaps Michael was among the estimated two-thirds of the local yeomen who were customary tenants rather than freeholders. Bailey and Culley (1794, 44) had noted

> a laudable anxiety in the customary tenants to have their little patrimony descend to their children. These small properties (loaded with fines, heriots, and boon days, joined to the necessary expense of bringing up and educating a numerous family), can only be handed down, from father to son, by the utmost thrift, hard labour, and penurious living.

Or, perhaps part of the land was held under customary tenure, the rest being freehold: hence the assertion that not more than half of Michael's land belonged to him. Patterns of ownership were often complex, and J.D. Marshall (1973, 212–15) gives some examples of the possible combinations. If Michael's father had been a freeholder, he might have mortgaged some of his property in order to acquire more, or to raise cash, leaving his son with the task of redeeming it. Wordsworth, as so often, avoids the implication that there might have been anything imperfect in the social system that brought this about, and concentrates instead on the efficient sense of ownership that has since come about.

Even more vague are the 'unforeseen misfortunes' that now oppress Michael's nephew, for whom he is 'bound/ In surety', and whose misfortunes now cost him 'but little less/ Than half his substance' (233). This is what forces the decision between selling land and sending Luke to the town, to the uncertainties of 'trade' and the temptations of the urban–commercial psychology (234). When Luke fails, the exact terms of the failure are again left unspecified:

> Meantime Luke began
> To slacken in his duty, and at length
> He in the dissolute city gave himself
> To evil courses: ignominy and shame
> Fell on him, so that he was driven at last
> To seek a hiding-place beyond the seas.
> (239)

We sense that it is the city that encourages this lapse, and that Luke *gives himself* to it. Without the frugal restraints and the benevolent discipline of the family, his sense of virtue cannot develop or survive. Thus it is *shame* as much as material distress that forces him overseas; his self-esteem is eroded beyond repair, so that the prodigal cannot return.[1]

As Luke's decline is related to a hostile environment, but also specified as a result of a self-elected gesture, so Wordsworth similarly minimizes the suggestion that the initial cause of this domestic tragedy might be related to the contradictions in the agrarian life itself. We have seen the evidence that this life was not always if ever a perfect commonwealth, so much as a somewhat unmellowed feudality. Wordsworth emphasizes that Michael has overcome whatever burdens he inherited; the ones that now afflict him are self-incurred out of fraternal loyalty, 'a fool at last/ To my own family' (233). In the same spirit, Wordsworth avoids any direct condemnation of the 'Stranger's hand' that possesses the land after Isabel's death. There is a suggestion of enclosure and 'improvement' – 'the ploughshare has been through the ground' (240) – but no more than that. No particular impropriety is attributed to the new owner's behaviour, despite the fact that, given what Douglas (1946, 150–5) tells us about the local record of the Flemings, we might suspect that the actual family would have been the objects of an overt policy of engrossment. Dorothy's journal reports a conversation with John Fisher in May 1800 as follows:

> He talked much about the alteration in the times, and observed that in a short time there would be only two ranks of people, the very rich and the very poor, 'for those who have small estates', says he, 'are forced to sell, and all the land goes into one hand'.
>
> (1952, 1: 40)

This suggests that Wordsworth's version of rural decline must be set in a context in which it was common to focus on the relations between the social classes as a cause of change.[2] The narrative that Wordsworth devises avoids any such implication, and may thus speak for a conscious or unconscious discomfort with the real background to the poem. Furthermore, Wordsworth apparently recalled, in 1836, that the poem had been partly based on a local episode whereby 'the son of an old couple' had 'become dissolute and run away from his parents' (PW, 2: 478). The order of events is interesting. If he had become dissolute *before* running away, then the image of perfect familial harmony in an ideal rural economy is at once fractured: Wordsworth's panegyric on the saving strength of the domestic affections may well have been out of tune with the 'facts'. Thus he relocated the principle of corruption in the urban environment.

We shall return to 'Michael' again in a moment. Meanwhile, it is worth remarking that the social and economic world impinging upon the drama of 'The Brothers' is equally unspecific about any tensions between the Ewbanks and the great local proprietors. The vicar reports that

> For five long generations had the heart
> Of Walter's forefathers o'erflow'd the bounds
> Of their inheritance, that single cottage,
> You see it yonder, and those few green fields.
> They toil'd and wrought, and still, from sire to son,
> Each struggled, and each yielded as before
> A little – yet a little – and old Walter,
> They left to him the family heart, and land
> With other burthens than the crop it bore.
> Year after year the old man still preserv'd
> A chearful mind, and buffeted with bond,
> Interest and mortgages; at last he sank,
> And went into his grave before his time.
>
> (LB, 142)

The passage bears close examination, for it is hard to decipher precisely. The Ewbanks had always worked hard to expand their property – not at all an ignoble ambition in Wordsworthian terms – but thanks to the ambiguous word 'yielded' we cannot be sure if they succeeded. They might have *produced* a gradual gain in the family holdings, and created debts to do it; or, their ambition might have driven them into *forfeiting*, bit by bit, what they already had. It seems not to matter, since Walter inherits the family ambitions, along with greater inhibitions than ever before. These inhibitions are not tithes, fines and heriots, the semi-feudal obligations that were the traditional encumbrances of the customary tenant; but bonds, interests and mortgages. Once again, it is clear that the Ewbanks, for laudable reasons indeed, have brought upon *themselves* the woes that now impinge upon the family. Wordsworth's emphasis deflects any suspicions we might have about the doings of the local gentry, and suggests that the Ewbanks have failed in some sort of 'free market' situation. Leonard goes to sea 'chiefly for his brother's sake' (145), but the logic of the narrative tells us that it is his own family legacy that makes this recourse necessary. Indeed, Wordsworth's account of this decision, added into the poem at some time after 1805, is a strange and strained reference to his own brother's fate, and almost suggests that Leonard might have been guilty of wilful folly in being

> tempted to entrust
> His expectations to the fickle winds
> And perilous waters.
>
> (*PW*, 2:2)

Wordsworth here sounds more like a sanctimonious vicar than the vicar himself. The echo of the opening scene of *The Merchant of Venice*, which has Antonio anxiously awaiting the return of his vessels, is telling, for Leonard too is afloat on the sea of trade, whose psychological profile is that of the pure desire that is intimated in the account of the calenture, where Leonard projects visions of his own upon the infinite and empty sea. This near-blaming of Leonard is consistent with the later logic whereby the Ewbanks are made responsible for their own misfortunes.

Thus, in both 'Michael' and 'The Brothers', the economic complexity of Lakeland society is pared down in order to locate the two families in a free space wherein their respective declines are the result of a high degree of self-determination. They are not blamed explicitly, since they are pursuing good Wordsworthian ambitions; but their failure is completely disconnected from any spectre of enclosing landlords or lordly neighbours. Of course, this strategy achieves the familiar Wordsworthian focus on immediacy, and on the emotional effects of living within broken families; but it also abstracts the protagonists from any place within a social contract that is not made up of people just like themselves.

The complexity of the social and economic narrative in 'Michael' is not simply to be looked for in the reported details of the shepherd's life and fortunes. For, to a degree that has only recently become the object of attention, this is also a poem about the poet who writes it. It would have been much more so had the manuscript drafts reprinted by de Selincourt (*PW*, 2: 479–84) found their way into the published poem, for they are denser in self-reference than the finished poem. In the 1800 text the most significant of such references occur in the first forty lines. Here, Wordsworth's introduction to the story of the sheepfold contains a rather startling confession:

> It was the first,
> The earliest of those tales that spake to me
> Of Shepherds, dwellers in the vallies, men
> Whom I already lov'd, not verily
> For their own sakes, but for the fields and hills
> Where was their occupation and abode.
>   (*LB*, 227)

This makes clear enough literal sense. As a boy, Wordsworth would have known little of the shepherds, who lived in the remoter vales and were perhaps a disappearing class; but he did know the fields and hills, and he could thus learn to sympathize, as he goes on to tell us, with 'passions that were not my own'. The life that he relates was not, we are told, known to him personally, but was already part of the traditional repository of oral culture. But what has come down to us of the sources for the poem suggests that the events that went into it might not have happened so very long ago, nor been so remote. The episode of the dissolute son does not seem to be a piece of remote history, and Rawnsley (1889, 100) has his local informant report that the cottage called 'Village Clock' is still standing in 1882, although the shepherd who used to live there has died. Not only does Wordsworth poeticize the cottage into the 'Evening Star' (230); he pushes it back in time and has it destroyed completely. (We might note also the appearance, in this domesticated form, of Wordsworth's later preoccupation with the evening star, already discussed.) Why did Wordsworth push the events of the poem further back into history than he need have done? The force of the example is in one sense strengthened by having the tragedy seem so final; but it is in another sense weakened in that it does not purport to address a present crisis. The letter to Fox *claims* a present application in describing 'the domestic affections as I know they exist amongst a class of men who are now almost confined to the North of England', and who are 'rapidly disappearing' (*EY*, 314–15). But the manufacturing economy and urban manners that this letter blames for their disappearance only register very inexplicitly in the poems themselves, in the form of peculiar self-determining ambitions; and, as I have stressed, 'Michael' takes place wholly in the past, and within an aura of idealism that Wordsworth elsewhere described as having become inapplicable at some time 'within the last sixty years' (*PrW*, 2: 206). Perhaps, in his poetic selfhood, Wordsworth sensed the need to remove the image of ideal owner-occupier existence *out of* the Westmoreland of 1800, where sons became dissolute before they ran away, and where gentlemen and statesmen were not subsisting in harmonious co-operation and mutual esteem.

We return now to Wordsworth's odd confession that he loved the shepherds 'not verily/ For their own sakes'. This does, as has been said, make literal sense; but it also invites a darker reading, one suggesting that he did not love them at all. Because Michael is the only shepherd mentioned in the poem, the implication is that his class is already part of the folk memory; but Rawnsley tells us that one at least survived until later times, and his cottage even longer. The writing-out of the present shepherds invites the suspicion of a thoughtful pun on 'verily'; for they, indeed, are not loved, nor are they mentioned. Wordsworth may be talking at once of past and present, with that peculiar honesty that so often invades his poetry. The boy might understandably have experienced love of nature leading to love of man; but the man makes no mention of a present man to love.

The play between the present and the past that a recovery of the contexts and sources for 'Michael' reveals is, as usual, eloquent. It presents the poem as the site of conflicts within the poet, within his subject, and within the relation between the two. In speaking of a world that has already passed away, the poetic self achieves a measure of distance and control, but the symptoms of uncertainty and insecurity remain. The poet will retell the tale

> For the delight of a few natural hearts,
> And with yet fonder feeling, for the sake
> Of youthful Poets, who among these Hills
> Will be my second self when I am gone.
> (227)

He sees only a small audience in the present, and perhaps an even smaller one in the future. As he is the medium for the transcription of the tale of Michael, putting it for the first time into the written culture, so he too will be but a memory to be revivified by later poets. The egotism is typically Wordsworthian, and typically complex, for it adds to the displacement back into history a displacement into a tenuous future: what, we may wonder, will these youthful poets write about, given the disappearance of the ideal virtues from modern life?

The invocation of the future does seem to offer Wordsworth something more positive than Goldsmith foresees for himself at the end of *The Deserted Village*; but, as with the 'Tintern Abbey' poem, there is here a

definite reluctance to face the present: in both poems, we can establish a
definite discomfort about working through the implications of what is
there. Wordsworth looks to 'youthful poets' in much the same way that
Michael looks to Luke, for a 'second self'. Michael sends his son out into
a world bedevilled by the urban mentality, as Wordsworth sends his poem.
But, while Michael does begin the poem with real property to hand down,
the product of undeniably hard and honest labour, Wordsworth can only
tentatively and wishfully imply the same for himself. Dorothy's journal
consistently describes her brother as working 'at the sheepfold', rather
than on the poem *about* the sheepfold (1952, 1:67–72), and he often
seems to have worked 'in vain'. It is hard not to infer that the fate of
Michael, beginning in hope and ending in despondency (if not madness), is
also that of the poet who tells about him. The appeal to 'youthful poets'
remains potential, but there is little in Wordsworth's vision of the future
that promises to make it actual. If Wordsworth is a Michael-figure, he is
also a Luke-figure, one who threatens to waste what he already has. The
financial circumstances of the Wordsworth family were extremely complicated, and I cannot fully describe them here. Suffice it to observe, none the
less, that Richard Wordsworth had been 'bonded' for William, in order
that the Calvert legacy should not be withheld on the grounds that it might
immediately be swallowed up by the debt William owed his aunt for his
educational expenses (*EY*, 131). William too was thus a potentially errant
nephew, just like Michael's nephew. Meanwhile, much of the Calvert
legacy was lent out to Montagu and to Charles Douglas (183). Montagu
lapsed in interest payments, and according to Moorman (1969, 297)
almost half of the legacy was in Montagu's hands by the end of 1796. The
principal was not finally paid off until 1814; meanwhile, Wordsworth's
brother John was consciously working for the financial support of the
family, and the poet himself was in various kinds of debt to his own
relatives (see *EY*, 180–200).

If Michael was 'a fool at last/ To my own family' (*LB*, 233), then
Wordsworth was perhaps doubly imprudent in being both a lender and a
borrower. The objective account of Michael's financial career is closely
related to some of the obsessive insecurities in the Wordsworth circle. Not
for nothing have several readers recently troubled the calm surface of this
poem with speculations about exactly what kind of legacy is handed on by
whom. Peter Manning (1977) has made good sense of the biblical allusions
(Luke as Isaac, as Christ, and as the prodigal son) in reading the poem as
an image of tension between the generations. Manning argues for Wordsworth's discomforting identification with the figure of the father, a figure
that is made much more strongly negative in John Bushnell's (1981)
reading of Michael as a dark, repressive presence, an extreme version of
the Abraham figure. Sydney Lea (1978) also explores the symmetry of poet

and protagonist in seeing in Wordsworth's 'passionate proprietorship of the pastoral vision' an analogue to Michael's relation to the sheepfold (67).[3]

To see Michael as a dark presence is, I think, to go too far, and to misunderstand his place in Wordsworth's image of the ideal rural economy. Similarly, the poem is not primarily or exclusively about its poet. These patterns do impinge on the poem, but they do not organize it in any complete or exclusive way. Wordsworth does seem to have been unsure about exactly how to present the material that finds its way into 'Michael', and in the drafts for a poem perhaps to be called 'The Sheepfold', published by Stephen Parrish (1970), there are hints that it might have been attempted in what the speaker himself calls a 'doggrel strain', of which the following is a fair example:

> Two shepeherds we have they're the wits of the vale,
> Renown'd for song satire epistle & tale
> > (Parrish, 1970, 72)

The exact relation of this material to what became 'Michael' has been debated and contested,[4] but we can at least suggest that in these early drafts Wordsworth was experimenting with a more self-consciously and perhaps ironically pointed version of the tale – or, of the sheepfold part of the tale. He was, at least, trying out different ways of relating the mood of the teller to the matter of the tale.

This account of 'Michael' has perhaps demonstrated that we can trace in the features and details of this uncontested masterpiece some of the same tensions and conflicts that appear in 'Gipsies'. This is not to render the two poems in any sense identical, but rather to show the applicability of the questions that 'Gipsies' raises to other and better-known cases. 'Michael' is of course the more conventionally 'finished' poem, in that it explores a fully delineated narrative and an 'empirical' instance of the themes of poetry, property and labour. Property and labour are described in great detail, while poetry is barely touched upon; thus the image of the empirical remains an aesthetically convincing one. But it too has been contrived, by displacing Michael into a vanished past, and by paring down the probable complexities and social interactions involved in the decline of the actual statesmen. What is offered as 'reportage' has been worked upon for reasons both personal and general. One has no sense, reading this poem, of an old shepherd who might have been living on in a cottage called 'Village Clock', or of a dissolute son running away from home, or of a local gentry taking over ownership of the landscape. These items of information do not of course undermine or disprove the poem; it remains polemically efficient as a transcription of how the ideal rural economy might indeed operate for its inhabitants. But, in making the family tragedy largely self-incurred, as he does again in 'The Brothers', there is no doubt that Wordsworth is avoiding mention of a number of other and perhaps more likely possibilities. One should not make the point too strongly; but it is hard to avoid at least a lurking suspicion that both Ewbanks and Michaels are being covertly blamed for their imprudence, even as their desire for property is entirely laudable and perhaps economically inevitable. It is, at least, finally unclear *who* is to blame for the decline of the rural statesmen. Michael, of course, could hardly have done otherwise than help his kinsman; but Wordsworth chose to plot the poem that way, and not in others.

The poet as patron

I turn now to another representation of rural poverty, one that will be found to be even more revelatory of hitherto unnoticed personal–historical anxieties: 'Simon Lee', first put before the public in the 1798 *Lyrical Ballads*. Much of the commentary on this poem has concentrated on the way in which it is a 'test' of the reader's ability to sympathize with a poetry devoid of gaudy and inane phraseology and loudly declared messages.[5] This critical emphasis is entirely consonant with Wordsworth's own, as he speaks of 'placing my Reader in the way of receiving from ordinary moral sensations another and more salutary impression than we are accustomed to receive from them' (*PrW*, 1: 126–8). Challenging us with the declaration that the ideal reader will find a 'tale in every thing' (*LB*, 62), 'Simon Lee' seems to fulfil Wordsworth's anti-authoritarian mandate in transcribing a poet who is a man speaking to men, rather than a sage gifted with superior insight. Invited to 'make' our own tale out of the raw materials of this incident, we at once accede to a creative stature and admire a poet who is prepared to record events that are inconclusive and even potentially inconsequential. In his assertion of the ordinary event as of great poetic importance, Wordsworth is mounting the sort of attack upon decorum that offended so many of the readers of his early work, and still offends others today.

We may wonder, none the less, whether Wordsworth is here making virtue of necessity, and inviting the reader's response as a way of displacing something that is not, in the last analysis, open to any comfortable aesthetic or moral control. This question must be pursued, once again, by tracing the clues that lead to the unfolding of a social and historical density to the images that Wordsworth as speaker seems to seek to evacuate or to displace. We may begin with Isabella Fenwick's account of the poet's recollection of the raw materials that gave rise to the poem:

This old man had been huntsman to the Squires of Alfoxden, which, at the time we occupied it, belonged to a minor. The old man's cottage stood upon the common, a little way from the entrance to Alfoxden Park. But it had disappeared. Many other changes had taken place in the adjoining village, which I could not but notice with a regret more natural than well-considered. Improvements but rarely appear such to those who, after long intervals of time, revisit places they have had much pleasure in. It is unnecessary to add, the fact was as mentioned in the poem; and I have, after an interval of 45 years, the image of the old man as fresh before my eyes as if I had seen him yesterday. The expression when the hounds were out, 'I dearly love their voices' was word for word from his own lips.

(PW, 4: 412–13)

The Fenwick note pays homage to many of the archetypes of Wordsworth's poetics. The emotion is recollected in tranquillity, but becomes almost as intense, after an interval of forty-five years, as if it were being experienced in the present. And Wordsworth authenticates the diction of the poem as in part a transcription of what the old man actually said, which is thus reported without the deviant glosses of poetic diction.

But this more or less exhausts the claims to documentary exactitude that can be made for this poem. Mark Reed dates its composition to the period March–May 1798, and the meeting with the old man to the autumn of 1797 (1967, 32, 202). The Wordsworths were a long way from Cardigan, and were in fact living at Alfoxden House, in Somersetshire; and the old man's name was not Simon Lee but Christopher Tricky. Moorman (1969, 329) reports that Tricky and his wife lived at the dog pound just outside the grounds of the house, and that the Wordsworths first made his acquaintance by asking him about the navigability of the local rivers, thus contributing to the spy rumours that were circulating in the neighbourhood about the new tenants and their odd friends – Poole, Coleridge and, most notoriously of all, radical John Thelwall, who visited the Wordsworths between autumn 1797 and the writing of the poem. Thelwall actually had plans to settle near Alfoxden, but was dissuaded from doing so as a result of the Wordsworth circle's concern about the spy rumours: he moved on to Llyswen Farm, in Brecknockshire.

The Wordsworths were not, then, at all comfortably integrated into the local community of which Christopher Tricky was the most closely contiguous representative. It was a time of national paranoia, focused on the possibility of a French invasion, and it is not surprising that the educated democrats from afar should have been the objects of gossip and suspicion. Exchanges between the Wordsworths and the Trickys must have been somewhat tense and embarrassed.

So: the real Christopher Tricky became the fictional Simon Lee, renominated into a generic, pseudo-biblical identity (his wife's name is Ruth), rehoused in his cottage (if he had ever had one – the Trickys were living at the dog pound), and shunted out of the Alfoxden landscape into the 'sweet shire of Cardigan' (*LB*, 60). Why Cardigan? The simplest explanation of such a displacement would rest with the shared syllabic patterning of Alfoxden and Cardigan, and invoke the principle of casual poetic licence. But there are a good many clues that suggest a more coherently motivated choice of location.

To the best of my knowledge Wordsworth had never been in south-west Wales; but in his account of the Celtic revival, David Solkin has pointed out the implications of the image of Wales for eighteenth-century men of letters (1982, 86f.). Among them was a strong tradition identifying Wales as a bastion of that much-vaunted entity, 'British liberty'. As the Welsh mountains had once kept out the invading Romans, so they were, from the 1760s, imagined to be keeping out also the more subtle modern corruptions of commerce and luxury. Wales became the locus of a picturesque feudalism, what Solkin (102) calls the 'patrician rural ideal'. As one might expect, this image persisted in despite of evidence that the actual economic condition of Wales was one of extreme poverty and hardship. (We have already seen that the Lake District was to provide Wordsworth with some of the same images.) Solkin quotes John Shebbeare, writing in 1756:

> Not long since on a journey into … Wales … I found more remains of ancient vasselage amongst the common people, and a greater simplicity of manners, than is to be met with in England … The peasants, as free by law as those in England, yet retain a great deal of obedience to their landlords, which was paid the Barons of old.
>
> (101)

This is a more explicitly hierarchical image of rural society than that Wordsworth was to claim as typical of the Lake District, but it speaks forth the same virtuous traditionalism. As Prys Morgan (1984, 45) has put it, the 'image of Wales was of a quaint back-of-beyond where gentlemen with hardly a shirt to their backs reeled off endless family trees going back to Aeneas from Troy'. Morgan suggests that the Welsh were very far behind with fashions, still wearing in the 1790s what had been current in England in the 1620s; and that the atmosphere in Wales in the 1790s was fiercely anti-revolutionary (60, 80). At the same time, things *were* changing owing to the attractions of the metropolis and the abandonment of the old ways (49–50).

This explains something of the implications of Wordsworth's removal of Simon Lee's cottage to the 'sweet shire of Cardigan', a place that was the site of the first recorded eisteddfod (Morgan, 1984, 56) and thus perhaps closely associated with the old traditions. In his mention of 'pleasant

Ivor-hall', moreover, Wordsworth seems to have been calling up a precise literary allusion. Morgan's account is worth quoting at length:

> Iolo Morganwg [a Welsh poet of the late eighteenth century] was responsible for turning many obscure figures into national heroes ... Iolo was farming in the 1780s in the marshland between Cardiff and Newport, where he came into contact with Evan Evans, then a drunken, threadbare curate at Bassaleg, and they both visited the ruins of the fourteenth-century hall of Ifor Hael (Ivor the Generous), who, tradition stated in a vague and uncertain way, had been the patron of the great fourteenth-century poet Dafydd ap Gwilym. Evans wrote a fine romantic poem about the ivy-clad ruins, and Iolo set about his first important forgeries, the imitation of the love poems of Dafydd ap Gwilym, which contained subtle little references to Glamorgan and to Ifor Hael. Iolo in his subsequent writings did much to make out Ifor as the greatest patron of Welsh literature. Ivor became a popular name in Wales, a household word for generosity. The most Welsh of the workmen's benefit societies, the Order of Ivorites, took their name from him; the inns where many of their lodges met were called Ivor Arms, and many of these still survive to this day.
>
> (85)

It is tempting to speculate that Wordsworth might have known something of this. I have found no record of his meeting or reading the works of either Evan Evans or Iolo Morganwg (Edward Williams), but he is likely to have known them. Evans (1731–89) the author of *Some Specimens of the Poetry of the Ancient Welsh Bards* (London, 1764), was born and died in Cardiganshire, a drunkard and a failure; as a writer, he had failed to make his way in the world, a predicament perhaps not too remote from the inner thoughts of the young William Wordsworth in the Alfoxden period. Morganwg, or Edward Williams (1746–1826), was a Unitarian and a member of the radical circle of Priestley and Wakefield. The author of *Poems, Lyric and Pastoral* (2 vols, London, 1794), he must surely have been known to Thelwall, as he was known to Coleridge and thence perhaps to Wordsworth. Coleridge met him in 1796 (1957, 174 n.16), and owned a copy of the poems. The name 'Ifor Hael' (Ivor the Generous) is very close to Wordsworth's 'Ivor-hall', which may thus be a convenient mistranslation, or coinage by association. Ifor Hael, according to Morganwg, lived in Glamorganshire, but it is the unfortunate Evan Evans's locality, Cardigan, that Wordsworth makes the site of his Ivor Hall. The displacement thus expresses both his wishful fantasies and his fears. In placing the incident, and thus himself, in Cardigan, he identifies himself with Evan Evans, the failed poet. And in invoking the name of Ifor Hael as Simon's former master (occluded, that is to say, by the name of the house), he laments at once the plight of the old man and his own condition as a poet without a patron. Morganwg (Edward Williams) had made much of the liberality of Ifor Hael, whom he called 'Ivor the Liberal':

> Thy ample gate, thy ample hall,
> Are ever op'ning wide to all ...
> The poor from thee with joy return,
> They bless thy name, they cease to mourn
> (1794, 1: 193)

Nor is it just the conventional poor who are favoured, for Gwilym himself has received the gift of a pair of gloves crammed with gold:

> Thy Bard, esteem'd the nobler guest,
> Was with distinguish'd bounty bless'd.
> (194)

The momentary social contract between Wordsworth and his Simon Lee thus conceals an identity within its apparent difference; in familiar Wordsworthian style, the stylistic and semantic instabilities of the poem emanate from a complex interrelation of self and other. The poet is able to come to the old man's aid, but his discomfort at so doing is a function of his own sense of displacement as well as of his guilt or embarrassment at being in better health and fortune. At the same time, he is better off than Simon, and is in this way a sort of 'proxy' of the vanished owner of Ivor Hall, able to dispense the assistance that Simon is now sorely missing. The incident thus appeals to a wishful fantasy in Wordsworth: that he himself is not in need, but in a position that enables him to dispense charity and patronage. The predicament of the apprentice poet in a world without patrons is momentarily eclipsed by an act of contingent condescension.

The odd mixture of emotional release, honest sympathy, condescension and embarrassment that critics have often found in the climactic moment of the poem can thus be coherently related to the conflicting aspirations and anxieties in the Wordsworthian psyche. Chopping the tangled root offers the poet a moment of freedom from an ongoing predicament that is all too similar to that of the old man – the predicament of one who cannot earn a living on his own.

Let us look more closely at the circumstances, apart from those of youth and good health, that enabled the poet to come to the aid of the struggling old man. The former squire of Alfoxden had maintained, we assume, his 'running huntsman merry', Christopher Tricky. But the house is now owned by a minor, and is no longer owner-occupied but let out to tenants – none other than the Wordsworths. The poet quite literally substitutes for the squire by living in his house. Alfoxden House, moreover, was not just any old home – it was by a long way the grandest place that the family would ever occupy. Moorman rather modestly calls it 'a charming middle-sized country house' (1969, 325), but Dorothy's account is much more rapturous. Having begun only with 'some dreams of happiness in a little cottage', she describes her residence as follows:

> Here we are in a large mansion, in a large park, with seventy head of deer around us ... The house is a large mansion, with furniture enough for a dozen families like ours ... Wherever we turn we have woods, smooth downs, and valleys with small brooks running down them through green meadows, hardly ever intersected with hedgerows, but scattered over with trees.
>
> (*EY*, 190–1)

Here are the Wordsworths enjoying the aesthetic gratifications of living in the house of the lords of the manor – long, uninterrupted views unmarked by signs of labour or human proximity, and a deer park. Deer had become property rather than game, in the eyes of the law (see Munsche, 1981, 107f.), and symbols of rural gentility. Of course, the house is now owned by a minor, so that the Wordsworths are not occupying the place of an active squirearchy; but the sight of Christopher Tricky's poverty and physical decay could hardly have failed to make William feel uncomfortable about his own tenure of the house that had once maintained him. Perhaps, in the severing of the 'tangled root' (*LB*, 63), we may see some grand, relieving gesture of making amends, as if the tangled roots of the poet's own social anxieties could similarly be struck away in a moment of resolution and independence. For Tricky, Wordsworth's timely appearance perhaps registered as the image of a long-vanished condescension from the master of Alfoxden House. Fond memories of interaction between master and man, as well as his own physical decay and the suggestion that he is all too seldom in receipt of such attentions from his other neighbours, may explain what the poem's speaker registers as an excessive gratitude. The 'long blue livery-coat' that Simon wears suggests a perfect accord of virtue and necessity. It may be the only garment he has left, in his abject poverty, but it is also the sign of his former place in the vanished social system, and of his 'belonging' to the house. As he clothes his back, he may also feed his memories and maintain his self-esteem. Of course, the Wordsworths were merely tenants, paying £23 a year for the privilege of occupying the centre of the landscape; but it is hard to imagine that William would not have felt uncomfortable at the interaction with Tricky, most of all at the time when he was very actively discussing the brotherhood of man with man in the company of Poole, Coleridge and Thelwall. The old order has changed, and the poet seems to have at least a lurking sympathy for its idealized features; but there is no new order yet apparent to relieve the neglect of its displaced members, nor indeed the needs of those who now function symbolically as proprietors. Being able to help an ailing working man must appeal to Wordsworth's democratic imperative, but the form and the traditions of assistance make him the symbol, only partly unwilling, of a vanished feudal order. The instability of his position makes him at once a man of the people – a man assisting a fellow man – and a proxy of the old hierarchy. Wordsworth occupies the classic bourgeois site, an unstable and amorphous middle ground which disables him from validating *any* orthodox social role in a wholehearted manner.

Once again, this is not to be seen simply as a 'generic' example of a conflict determined exclusively by social–historical conditions. As we accord these conditions a prominent causal role, we must also be aware of their compatibility with the idiosyncratic factors that had made up Wordsworth's particular life-experience. The traumas of not belonging and of disconnection must have been especially urgent to a poet who lost his mother when he was 8, and his father when he was 13. From his father's house he might even have recalled the presence of a liveried servant (Moorman, 1969, 9, 11), an image of the bourgeois aspiration to the genteel life. The bizarre mistranslation or coinage of 'Ivor-hall' may then also be a homophonal pun, 'I've a hall', a wished for, if uneasy, restitution of what he had lost – place, parents, and property. Against this paradigm of restitution, we may set the more recently acquired republican sentiments that, in the revolutionary spirit of new beginnings, might have made the ideology of *disconnection* – from place, parents, property – an appealing one. For it was precisely in its replacement of the language of inheritance, paternity and tradition by that of fraternity and equality that the rhetoric of 1789 was most striking. Wordsworth strikes through the tangled root that separates man from man in the social as well as the physical order; none other than Tom Paine, in his *Rights of Man*, had appealed to his reader to 'lay then the axe to the root, and teach governments humanity' (1976, 80).[6]

The conflict of desires and aspirations that are built into this poem is then to be understood in both personal and generic terms, each indeed informing and modifying the other. And, as Wordsworth's ideological and psychological personalities were thus divided within themselves, so too was his economic psyche. He was not an Evan Evans figure, completely unknown and unrewarded; but neither was he a Dafydd ap Gwilym (in Morganwg's reconstruction of him), sheltered by the generous attentions of a wealthy patron. The Calvert legacy had left him a sizeable £900, though much of it had been lent out again in an imprudent fashion. Alfoxden was not a cheap place to live, and might have seemed something of an extravagance to the Wordsworths themselves. The rent was £23 a year, almost three times as much as the £8 a year they would pay for the cottage at Grasmere shortly thereafter (Reed, 1967, 281). This was at a time when the agricultural workers of Somerset and the Vale of Gloucester were making between 1s. and 1s.6d. a day, depending on the season, i.e. between £15 and £22.10s. a year, based on a six-day week for fifty weeks.[7] The much-debated Speenhamland provision of 1795 had proposed that every poor and industrious man should have 3s. weekly, (£7.16s. p.a.), either from his own and his family's labour or from the poor rates, with an extra 1s.6d. a week for the support of his wife and any other family member (Hammond, 1978a, 109). The Wordsworths' expenses for a twelve-month period spanning 1797–8 were, according to Dorothy, £110 (Moorman, 1969, 399). The same sum would be advanced by the Wedgwoods to finance the Wordsworths' and Coleridge's trip to Germany, which they could not otherwise have afforded (409). Wordsworth repaid the loan in 1800. Alfoxden House was clearly not a comfortable symbol of the Wordsworths' financial condition, either actual or imaginary. Wordsworth and Coleridge were to receive thirty guineas from Cottle for the copyright of the first edition of *Lyrical Ballads*; but even as late as 1807, as we have seen, Wordsworth was to cast the then all too predominant sonnet form as his 'scanty plot of ground' (*1807*, 133), an almost exact recall of the 'scrap of land' (*LB*, 62) that Simon Lee had enclosed.[8]

There is one more major element in the iconography of 'Simon Lee' that requires some attention: his identification as a 'huntsman', the right-hand man of the master of hounds, who would usually have been the squire himself. Wordsworth seems quite sensitive to the technical vocabulary of fox hunting. The midland counties of England, where fox hunting was becoming more professionalized by about 1800 (see Itzkowitz, 1977), were commonly known as 'the shires', and Wordsworth places his poem in a 'sweet shire'. Simon's 'long blue livery-coat' may derive from the blue coats worn by the graziers who followed the Quorn; and in Devonshire a 'cry of hounds' was the technically correct term for the pack (Carr, 1976, 85; Itzkowitz, 1977, 34, 47).

Under the laws of the land the fox was classed as vermin rather than as game. This meant that fox hunting was in principle open to all, and not limited to those who owned a certain amount of land. It was, in other words, not subject to the game laws which were perhaps the single most divisive presence in the English legal system, at least in rural areas. E.P. Thompson, in *Whigs and Hunters* (1975), has shown how the rights to game were contested as part of the struggle between Whig magnates and Tory squires some years before Wordsworth was born. But right through the century, there were violent confrontations between poachers and gamekeepers, the haves and the have-nots. Blackstone (1979, 4:409) opined that whereas 'the forest laws established only one mighty hunter throughout the land, the game laws have raised a little Nimrod in every manor'. As such, he calls them a 'bastard slip' in the English legal system. The Hammonds (1978a, 133f.) and Chambers and Mingay (1982, 138) are eloquent about the intensity of the disputes over game; Dorothy Marshall remarks that 'no single factor caused such bad blood and bitter resentment in the countryside than the determination of the landowners to enforce the game laws in all their savagery' (1982, 62).

Relations between landowners and tenants were, then, particularly contentious on the matter of the game laws. These laws seem to have gone through a particular state of crisis in the 1790s, when their enforcement came to be, for the landowners, the public symbol of an anti-Jacobin platform (see Munsche, 1981, 123f.). In Wordsworth's poem, Simon Lee is not only shifted out of Alfoxden into Cardigan, but he is upheld as an emblem of the least socially divisive element of the traditional life of the gentry. Fox hunting stands as an ideal image of co-operation between the social orders in the English countryside. The potentially inflammatory charge that the livery coat of subservience to the squirearchy might have had for some readers of 1798 is diminished by its specification as a relic of fox hunting. If the squire of Alfoxden had ever been a 'little Nimrod', then nothing in the poem hints at such a possibility.[9]

The career of 'huntsman' is a part of Simon's past, an element in that 'mellowed feudality' of which Wordsworth was so fond. Rather more puzzling is his role in the present. He functions now as an owner-occupier, one of that class of persons whom Wordsworth frequently idealizes (in 'Michael', for example) as perfect citizens, and the desired analogues in ordinary life of the poetical character when it is most true to itself. Christopher Tricky had lost his cottage, if he ever had one, but Wordsworth restores Simon Lee to his, though we must wonder why. Simon can hardly stay alive, let alone work, so that he is not a very efficient image of economic self-sufficiency. Wordsworth does not play up his potential as an emblem of persistence in adversity, but rather seems to stress the pointlessness of it all. Simon's function in Wordsworth's economic ideal is thus not very clear; though we might note the ambiguity whereby the poet's gesture of unofficial charity and one-time assistance both compensates for a proper welfare provision (this would be the Burkean-Malthusian argument) and implies its necessity – for Simon's excessive gratitude surely results in part from the fact that he receives so little help of any kind from anyone. Nor should we forget the subjective appeal of this incident to the poet's imagination. Wordsworth is able to make a 'work' out of working, and this moment of climactic physical activity, of doing something whose validation is immediately apparent and beyond doubt, must have afforded him considerable psychological relief. If the hyperbole of 'Gipsies' was in part a result of the self-esteem attendant upon the glow of honest labour, then 'Simon Lee' chronicles the act of labour itself.

If this account of 'Simon Lee' and its coming into being carries any conviction, then it is not surprising that literary critics should have found themselves worrying over oddities of style and diction, which then become the formal manifestations of a serious turbulence and insecurity in Wordsworth's mind, and in the public languages available to it. Hartman (1977, 148) finds that Wordsworth 'has trouble with the tone', although John Danby (1960, 38−47) makes a good case for the purposive conversion of jest to earnest at the end of the poem. Andrew Griffin, in the most thorough of the available studies of 'Simon Lee', sees in its conclusion a 'characteristically fumbling apology', and suggests that in the later revisions Wordsworth loses 'confidence or interest in the burlesque aspects of his loquacious narrators' (1977, 399−400). This does seem to have been the most tangled of all the roots in Wordsworth's shorter poems, and he worked on it constantly over the years (see *PW*, 4: 413). It never achieves the comfortable mock-heroic tone of similar passages in, for example, *Benjamin the Waggoner* (*BW*, 108−10), but always retains elements of strong contrasts and even conflicts in style. How can this be explained, if at all?

As Danby has observed, the opening descriptions of the old man and his environs are platitudinous to say the least. Such phrases as 'sweet shire', 'pleasant Ivor-hall', 'huntsman merry' and 'cheek ... like a cherry' have often been judged to be intrinsically vapid, at best an uncomfortable participation in the language of naïve ballad conventions, at worst a total failure of poetic intelligence. The poem passes on to a more detailed description of Simon's physical predicament, so that a contrast appears between the first and second halves. This also corresponds, as we have seen, with the distinction between the 'invented' and the reported parts of the poem's plot. But what can we make of this? Is the poet in control of these shifts? A case could be made for the fictionalizing motifs of the first half as part of a parodic purpose whereby Wordsworth alludes to the 'fake' poetry of Edward Williams to expose the absurdity of middle-class ideas about what ballads are. Are we invited to mock romantic feudalism only to be later made aware that real people do suffer in real places? Or is Wordsworth totally under the sway of his own inner insecurities that motivate the complex play upon 'Ivor-hall' in the ways that I have already described?[10] This question seems to me genuinely insoluble, and not least because of the point made in various ways by the likes of Freud, Lacan and Derrida about the implausibility of any absolute distinction between the conscious and the unconscious, most of all in the realm of language. If both are motivated energies, then patterns of coherence are going to emerge, and as such they were 'meant', and meant by Wordsworth, whether he knew it or not. And yet the 'covering over' or displacement that the poem performs has proved very efficient, as it has in the case of 'Gipsies'. Wordsworth clearly did not mean his readers to have biographies and chronologies to hand for the deciphering of his meanings.

'Simon Lee' does not clearly and openly transcribe a subject in a state of historical and biographical crisis. Not only does it continue to foreground the questions raised by the 'objective' dimension, the old man's decay and excessive gratitude; it also displaces the production of meaning onto the alerted reader. But that crisis is there none the less, and its terms are available to a careful inspection. The names of the authors did not appear on the title page of the first edition of *Lyrical Ballads*; it is significant, then, that 'Simon Lee' alludes to an idealized, pre-alienated culture in which the production of poetry by gifted individuals is rewarded by lavish recognition, reputation and wealth.

We have, thus far, looked at three of Wordsworth's shorter poems in considerable detail. 'Gipsies' has been usually judged a failure, 'Michael' a masterpiece, and 'Simon Lee' something in between. All of these poems, upon close inspection, reveal complex interactions between the subjective and objective; as they address the objective features of the rural life, so they also dramatize the unstable position of the poet reporting upon them. Christopher Tricky and the band of gypsies lived and breathed, and their reality impinges upon the messages of Wordsworth's poems, even as they are variously refigured into shapes that Wordsworth found more manipulable, comfortable or polemically convenient. The discourses that Wordsworth was addressing by way of these refigurings also had actual consequences and implications. While it is possible to establish differences of degree between the public and the private references that Wordsworth's language brings forward, it is not either possible or useful to try to create absolute distinctions of kind. The self inspecting itself in language, and putting itself forward as a poetic speaker, is already in part contemplating a third person. These poems do not faithfully *reproduce* a simple external reality, but they inevitably *reflect* it, and comment upon it. Nor, at the other extreme, do they tell us 'just' about Wordsworth. In the realm of language, and exclusively conceived, there is no such person. The subject is always and inescapably intersubjective, and the forms of that intersubjectivity can be effectively objective, active elements in a shared world and a common public space. The same is true of the poems in which Wordsworth creates or reports encounters with beggars or vagrants, to which we now turn.

6
Poets, paupers and peripatetics: the politics of sympathy

'Simon Lee' is the first of the poems discussed in detail so far in which Wordsworth reports upon a direct encounter with a member of that large class of paupers and vagrants that was such a feature of the contemporary social landscape. The details of this encounter are indeed partly fictionalized, and removed in time and place, but it is not reduced to a passing observation, as it is in 'Gipsies'; nor does Wordsworth resort to a traditionary tale, as he does in 'Michael'. Simon, at least, has a perpetual place, although his hold upon it, as upon life itself, is tenuous to say the least. Wordsworth's poetry is also significantly preoccupied with those who do not have such a place, whether because they have lost property and domestic identity, or because they never had it to lose.

Dorothy's journals continually testify that there were a great many such people to be met in the lanes and byways, or to be heard knocking at the door. And as we might expect from what we have seen of the contexts for 'Gipsies', they were obsessively commented upon by social theorists of all shades of opinion. Those among Wordsworth's poems that are about vagrants and beggars thus need, once again, to be understood in terms that are both personal, or biographical, and general, or historical. And within this second category, we must be aware not only of the political economists but also of the fictional conventions, deployed by such writers as

Sterne, Mackenzie and Thelwall, within which the experiences of sentimental fellow-suffering or disapproval had been variously mediated to the reading public.

Wordsworth's experiences of and meditations upon the vagrant poor are, once again, implicated within the same preoccupations with property and labour that we have seen to figure so largely in his moral and aesthetic doctrines. The vagrant, or beggar, is either a person who does not aspire to, and perhaps threatens property, as true gypsies were often thought to do; or he is a person who has been dispossessed, or who has tried and failed to acquire the substance necessary to gain a settlement in a particular parish. Such 'settlement', or evidence of sustained and stable participation in a particular community, was a necessary qualification for any person to obtain parish relief. Parishes were thus especially reluctant to encourage vagrants to remain, lest they should do so for long enough to have an eventual claim on the funds (see Poynter, 1969, 3–7, etc.).

Both vagrants and paupers – who were incipient vagrants in so far as they tended to be on the point of losing what little they had – were the objects of constant analysis in terms of their labour, or potential labour value. Do they remain as they are because there is no work for them, or because their wages are too low for simple subsistence? Or are they the victims of their own idleness, too lazy and unscrupulous to want to earn a steady living? These questions were raised even more compulsively in 1800 than they are in 1987; and in each case the inquiring spirit is significantly motivated by what we might call ideological preferences. Wordsworth's poetry, as we might expect, charts its way through a complex middle ground in which the speaker's own good faith is as frequently challenged as is the integrity or honesty of those he encounters.

In Wordsworth's earliest poetry, the image of the vagrant tends not to be especially complicated. As, in the unpublished letter to Llandaff, he allows himself the somewhat Utopian hope that 'the class of wretches called mendicants will not much longer shock the feelings of humanity' (*PrW*, 1: 43), so the earliest poetic representations of that class are contained within a relatively comfortable vocabulary of 'social Gothic'. The vagrant woman of *An Evening Walk* (1793) is a striking image of suffering and forbearance; her condition questions the social order, indeed, but not the integrity of the narrator describing her. We can feel secure about Wordsworth's sympathies for such suffering (see *EW*, 60–6), which the reviewers found 'affecting' and 'pathetically delineated' (304). Similarly, in *The Borderers*, the beggar woman is an example of poverty corrupted and exploited by the promise of reward to act against conscience (*B*, 164, 280). She is not a complicated poetic personality, nor does she raise any awkward questions for the reader or the protagonists.

The uses of poverty: 'The Old Cumberland Beggar'

It is in the 'encounter' poems, to use Frederick Garber's (1971) term, that such questions tend to be raised. I have argued for a level of discomfort in the writing of 'Simon Lee', although this is a poem that has not so troubled all its readers. Few, however, have failed to register some measure of embarrassment or outrage at 'The Old Cumberland Beggar', the poem that, along with 'Michael' and 'A narrow girdle of rough stones and crags'[1], comes closest among the ballads of 1800 to continuing the themes implicit in the poeticizing of Christopher Tricky's physical labours. Cleanth Brooks sums up a large body of criticism past, present and to come in finding something 'shockingly candid' in Wordsworth's depiction of the old man's physical condition, and in his creation of 'a kind of inverse scapegoat' (1965, 376, 377). However aptly and ingeniously we may seek to explain the poem as the emanation of an attitude more common in its own time than since,[2] it is likely that some readerly dismay will continue to arise over its images and allusions. There is something uncomfortably harsh in the association (even as it is no more than that) of the old man with the 'dullest and most noxious' of created forms (*LB*, 207), as if extreme old age partakes of some of the daemonic or chthonic qualities that it has in *Oedipus at Colonus* and perhaps, at less apparent levels, in *King Lear*. At the very least, the sight of such physical decay functions as a powerful reminder of one's own mortality; Wordsworth's focus is very much upon the material details of such decay, unredeemed by consolatory social relations.

Jonathan Wordsworth (1969, 72–5) reminds us that Wordsworth was frightened at the sight of the discharged soldier (*Prelude*, 4: 400f.), and found an apt 'admonishment' in the meeting with the old leech gatherer (*1807*, 128). These figures of old and lonely men do seem to have had a disciplinary effect on the errant imagination of the more privileged poet, recalling him both to the facts of physical life and the less fortunate social predicaments of others. As I have said before, Kenneth Johnston (1984, 5–6) has suggested that the draft passages that eventually became 'The Old Cumberland Beggar', 'Old Man Travelling' and the 'discharged soldier' episode of *The Prelude* were central to Wordsworth's early schema for *The Recluse*. This implies that the interaction of poverty and mendicancy with polite values and perceptions was to be one of the originating preoccupations of the poet's grand plan. But in the published version of 'The Old Cumberland Beggar', there is no explicit signal of the poet's discomfort. What is at first sight shocking is the inflexible materialism of the poem's description of old age. The beggar's 'palsied hand' can scarcely hold the 'scraps and fragments of his diet', and he looks around 'never knowing that he sees' (*LB*, 206, 207). He is never conventionally integrated into human society, whether by speech or by physical proximity: 'his age has no companion'. It is Wordsworth's insistence that the old man is so close to death that he has ceased to be conventionally 'human' that is so unusual and challenging. Most of the poem's readers will be alert, articulate, and sociable; the beggar is none of these. As such, he is a direct threat to the assumption of common humanity – an entity Wordsworth threatens in many other ways, as in his analysis of the negative results of the urban life. Nothing in the beggar as a person *in himself* reflects or validates our images of ourselves. He has no inner life – or none that is apparent to the observer.

The argument of Wordsworth's poem suggests that it is the so-called polite reader, rather than the village poor, who is likely to be most threatened by or censorious of the old beggar. The 'abject poor' (209) keep him fed, while the 'statesmen' and the middle-class interests that they represent want to tidy him away, with a 'broom' (207), and make him industrious. To put the beggar out of sight is also to put him out of mind, and to evade the constant challenge that his existence presents to both physiological and social self-images. However, the comfort of this explanation of the poem is subverted by the details of the desired alternative to the workhouse:

> let his blood
> Struggle with frosty air and winter snows,
> And let the charter'd wind that sweeps the heath
> Beat his grey locks against his wither'd face.
> Reverance the hope whose vital anxiousness
> Gives the last human interest to his heart.
>
> (210)

Despite the sense that Wordsworth here employs a species of ventriloquism, voicing the arguments of the 'reformers' against themselves ('let his blood'), and despite the familiarity of the emphasis on 'vital anxiousness' as a life-enhancing experience that is in the Wordsworthian scheme of things integrally connected with the capacity to feel pleasure (as in *LB*, 117, where he wants the 'misty mountain winds' to blow against Dorothy), there is still something over-determined in this passage, and others like it; as if Wordsworth does yet more than he needs to do to make the points I have just made. It is appropriate to the description of extreme senility that the beggar does not speak or register any personal responses to those who feed him, but it is also part of a familiar Wordsworthian paradigm that he has no right of response. However insensible he may be 'in himself', it is hard not to suspect (even as it is impossible to prove) that he is not further anaesthetized by the speaker's perspective. There are a number of ways of explaining this, none of which is conclusively proffered. Perhaps the poet's own discomfort is alleviated by making the beggar insensible to conditions that would to most people be felt as extreme hardships – homelessness, loneliness, and the rigours of the climate. Wordsworth comments thus on the impoverished artisans described in *The Ruined Cottage:*

                                    happier far
   Could they have lived as do the little birds
   That peck along the hedges, or the kite
   That makes her dwelling in the mountain rocks.
                                    (*RC*, 54)

The same indifferent birds appear in 'Old Man Travelling', and the leech gatherer is imaged in a state 'not all alive nor dead' (*1807*, 126). In 'A slumber did my spirit seal' (*LB*, 154) this tendency to reify human life into insentience constitutes a notoriously complex moral meditation.[3] It is not anomalous to notice of the small celandine, as Wordsworth does in the poem of that name, its 'necessity in being old' and its inability to 'help itself in its decay' (*1807*, 210). The dying flower may speak to us of life in general, but it is not itself a human organism. When the same language is applied to old people, the effect is inevitably more disturbing, especially when the speaker's account lacks any expressed sense of sympathy or fellow feeling. The village poor who feed the beggar are impelled and trained to 'acts of love' (*LB*, 208), but the narrator claims no such distinction for himself. Once again, it seems as if the Wordsworthian speaker is located in some ambiguous middle ground between the village poor, of whom he approves, and the socially distant 'statesmen', of whom he does not approve. In his analysis of the moral and social benefits of the old beggar's role, the speaker does not situate *himself*. Once again, we may see here a symptom of Wordsworth's own displacement. In his 'Reflections on Having Left a Place of Retirement' (1980, 106–8), Coleridge makes a distinction between those rational spirits who do good 'with unmov'd face', and those who feel for others with the strong engagement of a 'brother man'. In Wordsworth's poem, it often seems as if the narrator is neither of these things, but something in between, or outside.

   The peculiar identity of Wordsworth's speaker becomes clearer when we set the poem against what seem to have been the dominant conventions for representing such subjects. Mayo (1954, 500) has noted that there was a plethora of magazine poetry dealing in beggars, and much of the fiction of the previous forty years had included encounters between persons of means and sensibility and the vagrant poor. Smollett's Matthew Bramble, in *Humphry Clinker* (1771), can seldom refuse the urge to give alms, and he does so modestly and without sanctimony. Sterne's *A Sentimental Journey* (1768) had undertaken a much more searching analysis of the same instinct, and of its place in the sentimental traveller's insatiable appetite for good feelings, themselves disturbingly remote from ever being implicated in sustained human relationships. Yorick's encounter with the monk teaches him the impropriety of trying to make (usually hypocritical) distinctions between the deserving and the undeserving beggars, and once begun he cannot stop giving:

> When man is at peace with man, how much lighter than a feather is the heaviest of metals in his hand! he pulls out his purse, and holding it airily and uncompressed, looks round him, as if he sought for an object to share it with.
>
> (Sterne, 1967, 28)

Without ceasing to admire the act of giving in itself, Sterne's novel persuades us to ponder its place within Yorick's compulsive quest for brief and sentimental experiences. One of Dorothy's journal entries suggests that the Wordsworths were not reluctant to derive 'interesting feelings' from 'melancholy' people, and from objects 'connected with man in dreary solitariness' (1952, 1:213); but in general the poetry images such feelings rather less light-heartedly than Sterne purports to do.

A good example of the kind of approach that Wordsworth does not choose can be found in Henry Mackenzie's popular *The Man of Feeling* (1771). Here, after the giving of alms, beggar and donor sit down together in harmonious picaresque fashion to discuss the state of society. Common feeling is established, and we learn that not all beggars are constitutionally idle, and that not all who give alms are genuinely charitable (Mackenzie, 1958, 12–14). Some of the same slightly platitudinous (albeit admirable) curiosity about and concern for the plight of the poor informs John Thelwall's *The Peripatetic*, a work much closer to Wordsworth and the probable model for some of his poems. Thelwall's narrator makes the same mistake as Yorick did with the monk; he refuses charity because of his conviction of the man's dishonesty, but then realizes otherwise and has to make amends (1793, 1:24f.). Like Mackenzie's Harley, Thelwall's peripatetic holds it as a maxim that 'there is no human being with whom it is not worth while to spend a quarter of an hour' (44–5).

After reading Mackenzie and Thelwall, we do not come away with any doubts about what to conclude concerning the predicaments of the various protagonists. This is seldom the case with Wordsworth's poems about the poor and vagrant. In 'Old Man Travelling', a poem made out of material that was originally part of the draft for 'The Old Cumberland Beggar' narrative, the speaker's exchange with the old man answers fewer questions than it raises. The man's reply to the speaker's question, modified in 1800 and in 1802 and omitted entirely after 1815, neither affirms nor denies the speaker's earlier speculations about the old man's 'settled quiet'

(*LB*, 107). It does something of both, and therein lies its challenge. Like the Cumberland beggar, this old man seems to belong to another world; he is a spectral presence who does not even scare the birds.[4]

A comparison of Wordsworth's poems with some other literary representations of mendicancy does not make 'The Old Cumberland Beggar' 'better' in some literary or moral way, but it does bring out the oddity of his approach. The question of the speaker's integrity is certainly raised, but there is too little information of the sort that would allow us to decide firmly about it. So far, I have argued against assuming that the speaker is a mere heartless observer by trying to take seriously his record of the material decay that accrues with extreme old age; this does not prevent the village poor from responding charitably, though it perhaps does alienate the middle-class reformers from wanting to be reminded of his presence. But this distinction cuts two ways, and Wordsworth does enough in the poem to make us wonder whether we ought at least to consider the possible benefits of a sedentary life in a warm place. Some consideration of the contemporary debate about the 'schools of industry' might help us here.

In the Fenwick note, dictated of course many years after the publication of the poem, Wordsworth recalled that

> The political economists were about that time beginning their war upon mendicity in all its forms, and by implication, if not directly, on Almsgiving also. This heartless process has been carried as far as it can go by the AMENDED poor-law bill, though the inhumanity that prevails in this measure is somewhat disguised by the profession that one of its objects is to throw the poor upon the voluntary donations of their neighbours; that is, if rightly interpreted, to force them into a condition between relief in the Union poor-house, and Alms robbed of their Christian grace and spirit, as being *forced* rather from the benevolent than given by them; while the avaricious and selfish, and all in fact but the humane and charitable, are at liberty to keep all they possess from their distressed brethren.
>
> (*PW*, 4: 445–6)

In this account, we may limit ourselves to the features of the debate before 1800, when the poem was first published; Kenneth Johnston (1984, 5) has pointed out that the 'discursive political commentary' that takes up so much of the poem was written a few months after the completed first draft, so that we may suspect that it had its origin in Wordsworth's response to an immediate contemporary crisis. As an introduction to the details of this crisis, some general observations are in order.

It would be hard for a modern reader to overestimate the 'concern' for and about the poor in the society in which Wordsworth moved. This concern was variously compassionate and disciplinary, and sometimes both at once. In Burn's *The Justice of the Peace*, the entry under POOR is by far the longest in the book, amounting to some 500 pages (1800, 3: 342–884). Sir Frederick Eden's (1797) bibliography lists 142 items published between 1758 and 1797 on the subject of poverty. Some writers, like Eden himself, called for a drastic curtailing of the whole system of poor relief, because of the 'ready encouragement which it offers to idleness, improvidence, and immorality' (1: 471). He blandly reports that

> the miseries of the labouring Poor arise, less from the scantiness of their income (however much the philanthropist might wish it to be increased) than from their own improvidence and unthriftiness.
>
> (1: 495)

Joseph Townsend is even more ruthless, arguing for the entire abolition of relief:

> Their hopes and fears should centre in themselves: they should have no hope but from their own sobriety, diligence, fidelity, and from the well-earnt friendship of their employers.
>
> (1786, 18)

There must always be poverty in society, so that 'the only question will be this, Who is most worthy to suffer cold and hunger, the prodigal or the provident, the slothful or the diligent, the virtuous or the vicious?' (37). Arthur Young (1767, 1801) wanted, as we have seen, to give all paupers and potential paupers a small plot of land, so that they might experience material self-sufficiency and develop an interested attachment to the institutions of government. George Dyer (1793, 61–2) wanted to replace the current system by a national charity scheme. And so on. In this highly politicized debate, in which extremes of hard-heartedness seem to have been more common than excesses of tenderness, Wordsworth's poems seem to occupy a complex and even confused position. The case for poverty as an inevitable part of 'nature's law' was mostly made from the Malthusian perspective, although in the first version of his notorious *Essay on the Principle of Population* (1798), Malthus himself did allow for the retention of workhouses to accommodate cases of 'extreme distress' (1970, 102). One of the most uncompromising tracts in this tradition was written by Burke, in his *Thoughts and Details on Scarcity* (1795). Here, Burke opines that

> To provide for us in our necessities is not in the power of government. It would be a vain presumption in statesmen to think they can do it.
>
> (Burke, 1906, 6: 3)

The rhetorically dishonest 'us' asks the reader to accept Burke himself as one of the needy. The poor, who are described as 'them', are recommended to the comforts of 'patience, labour, sobriety, frugality, and religion' (5). Relief is to be discouraged, and only charity encouraged, along with the drinking of gin to provide the necessary minimum of nourishment in the absence of other sources of nutrition. For Burke, government, in a phrase that has certainly resounded through the subsequent decades, should never interfere with 'the subsistence of the people' (32) – by which he means the rights of employers to pay as little as they can get away with.

The 'progressives' were arguing for precisely such interference, but often in the utilitarian terms that Wordsworth opposed. The exponents of the workhouses were also the exponents of a highly coercive system of social discipline. Even without the particular sensitivity to such systems that the work of Michel Foucault has bequeathed to modern historians of the Enlightenment, it would be hard not to sense something uncomfortably impersonal in Jeremy Bentham's proposal, first published in Arthur Young's *Annals of Agriculture* in 1797–8, to build the workhouses after the design of the famous panopticon. Among the advantages of this, Bentham lists:

> 14. Universal *transparency*. 15. Simultaneous *inspectability* at all proper times. 16. On the part of inspectors, the faculty of being visible or *invisible* at pleasure.
>
> (Bentham, 1812, 28)

It is Bentham, with his startlingly rational intelligence, who focuses the problem of beggars with the greatest precision and, I suggest, with the greatest relevance to the addresses of Wordsworth's poem. This, one suspects, was the immediate crisis that Wordsworth might have been responding to. Bentham enumerates the 'mischiefs' produced by the phenomenon of begging as follows:

> 1. In the instance of passengers in general, considered as exposed to the importunity of beggars – to same, the pain of sympathy: – no pain, no alms-giving; – begging is a species of extortion to which the tender-hearted, and they only, are exposed. 2. Disgust; which may exist where there is no sympathy: – the sympathy experiences a sort of relief by giving; the disgust finds no relief. – From the disgust excited by the presence of a filthy beggar, none but the equally filthy stand exempted. The multitude of the persons subject to this pain of sympathy, or to this disgust, considered, there can be little doubt but that the sum of these pains taken together is greater than the difference to the beggar in point of comfort between begging and working. 3. Discouragement to industry. Every penny spent, is the reward of industry: every penny given, a bounty upon idleness. – The luxuries seen in many instances to be

enjoyed by beggars, are a sort of insult to the hard-working child of industry: by holding him out as a dupe, who toils and torments himself to earn a maintenance inferior to what is to be earned by canting and grimace. 4. Facility afforded to real crimes. – Mendicity, by the removal of shame, removes one of the chief safe-guards to honesty ... 5. Unfavourable influence on happiness, even in the instance of the begging tribe itself, taking the whole together ... for one prosperous and happy beggar, there are probably many unprosperous and miserable ones; wretches who, notwithstanding, keep lingering in their wretchedness; sometimes for want of power, sometimes for want of resolution, to emerge from it.

(1812, 141–3)

In his account of the effects of begging upon the *givers* as well as upon the receivers, Bentham is engaging some of the issues raised in Wordsworth's poem. But Wordsworth resolves the 'pain of sympathy' in a quite different way. He presents an unprosperous and therefore potentially 'miserable' beggar and shows him, not as one racked by an impossible aspiration, but resigned or indifferent to a gradual decline into death. Far from appearing as an insult to the 'abject poor', and discouraging their industry, he has the opposite effect. Indeed, he is almost a stimulus to exertion, making the poor *more* grateful for their relative comfort, and more able to give 'with exhilarated heart' (*LB*, 210). Whatever 'pain of sympathy' might be latent in the situation is metamorphosed into an entirely positive sense of self-esteem, and an appreciation of relative good fortune (not discounted by the potential for reactionary mystification that is also to be traced in this interaction). It is the 'polite' or middle-class reader or 'statesman' who is more likely to be disturbed by the pain of sympathy, perhaps because he will be conscious of a greater gap between himself and the beggar, and will thus tend to feel guilty at not giving more than he does. Wordsworth here accepts the force of self-interest, which was the standard utilitarian first principle, but turns it against Bentham's case. Wordsworthian self-interest is not something that excludes concern for others, but rather includes it; it becomes dignified and positive.

A similar emphasis may be found in 'The Mad Mother' (*LB*, 84), where the woman cries out:

Then happy lie, for blest am I;
Without me my sweet babe would die.

It is also evident in 'Michael', where the 'certainty/ Of honourable gain' (*LB*, 228) makes Michael a better citizen than he might otherwise be. In 'The Old Cumberland Beggar', Wordsworth does not presume to speak of the beggar's own happiness; he avoids the subject altogether, by presenting him as beyond such considerations, at least as far as they are apparent to others. But he makes it clear that the community is maintained rather than threatened by the sight of suffering and need and the experience of sympathy. In despite of middle-class politics and reformist theories, the poor villagers are dependent upon the beggar for a creative sense of self-respect, of the sort that they would otherwise find hard to experience. The effects are almost inadvertent; they can no more refuse the old man than the beggar himself can prevent the crumbs falling from his 'palsied hand' (206) and feeding the birds that peck around his feet. Generosity, in the poem's schema, exceeds itself. The poem is a clear challenge to Bentham's assumption that the natural 'human' reaction to beggars must be one of pain and disgust. Wordsworth argues against Bentham that charity produces the greatest good for the greatest number of beings, birds included.

Bentham's plan for the panopticon house of industry was in fact dependent upon the removal of beggars – the very aspiration that Wordsworth's later note attributed to the political economists. For, says Bentham, if begging were to be tolerated, then no one would consent to be kept in the schools of industry. The sight of others who continued to subsist by doing nothing would discourage the inhabitant from working (1812, 141). He cannot foresee imposing penalties for the giving of alms, but he does want to create a situation where 'nobody durst take', so that 'nobody could give' (146). Whether or not Wordsworth knew of the exact details of Bentham's plan is unclear, but he would probably have been aware of its general priorities. In particular, Pitt's bill for the reform of the poor-law system, introduced in 1796 and abandoned in 1797 after extensive and controversial discussion, would have been impossible to ignore, and it shares Bentham's emphasis on the 'schools of industry'.[5]

The details of the proposed reform are reprinted in Eden (1797, 3: cccxiii–cccxxxviii). It is characterized by a strong determination to make the poor industrious. So-called 'schools of industry' would be set up for children, and for those among the poor who could not work at home. No one refusing to enter the schools would be entitled to relief, nor would anyone not having 'lawful settlement'. Impoverished property owners could, however, qualify.

One of the most striking features of Pitt's bill was its attempt at a near-total reform of the bureaucracy of poor-law administration, and its coercive attitude toward the creation of the schools of industry. The considerable funds necessary to finance such reforms were to be raised 'by taxation of the owners and proprietors of all estates, which are liable to be assessed for the relief of the Poor' (cccxvi). Justices were to be allowed to force reluctant parishes into compliance. In other words, one of the major implications of this bill was its cost – and this at a time when the problem of the poor was exceptionally urgent owing to the bad harvests of the mid-1790s. As Thomas Ruggles (1797, 376–7) put it,

> The summer of 1795 ... introduced this kingdom to the experience of such a scarcity and extravagant price for corn, as the oldest man cannot before remember; nor has the history of the last century informed us of.

An act of December 1795 had already made provision for the guardians to increase amounts charged on the parish, in an attempt to keep up with the needs of the poor (Eden, 1797, 3: ccxxv–vii). Not surprisingly, then, much of the most dogged opposition to Pitt's scheme came from the middle class, the taxpayers who would be forced into paying for the construction of the schools of industry. Although the parishes were meant to keep the profits of the labours carried out therein, the initial expenses of construction would have been considerable.

The question then arises: if Wordsworth's poem stands out against the terms of Pitt's bill, as of Bentham's panopticon scheme, does it then do so in sympathy with the financial worries of anxious lower-middle-class property owners? Such an option goes entirely unmentioned in the text, but this does not render it irrelevant. For Wordsworth's argument is not offered in support of public relief, but in favour of private charity, and against involuntary incarceration. There is no statement to the effect that the *parish* should support the beggar, and others like him; his needs, it is implied, may be appropriately met by the habitual donations of the villagers whose doors he passes by. The rhetoric of the poem bears little resemblance to that of a Burke or a Townsend, who regarded charity as the only species of assistance ever to be extended to the poor as a whole, whether aged vagrants or declining property owners. Townsend's case is explicit in its intention to preserve social discipline:

> When the poor are obliged to cultivate the friendship of the rich, the rich will never want inclination to relieve the distresses of the poor.
>
> (1786, 99)

No such cultivation goes on in Wordsworth's poem; indeed, what is most striking about it is the total *absence* of expressed articulation or interaction between givers and receiver. But at the same time, Wordsworth does not seem to envisage anything other than private charity as a response to the old man's needs. Wordsworth's ideal microsociety might indeed have maintained such a system of support for this one old man, but the public 'message' of the poem is surely weakened by its failure to suggest what might happen in cases where the community does not rally round as conscientiously, or where the number of beggars exceeds the capacities of the villages to give alms. It is coherent in its negative address to the utilitarian aspirations clear in Bentham's scheme and Pitt's bill, even though it is far from explicit about its opposition to the idea of turning the poor into an incipient factory labour force. But it is not so coherent in its analysis of the general fate of the vagrant poor. Of course, Wordsworth is not claiming to encompass in his poem the entire subject of poor relief on a national scale; he is simply writing about a single recollected example from his own life. But, in as much as this example is put into a public language, it does inevitably address itself to the larger questions that were so intensely debated at the time. The poem is entirely lacking in a sense of what would happen in situations where the poor cannot be relied upon to look after each other in this way; where they have become so brutalized or corrupted that they no longer experience the desire to give, and no longer care for the sense of self-esteem that comes with it.

It is with some credibility, then, that James Chandler (1984, 84–92) has recently made the case for this poem's affiliation as a Burkean one. Wordsworth is far more subtle than Burke. He maintains, as I have said, a strong distinction between different forms of self-interest, some of which are positive, and he does not suggest that the beggar is being offered Burke's pompous consolations of 'patience, labour, sobriety, frugality, and religion' (1906, 6: 5). Moreover, in his reluctance to accord the beggar any visible personality, Wordsworth renders irrelevant the habitual contemporary attempt to distinguish the deserving from the undeserving poor; an attempt typified by the behaviour of Sterne's Yorick and of Thelwall's narrator, at least in the first instance. But the Burkean logic, divorced from its rhetoric and from its totally *laissez-faire* spirit, is indeed to be traced in the poem. Wordsworth explores the socially bonding and morally self-validating implications of charity, and he posits these phenomena as available to the abject poor in a manner that is not open to the distanced middle class likely to experience something between disgust and the pain of sympathy. It is this second class that will want to tidy the beggar away, into a closed space where he can be put to work and where his presence is never a challenge to be constantly faced by the affluent traveller. None of Wordsworth's finer points figure in Burke's argument. At the same time, it is open to us to suspect that what these finer points *amount* to, closely considered, is a contribution to the lobby that was actively seeking to *deny* public relief to the vagrant poor.

This is not to say, of course, that Wordsworth consciously conceived the poem this way. His major polemic, I have suggested, can be identified as anti-Benthamite. But this polemic also enables his argument to sit comfortably enough with those who did not want to raise the demand on the poor rates, whether by extending relief to the vagrant class, or by building expensive new 'schools of industry'. The poem does not express support for these concerns, but it does not contradict them either. I suspect that, in his eagerness to explore the particular example of the old beggar, and to face his polite readers with the challenge that the materialism of old age presents, as well as to bring to light the recognizable moral dignity of the poor, Wordsworth might have been unable to resolve his poem in terms of its precise ideological affiliation. I say this not simply to 'excuse' him of some moral shortcoming, but because there is evidence even in Wordsworth's later writings that he did *not* endorse the Burkean credo. He does indeed write to Lonsdale, in February 1821, that 'the more you encrease the facilities of the poor being maintained at other people's expense, the more poor you will have' (*LY*, 1: 39), and he expresses a near-Malthusian disgust at the imminent marriage of a local pauper woman to a drunken shoemaker. But a later letter softens this position considerably (*LY*, 2: 405–6), and the 1835 *Postscript* is unambiguous in its declaration that '*all* persons who cannot find employment, or procure wages sufficient to support the body in health and strength, are entitled to maintenance by law', even those who are 'wandering about as strangers in streets and ways' (*PrW*, 3: 240–1). Here Wordsworth goes on to deny the propriety of any attempt to distinguish the deserving from the undeserving poor. It is better that 'ten undeserving' should be assisted than that 'one morally good man, through want of relief, should either have his principles corrupted, or his energies destroyed' (246). This argument of 1835 is in flat contradiction of Burke's in 1795. Wordsworth too talks of preserving 'ancient habits of independence' (245), but for him this is not to be done by the 'presumption' that 'it is a labouring man's own fault if he be not, as the phrase is, beforehand with the world' (246), nor by counselling one's fellow subjects to the 'necessity of looking upwards only' (243) for relief. One could of course explain this case as part of the standard Tory rhetoric of prevention; and there were, by 1835, a number of concerned reactionaries who sought to prevent a possible social revolution by a timely measure of kindness, rather than by leaving the poor to the ruthless laws of nature. But Wordsworth was not merely one of these; he goes further than he needed to go to prove this point. And in 1835 he was certainly not, it must be said, a Burkean.

   This should lead us to suspect, I think, an element of real confusion in the writing of 'The Old Cumberland Beggar'. The Burkean affiliations of this poem, while they are surely there, are not its major argument; or at least, they subsist along with other arguments of alternative emphases. It must be further emphasized that Wordsworth was writing for a generation in which many were in favour of abolishing beggars altogether, not out of a desire for an improved society (in the spirit of the poet's early letter to Llandaff), but because beggars were non-industrious or disgusting. Bentham, as we have seen, could not see his scheme for the schools of industry working at all as long as there remained a significant class of vagrants (1812, 141). Arthur Young, who had some sympathy for the 'industrious' poor, had none at all for those he conveniently assumed the 'scum of the non-industrious poor'. Thus 'beggars, vagrants, gypsies, thieves, pickpockets' were lumped together in a class that Young wished to exclude from even statistical existence. By being taxonomically ignored, they were to be erased from the notice of the social planners: 'the only people that should come into the account are, the rich, and the industrious' (1770, 4: 563–4). The workhouses that Bentham and others were offering as a solution to the problem of poverty were not so different from the 'houses of correction' that had previously existed for the disciplinary detention of the 'idle and disorderly persons' that included a number of figures familiar as the subjects of Wordsworth's poetry: beggars, unlicensed pedlars, beggars imitating soldiers or mariners,[6] others 'pretending to go to work in harvest', and indeed anyone else 'not giving a good account of themselves' (Burn, 1800, 4: 451–4; cf. 2: 800). Wordsworth's image of the beggar is compassionate by comparison with some of these prototypes, even if it does not locate itself comfortably within the alternative of enacted human reciprocity of the sort described by Henry Mackenzie; and, in his refusal to entertain a rhetoric that concerns itself with distinctions between the deserving and the undeserving, Wordsworth is close to Thelwall (1793, 1: 24f.) and to Godwin, who questions the behaviour of those who 'assume to be the censors of mankind' by affecting such rhetoric (1797, 197), and who argues, as Wordsworth was later to do, that it is better to give in good faith than to withhold on potentially false and self-deceiving premisses. The tendency to such judgements is indeed analysed and upbraided in another poem of 1800, and exposed as the result of the 'happy idleness' of the privileged poet, rather than of accurate reporting of the lives of others (*LB*, 225).

Close inspection of the contemporary allusions and addresses that can be traced in the language of 'The Old Cumberland Beggar' leaves the poem, I have suggested, somewhat open and unresolved. The Burkean tendency cannot be denied, but there is much evidence of other priorities which, while they do not in themselves negate that tendency, yet imply that the poet was pursuing other terms of inquiry. To argue that the poem is *dominantly* expressive of support for Burke would entail the assumption that Burke's case was *the* primary object of public attention at the time of writing, so that any reference to it on Wordsworth's part, however implicit, would have instantly signalled the poem's allegiance. I doubt that Burke was, in this respect (and in contrast to his undoubtedly infamous thoughts on the French Revolution), the major focus of public attention, compared to, for example, the Benthamite implications of Pitt's bill. Detailed inspection of other Wordsworthian images of beggary and vagrancy may assist us in further clarifying the terms of the confusion, even if resolution is in this respect hard to envisage.

Versions of relief: 'Beggars' and 'Alice Fell'

The phenomenon of vagrancy is touched upon in several of the *Lyrical Ballads*, though never quite with the complexity that can be traced in 'The Old Cumberland Beggar'. Another version can be traced in 'Beggars' (*1807*, 113–16). The encounter that this poem describes actually happened to Dorothy rather than to William, and her journal records its details as having taken place some two years before the poem itself was written (1952, 1: 47–8, 122). The journal is obviously the major source for the poem, presumably along with Dorothy's reported recollections. But it is transcribed in the first person, and tells the tale of the speaker's encounter with a strikingly tall and graceful beggar woman, to whom he gives alms in spite of the apparent implausibility of her tale of woe. Further along his way, he meets two boys who are obviously the children of this same woman, but who beg from him after declaring that they are orphans. After a brief argument, the boys give up and run off to play.

What most impresses the speaker is the physical stature and beauty of the woman: 'Fit person was she for a Queen'. As such she appeals to his romantic imagination; he imagines her ruling over the Amazons, or living the life of a bandit's woman 'among the Grecian Isles'. In his revisions, Wordsworth first expanded this appeal, reporting how 'Luxuriant curls half veil'd her ample brow' (1828), but then (in 1832) reverted to a more modest address. But we do not need to know that Wordsworth himself never saw the woman to sense the degree to which this is a poem about the speaker's moods and imaginations.[7] The woman tells a tale of misfortune that he judges completely improbable: 'Such woes I knew could never be' (and again, the revisions first emphasize her dishonesty, and then opt for a less judgemental account). But he gives her alms none the less, because she is so beautiful, 'a Weed of glorious feature'.

Thus to describe the woman as a 'weed', however glorious, seems once again to reveal a poetic speaker who is given to the sanctimonious hyperbole that we have analysed in 'Gipsies'. It suggests that she is deemed fundamentally unproductive or superfluous, an unwanted albeit decorative plant. But once again, and far more explicitly than in 'Gipsies', we are here dealing with a literary allusion, noted by de Selincourt (*PW*, 2: 509), to Spenser's 'Muiopotmos' (line 213). Spenser's poem is subtitled 'The Fate of the Butterfly', and Bialostosky (1984, 146) aptly notes that 'the narrator ... has taken the attitude of the butterfly Spenser is describing; he has assumed the position of lord of nature'. But Spenser's poem in fact adverts to the *dangers* of thoughtless enjoyment and vainglory – the butterfly is trapped by a spider. If the narrator is indeed in the role of the butterfly, feeding without reflecting upon experience, then the hyperbole of the Spenserian allusion reflects as much on him as it does on the beggar woman. The boys themselves, later in the same poem, are chasing butterflies (as flies to wanton boys are we to the gods?), and on three other occasions in the 1807 volume (74, 203, 215) the same insect appears as the image of fragile mortality. In one instance, it was the young Wordsworth himself who was the destroyer (203); in 'Beggars', the adult poet is cast as feeding his fancy upon a glorious weed.[8]

If Wordsworth's speaker is indeed a careless butterfly, by which spider might he be trapped? Both mother and children are, in the simple sense, liars. Is it then the speaker's insouciant generosity, giving alms in spite of his conviction of dishonesty, that is being called into question, showing him as trapped by wily vagrants who happen to be physically appealing? Or is his generosity to be approved in the light of the way in which the doubled image of the butterfly (as poet, and as chased by the boys) asserts the frailty of *all* mortal life, so that we must appreciate what we can when we can, without seeking to impose divisive moral judgements? Wordsworth later told H.C. Robinson that he wrote the poem 'to exhibit the power of physical beauty and health and vigour in childhood even in a state of moral depravity' (*1807*, 407). But the poem does not demand the attribution of such 'moral depravity', even as it admits that the art of lying is at work. There is no philosophical reasoning of the sort that marked Godwin's and Bentham's meditations on the subject of begging, but Wordsworth is here casting himself as being charitable to those whom many of his contemporaries would have thought of as the 'undeserving' poor. We might choose to speculate somewhat critically about the kind of almsgiving that is dependent upon the good looks of the recipient, and the poem indeed suggests that it is the spontaneous appreciation of grace and energy that renders redundant any concern for conventional accountability or honesty. This is compounded when we recognize the Spenserian invocation as a possible allusion to the speaker's own mortality.

In 1817 Wordsworth composed a 'Sequel' to this poem, not in fact published until 1827, in which he speculates on the possible fate of the two boys, now presumably adult if still alive. He recalls how the 'genial hour' of the original meeting was able to banish those 'thoughts with better thoughts at strife' that are

> The most familiar bane of life
> Since parting Innocence bequeathed
> Mortality to Earth!
> (*PW*, 2: 225)

Here, he interrogates precisely the impulses to 'sterner judgment' (a phrase included in 1827–32) that the sight of the boys had so successfully put aside. The logic is highly compact, but seems to argue that the impulse to judge our fellows (and ourselves) came from the anxiety that was the result of man's disobedience and the fall into mortality. The prospect of death creates a desperate concern for our fate in the afterlife (we have seen a similar pattern of thought at work in Wordsworth's Luciferic meditations upon the evening star). This in turn renders our right behaviour in this life all the more critical, and fosters judgemental habits of mind. In recollected homage to his earlier suspension of disbelief, the narrator now hopes that whatever might have happened to them in this life, the beggar boys might be destined for 'mercy and immortal bloom'. His earlier thoughts are 'still endeared' to his heart, as he hopes for a literal realization of that earlier glimpse of a prelapsarian community wherein his awareness of the boys' 'daring wiles' did not divide him from them. Just as in 'Gipsies' (though far more elusively in that poem), Wordsworth is fastening upon a moment of admiration for, and longing to be among, a society in which social and psychological divisions do not exist. As the earlier years afford a mundane example of this, so the life to come may offer a prospective return. It seems not insignificant that in the final order of poems reproduced in de Selincourt's edition, 'Gipsies' is the next poem after 'Beggars' and its 'Sequel'.

The image of poet as butterfly that impinges upon 'Beggars' does then possibly imply his thoughtlessness in being deceived by attractive dishonesty; but it resonates much more fully as evidence (especially in view of the interpretation advanced by the 'Sequel') of the poet's own mortality, and the pleasurable relief that is experienced at such moments when divisive moral judgements are made redundant. In contrast to the somewhat microscopic materialism of 'The Old Cumberland Beggar', we have here a definite transcription of silent sympathy.

The other poem of 1807 in which Wordsworth engages with the relation between charity and vagrancy is 'Alice Fell' (*1807*, 120–3). Here again we have Wordsworth adapting into his own voice an encounter that in fact happened to someone else, in this case Robert Graham, who, Wordsworth was to remember, 'urged me to put it into verse, for humanity's sake' (408). Dorothy's journal entry for 16 February 1802, tells the story in some detail; and on 12 and 13 March Wordsworth wrote the poem, apparently composing the draft that became 'Beggars' immediately afterwards (1952, 1:114, 122).

'Alice Fell' is one of the poems that Coleridge thought would have been 'more delightful ... in prose, ... told and managed ... in a moral essay, or pedestrian tour' (1983, 2:69). Coleridge also included 'Beggars' and 'Simon Lee' in this class; and Wordsworth was sufficiently sensitive to this and other criticisms that he omitted 'Alice Fell' from editions after 1817, only restoring it after Coleridge's death (*1807*, 408). Like 'Gipsies', this poem has had very little attention from literary critics, and has most typically been received as a study in the obsessiveness of grief (for example by Hartman, 1977, 143). But it is also, like some of the poems just mentioned, a study of its speaker; and in the interaction between speaker and child we can trace once again a social and historical vocabulary that brings into play the contemporary debate about the rights and wrongs of charity as against a systematic public policy for the relief of the vagrant poor.

The poem reports, in the Wordsworthian first person, Robert Graham's encounter with a little girl whose cloak is caught in the wheel of the coach in which he is travelling. She is not a paying customer, but a poor vagrant sitting behind the chaise. Although her cloak is tattered and worn, her grief at its loss seems inconsolable, even after the speaker has taken her into the coach and tried to comfort her. He then leaves money with a local innkeeper to buy her a new cloak on the following day.

When asked about her place of dwelling, Alice replies: 'I to Durham, Sir, belong' (line 45). She is 'fatherless and motherless'. Perhaps she is on the books as an object of parish care, in some technical sense of 'belonging', perhaps not. For if she is being legally cared for by the parish, there would seem to be no reason for her to be on the road in the first place. Her notion of 'belonging' may then merely imply a loose association with a particular community, by virtue of a more or less regular presence. She may thus be obliged to survive by the same kind of irregular and casual charity as she receives from the speaker of the poem, having no assurance of regular food and lodging. The poem does not answer the question of her exact relation to Durham, for its speaker does not seem curious to know. He tells us that she is a 'little Orphan' (line 60), but this is an interpretation of her parentless state, for she might instead be illegitimate. The categories of orphan and bastard (to use the term then current) were imperfectly differentiated, both in speech and under certain sections of the law. Blackstone (1979, 1: 447) notes that the illegitimate person can '*inherit* nothing, being looked upon as the son of nobody, and sometimes called *filius nullius*, sometimes *filius populi*'. Alice's admission that she belongs to Durham may then be an idiomatic version of Blackstone's 'daughter of the people'. Bentham, we may note in passing, has a plan for those he termed 'children of the public', meaning to put them to work in factories from the age of 4! (see Himmelfarb, 1984, 81).

By leaving these implications somewhat vague, the poem manages to suggest both the irrelevance of such considerations to the act of charity (something similar happens in 'Beggars'), and also the speaker's somewhat sentimental detachment from the real circumstances of the child's life. He is thus to be queried as one who perhaps gives alms for the emotional *frisson* of witnessing gratitude, or in this case pride. I shall return to this question. Meanwhile, the most important reference to the charity debate occurs in the following stanza:

> She sate like one past all relief;
> Sob after sob she forth did send
> In wretchedness, as if her grief
> Could never, never have an end.
> (lines 37–40)

The speaker is trying to pacify the child, and finding that his kind intentions do not work. She seems to be beyond 'relief' – a very important word, for in contemporary discourse it was the one always used to describe the general, public enterprise of assisting the poor. (*The Oxford English Dictionary* records it as applying specifically to the Poor Laws and the parish doles, but only up to 1865.) The reader of 1807 would have 'perceived' the charge that this word carries; it is lost to the reader of 1987. At this point in the poem, the speaker is suggesting that Alice is as one beyond the reach of public assistance, as well as declaring more literally that he cannot ease her immediate pain. (The 1845 revision strengthens this double meaning as she becomes 'Insensible to all relief'.) In 1815 Wordsworth added the subtitle, 'Or, Poverty', which further underlines Alice's emblematic status. Are we being told here that the child is beyond the point at which public relief can help her, so that only the heroic speaker can make a difference (or not, as yet)?

   Having thus surreptitiously disputed the potential benefits of such 'relief' for Alice, and perhaps thereby for the vagrant poor in general, the speaker goes on to register how

> sitting by my side
> As if she'd lost her only friend
> She wept, nor would be pacified.
> (lines 50–2)

Here, we may undermine the speaker's naïve astonishment by taking his simile quite literally. Perhaps she *has* lost her only friend. That tattered cloak might indeed have been all that she had – Dorothy says that she 'had no other' (1952, 1: 113) – her 'only friend' and her single defence against the rigours of a harsh climate (it is raining in the poem) both physical and social. Even a tattered cloak is a more reliable support against the hardships of a wandering life than the occasional experience of assistance from kind gentlemen in coaches. As long as 'relief' is a subject of anxious debate between middle-class politicians, the poor must hang on to the little that they have and make the best of it.

   It is then quite understandable that the material source of the child's grief should only be open to a material solution: the new cloak. Here, Wordsworth may be implicitly responding, as he does elsewhere, both to the general argument for ignoring the poor and leaving them to their own devices, and also to the sanctimonious advice that the only worthwhile happiness is to be sought in the next life. Thus, in suggesting that 'Scripture is the only cure of woe', Cowper describes how

> The soul, reposing on assur'd relief,
> Feels herself happy amidst all her grief,
> Forgets her labour as she toils along,
> Weeps tears of joy, and bursts into a song.
>   (1787, 1: 96)

Alice's tears are those of inconsolable grief, but the cure for them is firmly within the life on earth. The poem insists that only a minimal level of material comfort can make possible for human beings the very virtues of self-respect that the poor were so often accused of lacking. The kind of 'property' that the new cloak represents is the only thing that makes Alice feel better; it is of real and enduring value, while the spontaneous comfortings of passing travellers are not.

The poem further suggests that a single act of charity, provided that it has a clear material content, *can* make a difference to the life of an orphan child. It thus refutes the notion that the poor should be left completely to their own devices, because any assistance from others will simply corrupt them and take away their independence of spirit. In this poem, one cloak fills immensity. Alice is restored not just to a condition of subsistence but one of pride: 'Proud Creature was she the next day'. She is not only objectively assisted; she derives a subjective sense of worth from the possession of a cloak that is at once a public symbol of substance and a material protection against the weather. Here, charity *produces* a new dignity of spirit; but not because it is charity, so much as for the fact of its material content.[9]

Wordsworth suggests that Alice was justified in being proud, and the speaker right to be pleased with himself. Does this amount to a Burkean approval of the practice of private charity over the case for public relief, of the kind that the speaker has already implicitly queried? Before answering this question, we must explore the fascinating matter of the name of the child. We know from Dorothy's account that Alice Fell was the child's real name, and not an invention. But it has the appeal of an invention, for it suits the themes of the poem in a very artful way. The word 'fell' has the meaning of 'skin' or 'fleece'; Wordsworth might have known the word from Shakespeare, Dyer, or Burns (see *The Oxford English Dictionary*), if not from his shepherding neighbours. The name also suggests an allusion to the landscape of northern England (*fell* as hill or mountain) and perhaps also to the pairing of two other senses of the word found in Milton: *fell* as 'fierce' or 'wild', and thus a description of the *fallen* state.

Alice is a child of nature perhaps, in the legal sense; and she is certainly travelling alone in wild places. She is also 'half wild' (line 35) with grief. The poem is about the loss and reinstatement of her protective covering, or fleece – the cloak. And this too is a subliminally polemical point, for the debate or choice between nakedness and clothing was a feature of the 'political' rhetoric of the times. Blake's image of joy, energy and revolution, for example, is often that of nakedness, a casting off of the deceitful appearances of social rank and moral shame; a return to life before the fig leaf. Rousseau similarly identified civic virtue with nakedness, invoking a familiar Spartan iconography. Burke, on the contrary, suggests that clothing is what makes us most creatively human, redeeming us as far as anything can from the indignity of our fallen state, of which it is also (as fig leaf) the primary signifier. Clothing turns necessity to virtue. It is also, of course, the public emblem of social rank and difference. Thus, in his case against the 'new conquering empire of light and reason' that he saw embodied in the French Revolution, Burke laments that

> All the decent drapery of life is to be rudely torn off. All the superadded ideas, furnished from the wardrobe of a moral imagination, which the heart owns, and the understanding ratifies, as necessary to cover the defects of our naked shivering nature, and to raise it to dignity in our own estimation, are to be exploded as a ridiculous, absurd, and antiquated fashion.
>
> (1976, 171)

Against the republican image of naked or minimally clothed virtue, apparent in the literature, art and fashion of the revolutionary period, Burke offers a recourse to the necessity of robes and furred gowns. In Wordsworth's poem, Alice has a brief experience of naked and shivering nature, and is restored to a dignity in her own estimation. Does Wordsworth here transcribe a Burkean allegory telling of the reclaiming of one potentially fierce and wild (*fell*) and fallen (as a human being) into the society of property, possession and self-esteem? Are we witnessing the conversion of a potentially exiled and accusatory figure, and thus a prototypic revolutionary, into a solid Burkean citizen?

These are, of course, improbably portentous messages to be deriving from Wordsworth's poem; if they are there, then they are a good example of how doctrine can be familiarized and simplified, so much so as to be scarcely apparent. But we cannot, I think, declare that such messages are *not* there, for they are part of the world in which the poem had its original being, and they do make strong logical sense of the narrative. The element of grandiloquence that the Burkean reading implies also contributes to the incipiently (as read) and actually (as composed) dramatic nature of the poem. Although Wordsworth adapts Graham's encounter into the first person, the poem can still be read as calling the speaker's attitudes (though not his deed) into question. Robert Graham wanted Wordsworth to record his good deed 'for humanity's sake', but the poem that was produced is not totally innocent of irony at its speaker's expense. We have seen in 'The Old Cumberland Beggar' that Wordsworth did not have a cynical view of the self-satisfaction that accompanies charitable behaviour; quite the opposite. And the speaker does not invoke the grand Burkean rhetoric in favour of a charity whose 'manner, mode, time, choice of objects, and proportion, are left to private discretion', and which is 'performed with the greater satisfaction' for being discharged in 'freedom' (Burke, 1906, 6: 14). But what is implied in the poem *is* the education of the speaker, from one who seeks merely to console the child (and is thus ironized) to one who sees the point of uncontingent material compensation, and who buys the new cloak. Alice, it must be stressed, does not give forth with expressions of gratitude; there is no moment of 'bonding' between the giver and the receiver, of the sort that was for many writers and readers the central climax of the act of charity. The speaker is denied this gratification, if he ever sought it (it similarly does not exist in 'The Old Cumberland Beggar'). Alice's pride is self-focused, and the more dignified because of it. To suggest that no one is beyond reclamation if proper incentives are offered, and to make clear that these involve such material factors as food and clothing, is to go well beyond the details of Burke's case, though Wordsworth remains very much within the general terms of his argument. It may be that, in the tentative though arguable gap that this poem opens between poet and speaker, we can see something of a Wordsworth who has things both ways, and who does not make it finally clear whether he endorses or ironizes the insight that Alice and others like her might be 'past all relief'. The 1835 *Postscript*, as we have seen, argues otherwise.

In each of the three poems discussed in detail in this chapter we have seen the representation of a complex social interaction between the 'haves' (however little they have) and the 'have nots'. These encounters invoke or allude to determinations that are variously particular to Wordsworth and of general import within his language; they also call into question the presence or absence of authorial or dramatic attitudes in the voices of the speakers of the poems. One could indeed say authorial *and* dramatic, for in each case (as indeed in 'Gipsies' and 'Simon Lee') Wordsworth's writing suggests but does not confirm a distance between the persona of the poet in charge of the artifice of the text, and the narrator who enunciates it. In the case of two of these poems, moreover, Wordsworth adopts incidents that happened to others as his own, or his speakers'; a gesture which implies both identification with and distance from the attitudes therein explored. The experience of reading these poems carefully is thus one of continual displacement and dislocation; we are constantly confused about the degree to which we are witnessing the transcribed limitations of others (as dramatic speakers) or being ourselves invited to occupy perspectives of authority.

In the 1802 preface, Wordsworth wrote of the poet's tendency to 'slip into an entire delusion, and even confound and identify his own feelings' with those of his characters and subjects (*PrW*, 1: 138). The confusion is considerable when this happens with narrators and protagonists at different times and in different ways. The famous note to 'The Thorn' *tells* us to be alert for a dramatic narrator, and even here some readers manage to continue to miss the point. More commonly, Wordsworth's poems do not give us such clues, but tease us with possibilities and partially intelligible schemas for a 'dramatic' interpretation. Not without some justification did Coleridge complain of an 'undue predilection for the *dramatic* form in certain poems' (1983, 2: 135), though he does not suggest that he is unsure about when and where this occurs. There are two extreme alternatives open to us in estimating the force and nature of this effect in Wordsworth's poetry; we may choose to see it as the result of an omniscient control or compulsion on the poet's part, so that the text exists as a system of informative traps for the unwary reader. Or, we may read it as evidence of some disabling incompetence, both technical and moral.[10] Neither of these extreme attitudes does proper justice to the problems of reading the poetry, though each of them is partly credible at various times. The spectrum of speaker–poet relations, or arguable relations, in Wordsworth's poetry is a very unstable one, and is best read as the evidence of a crisis that is often not resolved, rather than as the symptom of some hardened doctrinal affiliation. In all of the poems we have discussed in detail so far, a consciously and explicitly dramatic medium might have been the most fitting vehicle for the coherent examination of the conflicts and ideological options that the poems entertain. But Wordsworth was not the poet to produce such coherence. The poems *are* coherent, but at a different level from that of conclusive aesthetic constructions. We have to ponder the mutual interaction of the idiosyncratic and the intersubjective as a process that does not, in these cases, resolve itself into finished arguments or unambiguous positions.

In this way, the poetic investigations of charity and vagrancy that we have been examining do not so much articulate a decision as investigate a series of options. The decisions are there, eventually, but we have to work hard to recover them. 'Alice Fell' is not immediately intelligible as a piece of Burkean ideology; and, though this is what emerges as part of its meaning, much else is revealed along the way, so that the emergence of Wordsworth's doctrinal affiliation becomes both complex and qualified. Coleridge, as we have said, would have preferred such poems as 'Simon

Lee', 'Beggars' and 'Alice Fell' to appear in prose, as incidents experienced on a pedestrian tour (1983, 2: 69). It would be interesting to imagine what Coleridge's prose paraphrase might have amounted to! Blake's famous lines, declaring that

> Pity would be no more
> If we did not make somebody poor
> (1982, 27)

have been cited as a complex alternative to Wordsworth's so-called naïve refusal to investigate self-complicity (see Glen, 1983, 229, etc.); but this investigation occurs constantly in Wordsworth's poems, when we read them carefully. It is not always advertised, as it is in 'The Thorn' or in 'Simon Lee', where we are instructed in how to read, and in the need to make our own tales. For many of Wordsworth's poems do not appear as the result of a writer having *mastered*, in some conscious and conclusive way, the terms and implications of his own displacement (which is at once particular and general). Instead, they *reproduce* these terms, and do so in a frequently inconclusive way. Understanding this important aspect of Wordsworth's 'art' puts us in a good position to try to make sense of Wordsworth's most extended and famous attempt to deploy the dramatic mode. *The Excursion* has variously bored, outraged and frustrated its readers, at least of late. It is consequently one of the least understood or examined among the poems, published or unpublished. Full of apparent technical confusions (is Wordsworth the wanderer? the solitary? and so forth) and difficult doctrinal energies, whether embarrassingly clear or unfathomably obscure, it has stimulated very few critics to detailed response. The task of recovering the historical and intersubjective component of language is, for a poem as long as this, not to be attempted in a chapter. But beginnings may yet be offered, while the place of *The Excursion* within the Wordsworthian reproduction of displacement must be an important part of my argument.

7
Structuring a subject:
The Excursion

To the reader or student of Wordsworth who sets out with the standard assumptions about his characteristic excellences and defects, the fact that *The Excursion* was published as early as 1814 is likely to come as something of a shock. Even more of a shock is the realization that much of the poem was in draft form well before that time (see *PW*, 5: 369–72). What we call Romanticism was by no means over by 1814; Keats, Shelley and Byron had yet to write their major works. But received wisdom none the less has it that *The Excursion* is not only a 'bad' poem, but also a somewhat 'Victorian' poem. As Kenneth Johnston has aptly noted (1984, 291), Wordsworth 'gave his Victorian epic to the Romantics; his Romantic one, to the Victorians'.

Anthologies of the period are still more likely to reprint different versions of *The Prelude* than to present any portion of *The Excursion*. And yet, despite its prophetic recognition of the questions that were to preoccupy the muscular Christians and earnest philanthropists and disciplinarians of later generations, this is a poem that must be central to any coherent understanding of Wordsworth, and to any scrupulous account of what Wordsworth meant to his contemporaries. Its combination of didacticism and dramatic form has proved too much for many readers, starting with Jeffrey and Hazlitt. Of Wordsworth's two major long poems, it has been *The Prelude* that has been the subject of innumerable critical studies, and that has been used most commonly in the adjudication of various Wordsworthian cruxes. Most frequently read as a spiritual autobiography, *The Prelude* is also, as we have seen, full of allusions to and representations of social–historical phenomena in their conjunctions with poetic subjectivity, most obviously in its inscription of the French Revolution, and of the perceived relations between city and country. But in *The Prelude* these themes are woven into the autobiographical mode so easefully that it has proved possible for generations of readers to miss them altogether in their objective import. In *The Excursion*, on the other hand, the doctrinal and even didactic arguments are impossible to miss, so much so that readers are more likely to complain that the poem contains nothing else.

These arguments exist, I shall argue, as some of Wordsworth's most searching and anxious inquiries into the relations between poetry, property and labour, and into the potential in the agrarian life to respond to or modify the challenges of urbanization. *The Excursion* is thus a very important poem for the exploration of the themes of this study. Here, the dramatic form that seems to lurk but is never quite declared in such poems as 'Gipsies' and 'Alice Fell' is explicit – although such explicitness by no means solves the problems of attribution that the poem raises. Here, more fully than in any other poem except perhaps the unpublished *Home at Grasmere*, Wordsworth explores and expounds upon the tensions between social and individual restoration, and between small and large communities.

The Excursion has been very little studied. Judson Lyon, the author of one book-length account, predicted in 1950 (viii) that it might be about to become a new centre of attention in the Wordsworth canon. This has not as yet come to pass. Geoffrey Hartman (1977, 292–323), in what has proved to be the single most influential recent reading of Wordsworth, discussed the poem with real intelligence, but his account is premised on the sense that reading it is a 'massively depressing experience' (292). Among subsequent readings of the poem or its parts, that of Frances Ferguson (1977, 195–241) is exemplary for its subtlety and scope; but it is fair to say that the 'rebirth' has not yet happened.[1]

The Excursion went through seven editions in the poet's lifetime, though it was not much liked by that most eminent of Victorians, Matthew Arnold; but, given the familiar notion of the later Wordsworth as an apostate, one who turned his back on the radical doctrines of his youth (if he ever held them), it is worth remarking that neither Jeffrey nor Hazlitt, the poem's most influential and exact reviewers, make any mention of its politics, or suggest that its affiliations are unusual or questionable. Jeffrey finds the poem 'decidedly didactic', and a 'tissue of moral and devotional ravings' (Reiman, 1972, 2: 440–1) but he does not question the substance of the ravings. For him, the problems of the poem are literary ones; it is 'longer, weaker, and tamer' than anything else of Wordsworth's (439), and in particular it is lacking in decorum. He objects to the pedlar as a spokesman: a 'person accustomed to higgle about tape' should not be given an authoritative voice in poetry. Given that the pedlar has such a voice, his speech is unrealistic: 'A man who went about selling flannel and pocket-handkerchiefs in this lofty diction, would soon frighten away all his customers' (453).

Hazlitt's criticism is more complex (of which more later), but he too objects to Wordsworth's having made 'pedlars and ploughmen his heroes, and the interpreters of his sentiments' (Reiman, 2: 527), albeit that they are, for him, obvious projections of the poet himself. Even Coleridge, who defends the poem in general, and in particular against Jeffrey, regards its diction as a problem. The language is *not* that of 'the ordinary intercourse of spoken words', and thus nothing said by the Wanderer is 'characteristic of a *pedlar*' (1983, 2: 105, 134).

These reviews and reactions suggest that the major challenge of *The Excursion*, as of *Lyrical Ballads* so many years earlier, was to the idea of decorum. In 1814 Wordsworth is still remembered as the proponent of a poetry of ordinary language, and is now gleefully convicted of a contradiction, and of betraying his own mandate. It was, we must assume, still a threatening gesture to employ the characters of humble life as the bearers of poetic debate, even if they did speak an improbably complex language. Jeffrey, Hazlitt and Coleridge, in despite of their doctrinal differences, are also united in their dislike of the poem's dramatic format, in principle and in performance. Hazlitt and Coleridge both resolve the dramatic medium as a falsification of what they see as a solidified Wordsworthian subjectivity. Coleridge says that it is always 'clear that he himself is still speaking' (1983, 2: 100); Hazlitt that 'Mr. Wordsworth's mind is the very reverse of dramatic', so that the so-called 'dialogues' are in fact 'soliloquies of the same character, taking different views of the subject' (Reiman, 1972, 2: 523). Such an interpretation allows anyone who subscribes to it to avoid any following through of the possible objective elements of the various dramatic voices. If we do not take for granted Hazlitt's conviction that the whole poem is spoken by the same character, and concentrate instead on the dramatic propriety of its 'different views', then we will be better able to understand the complex image of subjectivity that I think this poem deploys. We can then return to that 'same character' in a different way.[2]

Talking through the rural life

The themes and arguments of *The Excursion* are, in a way that is very typical of Wordsworth, announced in a mode that is at once subjective and objective. The different doctrinal perspectives are dramatically appropriate to the various characters, as well as begging attention as incipiently Wordsworthian; and they are also generally responsive to and expressive of discursive priorities at the time of writing. Wordsworth claimed to have adopted 'something of a dramatic form' (*PW*, 5: 2); the question is, how much, and when? This symptom of sameness-in-difference may in fact be the perfect vehicle for a poetic subjectivity that we have already seen wandering between a range of positions and preferences that are not at all times coherent one with another. The historical identity of that subjectivity is, I think, to be discovered precisely in this confusion. We may begin to trace its terms by looking at what is perhaps the single most important theme debated in the poem: the nature of the rural life.

Some of the most memorable paragraphs in Hazlitt's review of *The Excursion* are devoted to his negative pronouncements on country life. Wordsworthians have long known about Hazlitt's own experiences in that sphere, modestly transcribed by Moorman (1969, 610) as 'some sort of escapade involving a girl'. We might thus incline to receive the following verdict as a strictly personal view:

> All country people hate each other. They have so little comfort, that they envy their neighbours the smallest pleasure or advantage, and nearly grudge themselves the necessaries of life. From not being accustomed to enjoyment, they become hardened and averse to it – stupid, for want of thought – selfish, for want of society. There is nothing good to be had in the country, or, if there is, they will not let you have it. They had rather injure themselves than oblige anyone else.
>
> (Reiman, 1972, 2: 528)

But Hazlitt too has an intersubjective identity, an expressed affiliation to a theory of civil society that is precisely opposite to that espoused by Wordsworth. Thus he declares that 'vanity and luxury are the civilisers of the world, and sweeteners of human life' (528). His remarks are not to be taken as empirical evidence, though that is what they pretend to be; they are the result of an 'urban' political economy that was the inheritance of what has been thought of as the 'Whig' mentality. Burke also subscribed to it in his preference for the body clothed over the body naked.

Hazlitt also remarks that the 'author himself lets out occasional hints that all is not as it should be amongst these northern Arcadians' (528). So indeed he does, and much more overtly and thoroughly than in any other of the published works. *The Prelude*, for all its darker qualifications – and there are many – generally maintains a strong contrast between the urban and the ideal rural worlds, the second populated by

> Man free, man working for himself, with choice
> Of time, and place, and object.
>
> (8: 152–3)

Perhaps because of the nature of *The Excursion* as a public poem, and enabled by its commitment to a dramatic form, Wordsworth here pushes his inquiry into the features and possibilities of the rural life to a much more sceptical point. The town, of course, remains an almost completely negative social environment. Those 'barricadoed evermore/ Within the walls of cities' (*PW*, 5:5) are as ever in the greatest need of the regeneration that the poem purports to offer. Coleridge wanted Wordsworth to adopt 'something of the Juvenalian spirit as he approached the high civilization of cities and towns' (*PW*, 5:364), and he does so. As the 'huge town' emerges from the germs of some 'poor hamlet' (*PW*, 8:119−20), so the labour patterns and consequent cultural profile of the factory economy replace the agrarian experience. The results of manufacturing industry are analysed by the Wanderer in terms that are almost proto-Marxist:

> Our life is turned
> Out of her course, wherever man is made
> An offering, or a sacrifice, a tool
> Or implement, a passive thing employed
> As a brute mean, without acknowledgment
> Of common right or interest in the end;
> Used or abused, as selfishness may prompt.
> (9:113−19)

The towns and cities thus remain as dangerous for the Wanderer as they were for the author of the 1800 preface to *Lyrical Ballads*; his remarks stand as a versified successor of that polemic (*PrW*, 1:128), and show an even more precise understanding of the conditions and preconditions of factory labour:

> The limbs increase; but liberty of mind
> Is gone for ever; and this organic frame,
> So joyful in its motions, is become
> Dull, to the joy of her own motions dead.
> (8:321−4)

Cut off from the experiences of the outdoor life, children grow up unable to sense and appreciate 'what there is delightful in the breeze' (line 329).

We have seen on other occasions in the course of this study that Wordsworth is able to be more coherent about what is wrong with the urban life than he can be about what is right about life in the country. Hazlitt was right to notice the qualifications of the rural ideal that *The Excursion* presents. The country life is now clearly tainted both from without and from within. We have seen, in the implied economic plots that underlie the events of 'Michael' and 'The Brothers', that Wordsworth for various reasons shows that rural smallholders tend to be responsible, in a large part, for their own undoing. In this later poem, the stresses within the rural ideal are much more apparent. In the familiar way, the long discourse (8: 148ff.) on urbanization and factory labour makes it clear that 'gain' is the 'master-idol of the realm' (line 184) and the foundation of the national economy, threatening the 'old domestic morals of the land' (line 236) with the strong possibility of total extinction. One of the forms of its supremacy is that it turns rural dwellers against themselves. Thus the driver of the timber wagon (7: 546f.) fells the trees that support the mines and the shipyards. Economic incentives, and often the demands of mere survival, force the inhabitants of less powerful social groups (then as now) to work against their own traditional and arguably 'best' interests.

These are the terms of the corruption from outside. But, perhaps more explicitly than ever before, *The Excursion* also suggests the degree to which the rural idyll is questionable in its own, intrinsic terms, regardless of the threats of ulterior vested interests. After the Wanderer's condemnation of the conditions of life in the factories and cities, it is the cynical but persuasive Solitary who asks whether there are not also 'multitudes' who have enjoyed every advantage of the rural environment, while remaining every bit as 'abject' and 'degraded' as the very worst of their urban contemporaries (8: 336f.). He refers not just to beggars and highwaymen, but to the kind of rustic imbecility whose admission ought to have delighted Hazlitt: the 'thriving churl' with his expression 'Wide, sluggish, blank, and ignorant, and strange' (8: 404, 410). The Solitary wonders

> What penetrating power of sun or breeze,
> Shall e'er dissolve the crust wherein his soul
> Sleeps, like a caterpillar sheathed in ice?
> (lines 417–19)

This is a significant challenge, not only to the Wanderer's neat sketch of the rival psycho-economic systems of town and country, but to the very notion of an 'environmental' determination of human character of the kind that I have argued to be consistently important in Wordsworth's writings. The image of the caterpillar sheathed in ice may indeed preserve some prospect of the emergence of a future butterfly; but the invocation of the thriving churl is clear in its suggestion of a residual element in human nature, or the nature of some humans, that can of itself prevent the growth of mind and moral sense. Some political economists, like Hazlitt, had always maintained that city dwellers were more alert and educable than their rural counterparts; prelapsarian shepherds had always jostled for space with country bumpkins in the literature of the country life. But the Solitary's argument suggests that *no* single environment can be thought of as an efficient nurturing place for a stereotypically ideal personality: good and bad examples will continue to abound everywhere.

The real challenge that the Solitary here mounts is thus to the very credibility of governmentally sponsored or contingent aspirations for the reform of human nature. He suggests himself, by default, as a Burkean, one who sees little prospect of altering what seems to be an inevitable mixture of the progressive and regressive in human society. Looking back to earlier Wordsworthian formulations of the relation between social (objective) and idiosyncratic determinations in the formation of individual character, we can in fact see that there was never a simple model of the personality as something entirely *made* by its environment and occupation. Even in the best instances, such as are imaged in 'Michael', it is clear that the maintenance of the ideal requires a strong disciplinary principle. There is implicit a 'fallen' tendency in human nature to wander into waste and idleness (as the 'prince of poetical idlers' knew all too well), unless it be restrained by the demands of life somewhere near the poverty line. The Solitary notes that the 'mutual aptitude of seed and soil' that produces humanity at its best is always 'rare' (5: 878–9), and much else in Wordsworth's writing supports this conviction. As early as 1802, Wordsworth wrote to John Wilson explaining that modern country life is already 'complex', so that its inhabitants are most likely to be responsive to nature when there is 'a peculiar sensibility of original organization combining with moral accidents'. Rural dwellers usually do love the country, and are to a significant extent formed by it, through 'the influence of climate, changes in the atmosphere and elements and the labour and occupations which particular districts require'; but a 'marked degree' of attachment usually depends upon something more than this (*EY*, 354). There is nothing naïve in Wordsworth's idea of the social–environmental determination of character, which fully recognizes the importance of individual modifications of general patterns.

At the same time, and on some occasions, forces outside the individual *are* seen to be responsible for the nature of behaviour. The soldier of 'Adventures on Salisbury Plain' is clearly brutalized by his experiences both of war and of the domestic society to which he returns. Even in the latest version of this tale, published as 'Guilt and Sorrow' in 1842, Wordsworth works up the degree to which the murderer has been brutalized by war, and makes this theme more prominent than it is in the source material (see *SPP*, 310, compared with 125, 229). Alternatively, it is consistently suggested in the various drafts of *The Borderers* that the villain's motives are 'founded chiefly in the very constitution of his character' (*B*, 67). Although his 'strange incontinence in crime' (204) is related to his previous experiences, it is not in any simple sense determined by them.

Even early in his career, then, we can find evidence of two different kinds of explanation of human behaviour in Wordsworth's writings. He accords a prominent place to the social determination of character, but also describes instances where it does not seem to operate. He does not suggest that all the details of individual personalities can be explained by reference to social and ideological forces; but neither does he rely upon innatist notions of moral identity. If Wordsworth's political beliefs had moved as steadily from the left to the right as some readers have assumed, then we would expect a corresponding shift between these two explanations, with the second displacing the first. What we find, on the contrary, is an apparent reluctance to proclaim allegiance to either theory in its most absolute terms. Once again Wordsworth differs in this respect from Burke, who strongly emphasized the irreducibly personal dimension of human nature, only modified in restraining ways by the traditions of custom and convention. For Burke, such conventions could domesticate the negative energies in mankind; but, like other conservatives anxious to argue against the credibility of what we now call a 'welfare' system, he could not afford to admit that social engineering might appreciably better our lot, or lighten the burden of suffering incumbent upon fallen beings. His notion of the customary was defined in terms of what was already there, and should not be disturbed; all change affecting the status quo was therefore discouraged.

Wordsworth seems not to decide these arguments at the level of general theory, but to focus instead upon particular instances. There are occasions, for example in 'Michael', where custom and habit does function to dignify potentially ungovernable desires; but he is also very much aware of the negative forces that are tending to break down these saving institutions. These forces emanate from other, rival formations within the status quo, which thus loses the unitary rhetorical identity that it tends to have in Burke. For Wordsworth, it is not the alien political theories coming from across the Channel that threaten to destroy the fabric of British society, so much as the tensions generated within that society by poverty, urbanization and the changes in patterns of labour and leisure. Various arguments in *The Excursion* point towards self-reliance as the single reliable principle in an unstable world, but this never takes the form of a dogmatically affirmed doctrine or theory. Wordsworth thus remains absolutely clear that there is a strong relation between poverty and brutality. Whatever we may or may not be innately, poverty *does* have a brutalizing effect on most of us. The declining shepherd of 'The Last of the Flock' (*LB*, 78) finds that he loves his family less as his flock disappears. Similarly, the portrayal of Margaret's husband in 'The Ruined Cottage' is marked by a complex awareness of the terrible effect of unemployment on the moral and domestic life. It is as significant a challenge to the present day apologists of the doctrines of self-help as it was to their precursors among Wordsworth's own generation:

> at his door he stood
> And whistled many a snatch of merry tunes

That had no mirth in them, or with his knife
Carved uncouth figures on the heads of sticks,
Then idly sought about through every nook
Of home or garden any casual task
Of use or ornament, and with a strange,
Amusing but uneasy novelty
He blended where he might the various tasks
Of summer, autumn, winter, and of spring.

(*RC*, 54)

As continued poverty and idleness brings on a 'petted mood' he starts to be cruel to his children, playing with them in 'wild freaks of merriment' that they cannot understand. There is in English poetry perhaps no more exact imaging of the psychological stresses resulting from prolonged unemployment than this of Wordsworth's. Love and cruelty intertwine as the children become both signals of the father's shame and competitors for his scanty resources. Parental altruism and material self-interest combine and conflict in unbearably perverse ways. From Margaret herself, the infant child catches the 'trick of grief' (68), so that its character is determined before it even leaves the cradle and assumes self-consciousness.[3]

The details of Robert's psychological disintegration and its effects on family life survive in the first book of *The Excursion* (1: 566f., 829–31), and are never revised out of it. They are thus part of the argument which the Solitary's question – to which we now return – is designed to test out. As such they remind us that, while some rustic personalities do seem to be beyond reform, others are responsive to changes in political, economic and environmental circumstances. Robert begins as an ideal vehicle of rural virtue, one 'Frugal, affectionate, sober, and withal/ Keenly industrious' (1: 522–3). It is the bad harvests and the wartime economy of 1795–6 that bring him down, not any fatal flaw in his own nature. It is of course possible that some, like the Wanderer perhaps, would have stood firm under pressure; but this does not make lesser humans out of those who do not have that strength. The story of Margaret's family represents a definite alternative to the image of social nature in the Solitary's invocation of the 'thriving churl'. It shows that external circumstances can be and have been crucial in the destruction of the best elements in social and human nature.

The force of the Solitary's example is however all the stronger for the fact that it remains unanswered for some 300 lines. The Wanderer rejoins the debate in book 9 (lines 153ff.) and confesses that 'tens of thousands' of such types exist, and in 'every country under heaven' (lines 178, 186). His explanation and response first suggests that such radical and obvious differences between man and man can only come 'from himself', since nature is open to all without 'reserve or veil', as is God's consoling prospect of immortal life. But he then goes on to argue that, in despite of such apparently unmodifiable differences, it remains the lamentable case that the gap between man and man has been widened rather than reduced by civil and economic institutions. Finally, he redirects attention to the 'brighter scene' imaged in the two children just beheld, and to the hope (for that is what it is) that education will be offered to all throughout the land.

While admitting that some distinctions do seem irreducible, the Wanderer thus claims that little has been done to diminish those that *are* open to modification. This is entirely consonant with what I have argued to be Wordsworth's view of the subject; that we are dealing with differences of degree rather than of kind in most cases. One thriving churl does not negate the potential for some worthwhile social reform. The Wanderer's prospectus is closely dependent upon education; until education is available to all, we cannot know how much or how little can be changed in human nature. Even the rustic blasphemer 'Declares his due, while he makes known his need' (line 320). We may of course interpret the Wanderer's argument in the same way that we read Coleridge's case for the educational function of the clergymen of the established church – as a form of social discipline rather than an encouragement of the intellect for its own sake. Indeed, the Wanderer confesses as much:

> Thus, duties arising out of good possest
> And prudent caution needful to avert
> Impending evil, equally require
> That the whole people should be taught and trained.
> (9: 355–8)

In the replacing of 'licentiousness and black resolve' by 'virtuous habit' (lines 359–60), education plays an important role, and as such is a political convenience as well as a moral obligation. General literacy is no longer cast as a threat to the entire social order, as it had been for many of the conservatives of the 1790s. It has now become acceptable, as long as it is directed to the consumption of 'worthy' materials.

In a rhetoric of optimism that is likely to be particularly uncomfortable for the late twentieth-century reader, the Wanderer goes on to discourse upon the virtues of colonialism (lines 363ff.). The ideal social life is something that it is Britain's duty to export; and, conveniently, the colonies are a suitable repository for any excess population that might otherwise threaten domestic security. The increasing accumulation of men in cities (*PrW*, 1: 128) can now, it seems, at least for the Wanderer, be countered by exporting the surplus to Australia. This is an argument against popular Malthusian doctrine, which used the concern for overpopulation as an argument against any form of compassionate social intervention, lest such benevolence encourage more efficient procreation among the poor. But it also partakes of a standard post-war Tory rhetoric according to which reform was seen to pre-empt the possibility of revolution, with the colonies as a convenient safety valve for excess population.

The degree to which the Wanderer here articulates views that we may assume to be Wordsworth's own needs to be investigated, though I shall not here take on that task. Meanwhile, the image of the rural life that *The Excursion* presents needs to be summed up. It is, as we have seen, a varied image. Between the mental agony of Margaret and her spouse and the inert faculties of the 'thriving churl' there lies an entire spectrum of examples about the relation of character to environment. Amidst such a range, it is implausible to suggest that the agrarian ideal is a potential solution for doing away with all forms of social disjunction and distinction. There is no doubt that rural life and solitude do, as the narrator says, 'favour most/ Most frequently call forth, and best sustain' the 'pure sensations' of both self-interest and the 'mutual bond' (4: 362f.). The social–aesthetic benefits of this life are as evident here as they were in 'Michael'. At the same time, and in a way that is consistent with the rest of Wordsworth's writings, it is never suggested that rural virtue exists either untroubled from within or unchallenged from without. The Solitary reminds us that his neighbours 'partake man's general lot/ With little mitigation' (5: 426–7). Any unified (or reified) image of the ideal country life is pre-empted in this poem: by the dramatic form itself, which invites us to regard each interpretation of events as the property of speakers with specific interests and priorities; by the objective contradictions which individual speakers themselves acknowledge; and by the fact that, in the long conversation in the churchyard that takes up so much of the middle of the poem, the various examples brought up by the Pastor are all case-specific. What is true for one does not pretend to be true for all. Wordsworth is thus as far from offering a naïve Utopianism as he always was. Just as the ideal life in 'Michael' was cast into a tragically vanished past, so in *The Excursion* the *most* perfect image of rural life is located not only in the past, but in the remote wilds of Scotland. That is where the Wanderer was brought up, within the 'keen, the wholesome, air of poverty' and on a 'small hereditary farm'. Here, thanks to a 'strictness scarcely known on English ground', he developed his 'habitual piety' (1: 109, 115–16, 306). In the earlier drafts of what was to become this first book of the poem, the figure who became the Wanderer was a native of Wordsworth's own English Lakes. That he was removed from thence in the revisions seems to suggest that his qualities are *not* to be assumed as available to all; perhaps they are not even to be thought of as desirable for all. Nor is he merely a creature of his environment, for the Solitary comes from the same background, but has developed a more speculative and restless disposition (2: 164f.). For those of us who do not have the Wanderer's particular blend of personal qualities and social training, the rural life is a mixed affair at best. The fact that so much of the information about it comes in the form of anecdotes suggests that no one case can be taken to speak for any other. There are always imaginable alternatives, leaving us with a rhetoric of stubborn specificities. As the Pastor declares that he will

> willingly confine
> My narratives to subjects that excite
> Feelings with these accordant; love, esteem
> And admiration
>
> (6: 646–9)

he is really telling us that his perspective is a selective one, polemically the more efficient as it is the less comprehensive and objective. Even then it has been argued (see Galperin, 1980) that his examples do not support the points he thinks he is making by invoking them. The potential of the ideal rural life as a principle of social regeneration is defended, as ever, but the qualifications are still there, and perhaps even weightier, significant enough at least to suggest that the remoter vales of northern England function more as places to hide than as models of a consistently alternative reality.

Education and religion

We must now question the thematic conviction and the historical identity of the Wanderer's responses (for they cannot be called resolutions) to the woes of a variable human nature suffering the developments of a modern manufacturing society. Of the vivifying effects of residence among the great and permanent objects of nature, enough has been said in the previous section. The Wanderer's views on the benefits of colonialism are an early version of an ideology that would become extremely popular later in the century, and sponsor a range of benefits and atrocities. The major initiatives that are emphasized in this poem of 1814 are, however, those involving education and religion.

These are the arguments that have most contributed to the poem's reputation as a didactic discourse. There are no versified details of the educational prospectus in the body of book 9, although Wordsworth's (1814) note refers us to Andrew Bell's system, opining that it is 'impossible to over-rate the benefit which might accrue to humanity from the universal application of this simple engine under an enlightened and conscientious government' (*PW*, 5: 473). Bell was the author of the so-called 'Madras' system, first published in 1797. It is a strange mixture of Rousseau and Gradgrind; enlightened self-dependence and utilitarian efficiency constantly support each other. On the one hand there is an emphasis upon treating children with dignity, and on making education a pleasant and creative experience (1807, v, 74–5). Children tutor each other, with the advanced teaching the less advanced, so that the 'sociable disposition' (5) is encouraged. The superintendent should respond to each child according to his particular 'temper, disposition, and genius' (10); and the students will be 'delighted with being, to every wise and good purpose, their own masters' (14). Thus far, Bell's scheme reads like a suitable implementation of many of the priorities we have come to recognize as 'Romantic'. But there are other priorities at work. A spirit of 'emulation' (7) and competition is to be maintained at all times, and having children teach each other is appealing not least because it can 'economise the time, the labour, and the expense of teaching' (88). This argument probably came straight from Bentham (see 1812, 73), and, as Bell's account develops, it becomes more and more Benthamite. He at least does *not* propose to teach the poor to 'write and to cypher' (although Wordsworth's Wanderer clearly does). For

> Utopian schemes, for the universal diffusion of general knowledge, would soon realise the fable of the belly and the other members of the body, and confound that distinction of ranks and classes of society, on which the general welfare hinges, and the happiness of the lower orders, no less than that of the higher, depends.
>
> (90)

For Bell, there is a danger of 'elevating, by an indiscriminate education, the minds of those doomed to the drudgery of daily labour, and thereby rendering them discontented'. To avoid this, the 'generality' should simply be taught 'to read their Bible and understand the doctrines of our holy religion' (90–1). Bell further calls for the consolidation of charity schools and schools of industry, so that useful profits might even be turned: 'more would be earned by each child than his education would cost, and an aid to the poor rates may be derived from this source' (93–4). As an example of how an efficient school might be organized, Bell offers the model of a military regiment, or a ship; exemplary instances of the 'grand principle of superintendence which pervades all the works of men' (106). Bell always preserves his case against the notion of an innate depravity in children; but his later writings further emphasize the utilitarian element. Thus he describes his system as

> a new *Organ* for the multiplication of power and division of labour in the intellectual, political, and moral world ... As, by material machinery, the number of skeins of silk or hanks of cotton which one man can spin is multiplied in a high ratio, so, by the intellectual machinery, is the number of scholars whom one master can teach.
>
> (1819, 29–30)

How much did Wordsworth know about Bell's scheme, and how much of it is he recommending in his note to *The Excursion*? He must have known quite a bit. Coleridge and Southey were both supporters of Bell, and the man himself visited the Wordsworths in 1811 and 1812. Moreover, Bell became known as the favourite of the 'church and state' Tories in response to the more liberal interpretations of the scheme published by the Quaker Joseph Lancaster (*PW*, 5: 473). We would assume that Wordsworth would be in favour of the 'Romantic' elements in Bell's writings, approving as he did the idea of 'voluntary and self-originating effort' and 'the practice of self-examination' (*PrW*, 2: 13), but evidence suggests that he not only approved of the system in its complete form, Gradgrindian principles included, but gradually came to find it *too* liberal (see Moorman, 1968, 176–81, 222–8, 474–7).

In fact, Wordsworth's thoughts on education are somewhat confused in their finer details and implications, even as his general priorities are clear. In a letter to Wrangham in 1808 (*MY*, 1: 247–51), he expresses doubts about the viability of any *national* scheme of education in a country where 'Heaven and Hell are scarcely more different from each other' than are Manchester and Westmoreland. Seeing little to hope for from a government that has no regard for the morals of the people, he advises making a beginning at the top of the social ladder, hoping that the rest might follow. By 1828, Wordsworth is writing to H.J. Rose (*LY*, 1: 685–6) and disapproving of the spirit of 'emulation' in Bell's system; but he is also suspicious of its tendency to discourage the poor from settling down to 'any kind of hard labour or drudgery'. In another letter to the same correspondent (*LY*, 2: 19–25), infant schools are criticized because they break up the family at too early an age, and because the education they offer is insufficiently imaginative. At the same time, Wordsworth worries about children knowing more than their parents, and failing to experience the proper 'gratitude' to authority as a result of free education. By 1829 he is stressing the need to educate 'the middle and upper classes' before trying to assist the poor (*LY*, 2: 99); and by 1830 'book learning' is dismissed in favour of 'the education of duty' (254). The later letters are consistently preoccupied with the necessary priority of religious education for the poorer classes.

Most of this is consistent with the 'trickle-down' model of social reform that characterizes much of Wordsworth's later thought. This is, generally speaking, a reactionary position. Confusion arises because Wordsworth is genuinely and articulately anxious to offer a positive prospect for wider education, but at the same time unable to suggest anything that might question the terms of the established social hierarchy, or set going the murmurings of revolution. Confusion on this subject was not uncommon. Even that evident 'man of the people' William Cobbett, who wrote a highly democratic grammar of the English language, could be found recommending that poor children be taught to reap rather than to read, since being 'habituated to labour cheerfully' might be their only reliable insurance against want (1979, 78–9). Patrick Colquhoun (1806, 140) argued that any scheme for a national education that was 'beyond a mere Channel for conveying religious and moral Principles would be mischievous and utopian'; and even the radical Henry Brougham, Wordsworth's enemy in the 1818 election campaign, contended that it 'is not necessary that all who are taught, or even any large proportion, should go beyond the rudiments' (1825, 10). In this general climate of educational ideology, it is the less surprising that Wordsworth's already conscious and somewhat extreme anxieties about the effects of urbanization should have led him to favour religious orthodoxy as the proper centrepiece of any prospectus for educating the poor.

However, in the various revisions of *The Excursion* that were incorporated after 1814, nothing is done to cast doubt on the Wanderer's appeal for a national education founded in the ideal of universal literacy. Of course, this is a dramatic voice, but it is not one substantially ironized on this occasion, except to the degree that it is an aspiration and not a prediction that is here put forward. It remains for us to question what kind of religion might have been at the centre of this national education, had it ever come about.

The longest exposition of this topic does not come from the Pastor, but from the Wanderer, in book 4. This is itself slightly disjunctive, given the authority that we might expect the poet to place in the man of fixed place and recognizable social status. It is the Pastor, and not the Wanderer, who should speak for the established church. Moreover, the terms of the Wanderer's faith seem remarkably basic and inter-denominational, so much so that they have been felt to approach heterodoxy.[4] There is little if anything in his speech that suggests a strong dogmatic affiliation to a single sect or faction. He emphasizes belief in a being of 'infinite benevolence and power' and in an idea of 'duty' that outfaces the anxieties of earthly mutability, being supplied by an 'abstract intelligence' emanating from a place 'where time and space are not' (4: 15, 75–6). It is the law of 'conscience' that is 'God's most intimate presence in the soul' and his 'most perfect image in the world' (4: 225–7). After this emphasis on that part of the mind that is *not* related to external nature, the Wanderer further commends active participation in the cycle of non-human nature. Any inclination toward dangerous introspection is to be avoided by rising with the lark, remaining busy all day, and sinking into 'sound repose' at night (4: 491f.). Such a routine will develop the 'mind's *excursive* power' (line 1263) as a force in sympathy with the active universe. As in the 'Ode to Duty' (*1807*, 104), Wordsworth is here suggesting a synthesis of nature and conscience that recalls Schiller's model of the *schöne Seele:*

> – So build we up the Being that we are;
> Thus deeply drinking-in the soul of things,
> We shall be wise perforce; and, while inspired
> By choice, and conscious that the Will is free,
> Shall move unswerving, even as if impelled
> By strict necessity, along the path
> Of order and of good.
>
> (4: 1264–70)

Wordsworth had been working with such a schema since he proposed a model of poetic spontaneity that synthesized deep feeling with profound thought (*PrW*, 1: 126). The Wanderer here seeks to reconcile the inner voice of conscience with the energies of animate and inanimate nature. In a similar spirit, the Pastor later describes our life as an 'energy of love/Divine or human' (5: 1012–13). This is correlative with the '*active* Principle' (9: 3) that the Wanderer describes as prophetic of a life to come. The experience of living 'by hope/ And by desire' (9: 23–4) is not only a form of religious assurance but also, as in *The Prelude*, a formal schema for describing Wordsworth's ongoing poetic intentions. Both propose 'something evermore about to be' (*Prelude*, 6: 542).

'A species of ventriloquism'

The religious debate in *The Excursion* is not, it seems to me, the subject of the same dramatic specificity as are the social and educational debates. There are no radical disagreements on matters of doctrine or emphasis; the Solitary, for whose edification much of the theology is intended, never enters fully enough into the argument for Wordsworth or the Wanderer to need to refine any precise, doctrinal positions. The major questions that we might ask of the poem's theology are thus arguably questions about its practical effectiveness: does it work, and if so for whom? When this question has been posed, it once again comes to seem that the dogmatic element in the poem calls for a contextual and particularized understanding of the sort that does not easily permit the reader's expropriation of a simple or definitive prospectus.

The Excursion is borne along by one major, confessed narrative intention: to educate the Solitary out of what is said to be a self-consuming melancholy and into a state of active acceptance or peace of mind. That the poem fails to do this, except by glimpses, is adequately evidenced by its conclusion. Despite the resounding claim of the heading of book 4, 'Despondency Corrected', the end of the poem has the Solitary leave the party with the case far from closed; its further exploration was to be the business of the poet's 'future labours' (9: 796).

The second character who is presented as the object of a religious education is, of course, Margaret, the former inhabitant of the ruined cottage. Critics have rightly focused on the end of the first book of *The Excursion*, and on the various draft manuscripts that preceded it, as one of the great points of crisis in Wordsworth's writings. This is another of those occasions on which it is very difficult to be sure of the degree of dramatic method; how are we to feel about the Wanderer? Reeve Parker makes the point well:

> As readers we share the perplexity of the narrator, moved by Margaret's otherness and unsure of our affinity with the difficult ideal of the wanderer's philosophic calm. The success of Wordsworth's poem is in the generation of that perplexity in the face of such disparate styles.
>
> (1972, 110)

The narrated events of the first book make up our most testing experience of the Wanderer's credibility as the voice of consolatory wisdom. On no other occasion does he dare to pronounce so fully on the relation between another's grief and his own happiness. It is not in itself shocking that a man of faith should find a way of coming to terms with the miseries in the world; but Wordsworth elects to work up this acceptance into what is almost a language of pleasure. The first draft, written in 1798, ends at what was to become 1:916. Margaret's death is reported, but there is no mention of the narrator's discomfort or the Wanderer's response (*RC*, 72). In the 1799 version, the narrator feels 'weakness' and the 'impotence of grief' (73), for which his companion tries to console him by telling of his own former accommodation with Margaret's tragedy. The associations of the ruined cottage with human love and courage have brought him to the point of being able to turn away 'in happiness' (75). Only in a cancelled draft does Wordsworth have the *narrator* confess that the trouble in his thoughts

> Was sweet, I looked and looked again, & to myself
> I seemed a better and a wiser man.   (257)

And only in the 1845 revision of *The Excursion* does Wordsworth add in the moralizing lines (1:934–40) explaining why we should not give way to grief, and expounding upon Margaret's Christian fortitude. This is what we would expect the Wanderer to think; but Frances Ferguson (1977, 216f.) has written well of the degree to which he too continues to be disturbed with the memory of Margaret's fate, and, in all versions of the passage written after 1799, the end of the account leaves very open indeed the question of the true status of Christian acceptance in relation to what has happened. That it produces not just acceptance but 'happiness' seems to suggest a disjunction between the events as seen by others (including the troubled narrator) and as received by the Wanderer. It is by no means clear that the Wanderer has passed his first test in trying to convince others (or even himself) of the sufficiency of faith as an answer to the problems of the earthly life.

Much of our uncertainty about how to read the end of the first book depends upon the degree to which the Wanderer has by that time already been particularized as a very unusual character. His upbringing has been marked by a 'strictness scarcely known on English ground' (*The Excursion*, 1: 117), so that we cannot assume that his particular construction of experience will be simply available to others. His training has rendered him immune to 'wild varieties of joy and grief', and has left him able to '*afford* to suffer/ With those whom he saw suffer' (1: 359, 370–1). He is indeed something of an ideal personality in Wordsworthian terms, but the cultural and environmental conditions that formed his character are themselves disappearing; the frugal subsistence economy is increasingly threatened, and the trade of pedlar is becoming scarce. Not even the narrator, let alone the reader, seems to be able to identify completely with this wisely passive old man. Wordsworth's later note may be quite precise in its claim that the Wanderer represents 'an idea of what I fancied my own character might have become in his circumstances' (*PW*, 5: 373); and *The Prelude* does indeed declare a poet who is 'withal/ A happy man, and therefore bold to look/ On painful things' (10: 869–71). But the poet's circumstances are not the Wanderer's, and this is not an adequate summary of the personality of the narrator of *The Excursion*. Furthermore, the dramatic identity of the Wanderer himself is at times pointed by moments of irony, and even comedy. The Solitary first appears in the poem immediately after the Wanderer has pronounced his epitaph: 'Behold the Man whom he had fancied dead!' (2: 497). Despite this implicit corrective, the flow of the Wanderer's funereal meditation is only briefly interrupted by this startling apparition, and readily transfers itself to another subject (2: 546f.). On another occasion, the Wanderer seems to undermine the illusion of dialogue by 'Answering the question which himself had asked' (4: 68). We cannot go so far as to argue that he is consistently presented ironically, and as the voice of a partial vision; but there are moments in the narrative where such seems to be the case. In a note to the first (1814) edition of the poem, Wordsworth specified the Wanderer as the representative of a type 'strongly disposed to enthusiasm poetical and religious' (*RC*, 479). The traces of such a personality are never erased to the point where he becomes a possible emblem of or model for a general human nature; he continues to have what Wordsworth elsewhere calls 'an external existence' (*PW*, 5: 373).[5]

The Wanderer's dramatic interactions with other characters do then give us cause to question his credibility as a voice of authority. Such questioning is also appropriate at such points where his personality does correspond closely with what Wordsworth elsewhere describes as that of the poet or man of imagination. Like the poet, he is largely removed from 'the freedom and power of real and substantial action and suffering' (*PrW*, 1:138), the sensation of which he must try to recreate by after-recollection. Such stability as he has achieved in his perspective on the tragedy of Margaret may well thus result from the passage of time. The ways in which the Wanderer derives meanings from experience, and his distinct tendency toward the transcendental, are admittedly very close to those attributed by the author of *The Prelude* to himself. Indeed, many of the draft passages describing the pedlar-wanderer eventually found their way into the autobiographical poem, but this neither proves nor disproves the 'identity' of poet and pedlar; instead, it calls into question the whole concept of identity. The Wordsworthian syndrome is such that almost all self-descriptive moments are implicated in both affirmation and negation. The youthful Wanderer is very like the youthful Wordsworth (as reported) in his development of an 'active power to fasten images/ Upon his brain' until they acquired the 'liveliness of dreams' (1: 145−8). But in the suggestion that the dream is livelier than the perception of everyday objects in the waking state, we are made to engage with the same problem of imaginative manipulation or modification that appears in the famous moments of empirical disappointment in *The Prelude*. Thus, for Wordsworth himself, the 'soulless image' of Mont Blanc is a poor substitute for the 'living thought' that had encouraged him to pursue it (6:454−5). This gap between the imagined and the actual is one that constantly appears in Wordsworth's encounters with both objects and human beings, and it is often, as we have seen, the source of moral crisis. The Wanderer too is visited by states of mind in which 'thought' expires in 'enjoyment', leading to an 'existence oftentimes *possessed*' (*The Excursion*, 1: 213, 221). The other figures in the poem function inevitably as questioners or critical audiences for such moments of insight. His assertion at the site of the ruined cottage − 'I see around me here/ Things which you cannot see' (1: 469−70) − does indeed ask to be heard as a claim to a superior vision and understanding; but it may also be taken as a sign of a transcendentalizing poet's tendency to find sermons in stones, and good in every thing. We should not try to make the Wanderer into an emblem of the extremer sorts of misapprehension that also figure in Wordsworth's writings; but we should also not try to exempt him from the scepticism that generally informs Wordsworth's analysis of the figuring of the real.

The dramatic quality of *The Excursion* is, of course, evident in the representation of all the other characters (see Lyon, 1950, 67−71). If readers have tended to assume too easy an identification of the Wanderer as the authoritative voice of the poet, then the Solitary has been too often misunderstood in the opposite way, as a figure with no credibility whatsoever. If there is much of Fawcett and Thelwall in this personality, then there is also much of Wordsworth, and much that we may choose to take more seriously than the Wanderer himself seems to. Incipiently an atheist or pagan, the Solitary yet has a dignity and humanity that is not at all contained within the Wanderer's prefatory account of him as one 'steeped in a self-indulging spleen, that wants not/ Its own voluptuousness' (2: 311–12). He too has his mountain vision, and his fit of poetic abstraction (2:834–81); and his response to the death of one he knew and cared for (2:729f.) does not contrast unfavourably with the Wanderer's tale of the sufferings of Margaret. He expresses, on two occasions, the same appreciation of the paradisally 'unappropriated earth' (3:538, 939) that Wordsworth himself so often celebrates; and, as the 'pale Recluse' (5:224) it is he who gives the title to the grand project that was to be Wordsworth's great work. It may be that Wordsworth intended us to realize that essential human nature never did disappear from the Solitary's mind and heart, and that it was eventually to be restored in full. But in the poem that we have, this also has the effect of legitimating his perspective by demonstrating that it is not just to be dismissed as the product of a disabled psyche. *He* has suffered not just by proxy but in the course of his own life, and the question of what might be a 'proper' response to the disappointments he has experienced is not one that the poem finally answers. By having the Wanderer completely exempted from suffering in his *own* person, Wordsworth inevitably puts into question the authority of his pious advice to others, and the frequent facility with which he reconciles himself to their woes.

The other significant personality (besides the Pastor, of whom more later) in *The Excursion* is the narrator himself. He slips in and out of dramatic engagement, and disappears entirely for long stretches of the poem. At the opening of book 6, he voices a strangely disembodied paean to British liberty and the established church; the lack of response to this makes him seem indeed the spokesman of authorial dogma rather than a participant in a dramatic exchange. But this is an exceptional moment, in that elsewhere the narrator does have a definite personality, and one that engages with the challenges and perspectives presented by the others. He is not at all the 'mere foil to the other characters' that Lyon (1950, 46) would have him remain.

The narrator is himself a part-time wanderer, one 'whose favourite school/ Hath been the fields, the roads, and rural lanes'. Thus he has a 'reverential love' for the Wanderer (2:28–30), even as he cannot become one with him. In fact, he demonstrates many of the same anxieties about property and vagrancy (of which wandering is a sanitized form) and idleness and labour that we have seen to mark the speaking voices of so many of the 1807 *Poems*. His appetite quickens at the sight of the Solitary's chosen vale – so like the one that Wordsworth intends for himself in *Home at Grasmere* – but it is immediately identified as tainted by a death-wish: 'Urn-like it was in shape, deep as an urn' (2: 333). This is appropriately confirmed by the 'funereal dirge' (line 376) that emanates from it. It is the narrator who seems most anxious to preserve the idea of a harmonious rural community (2: 607), and who is most reluctant to leave 'the spot that seemed/ Like the fixed centre of a troubled world' (5: 15–16). Despite his proclivity for wandering, he also desires to be 'fixed' in a 'still retreat' (5: 53), and thus projects the familiar schizophrenia that marks so many of the first-person speakers in Wordsworth's poems.

In a brief essay that might be the starting point for volumes of discovery, Stuart Peterfreund (1978, 174) has noted that *The Excursion* performs a precise reversal of *Paradise Lost*. The final lines of Milton's poem have Adam and Eve descending out of Eden to a plain parched with punishing heat; Wordsworth, who knew perfectly well that he was risking geographical incoherence to bring it about (*PW*, 5: 375), has his poem begin there, and moves from thence to a landscape that is, for the narrator, Edenic. We might also note, in the context of a theme that has preoccupied much of the first chapter of this study, that Satan *begins* his part in Milton's poem by repairing to a 'dreary plain' (having already crossed the 'torrid clime' of the 'burning marl') after which he will make *his* way intrusively into paradise (*PL*, 1: 180, 296–7). If *The Excursion* in one way reverses the order of landscape in *Paradise Lost*, then the narrator, as a Luciferic intruder, also duplicates it. After the Wanderer's strenuous advocacy of the active life, it is the narrator who applauds, as follows:

> How divine,
> The liberty, for frail, for mortal, man
> To roam at large among unpeopled glens
> And mountainous retirements, only trod
> By devious footsteps
>
> (4: 513–17)

These 'devious footsteps' are underpinned not only by the 'wandering steps' of Adam and Eve's exiled and 'solitary way' (*PL*, 12: 648–9), but also by Satan's previous and proleptic passage: 'Through wood, through waste, o'er hill, o'er dale his roam' (4: 538). The narrator is wiser than Lucifer in seeking to be what the angel should have been content with, 'an equal among mightiest energies' (*The Excursion*, 4: 532). But it is as much Satan as Adam that he invokes in seeking to support the attempt

> To lift the creature toward that eminence
> On which, now fallen, erewhile in majesty

> He stood; or if not so, whose top serene
> At least he feels 'tis given him to descry.
> (5: 298–301)

If the narrator's most consistent attempt at emulation is directed at the Wanderer, he is yet not immune to the Luciferic appeal of the Solitary's 'intense and glowing mind', and to his appearance as one 'All fire' (2: 474, 516).

The same divided self that registers in the drama of 'Gipsies' and in *The Prelude* is thus present in the persona of the narrator of *The Excursion*. As he celebrates the apparently perpetual motion of wandering, so he recognizes it as the trope of alienation and displacement, and finds himself longing for a place at the 'fixed centre of a troubled world' (5: 16), where one

> Might, by the promise that is here, be won
> To steal from active duties, and embrace
> Obscurity, and undisturbed repose.
> (5: 26–8)

This in turn resurrects the familiar anxiety about idleness and ineffectuality. Thus he must hope that such retreat might be 'Uncensured', and lead to 'principles and powers/ Discovered or invented' (lines 33, 40–1). He must be

> Sheltered, but not to social duties lost,
> Secluded, but not buried; and with song
> Cheering my days, and with industrious thought.
> (5: 54–6)

The paradigm of active retirement that is here put forward is exemplified by the Pastor, who has chosen to leave behind a successful worldly life (5: 110f.) in order to pursue it. However, the balance is possible only in small communities, of the sort that Wordsworth saw to be increasingly threatened. Here only can one combine 'private life/ And social neighbourhood', mingling with others while remaining 'self-governed, and apart' (5: 381–2, 385–6). The narrator aspires to a synthesis of the Edenic and the Satanic, a state of society that is more individuated than the paradisal unbroken knot, but less isolated than the demonic alienation. It is the Pastor's image of the small rural community that comes closest to fulfilling the conditions for such a life. Here, each is known personally to all, so that remaining differences may be tolerated, enabling the friendly co-existence of 'flaming Jacobite' and 'sullen Hanoverian' (6: 458–9), and the reintegration of the fallen woman (6: 1018f.), who is not cast out on to the streets as she might be in the city. This emphasis on the positive potential of small communities is consistent with other examples in Wordsworth's writings. In 'The Two Thieves' (*LB*, 175) the familiarity and practical harmlessness of the village kleptomaniac renders unnecessary any appeal to the laws of the land; and in 'The Thorn' (*LB*, 70), in a more ambiguous way, Martha Ray is kept from the hands of the law in a manner that is both cruel and kind.[6] The ideal adjustment of principle to practice that Wordsworth commends in such cases is possible only in small societies where habitual contact softens the otherwise impersonal operations of laws and factions.

The Pastor's image of the rural life is questionable in itself, as we have seen. And its sufficiency is further qualified by the fact that it is the Wanderer, rather than the Pastor (who has not yet appeared), to whom the narrator points as an example of the ideal balance of social and individual (5:387). This is striking in view of the fact that the Wanderer is *not* related to any particular place of fixed abode. The Pastor is the most obvious candidate for imaging as the Coleridgean patrician, using his role in the established church as a means of administering social control, enlightened or otherwise; but it is to the itinerant Wanderer that Wordsworth's narrator turns. As *The Excursion* reveals itself to be structured upon the familiar oscillations between the fixed and the fluid, participation and retirement, labour and idleness, and hence in the most general sense between integration and displacement, so it registers the same ambivalent reconciliation of these opposites as many of the earlier poems. Once again, there is an objective or economic aspect to this predicament. The preface tells us that *The Recluse*, of which *The Excursion* was to be but a part, is to have for its principal subject the 'sensations and opinions of a poet living in retirement' (*PW*, 5:2). In the voice of the narrator of the poem that we do have, this takes the form of a desire to wander within safe limits, having the best of both worlds, as in *Home at Grasmere*. But this is harder to achieve in a world where the conventions of patronage have disappeared. Thus he speaks fondly of the ancient minstrel

> wandering on from hall to hall
> Baronial court or royal; cheered with gifts
> Munificent, and love, and ladies' praise.
> (2:2–4)

We recall Wordsworth's (probable) allusion to 'Ifor Hael' in 'Simon Lee'. Such times have gone forever, giving way to 'these our unimaginative days' (line 24). In economic as well as theological terms, it may then be that Wordsworth's commitment to some form of wandering partakes as much of necessity as of virtue. This is the other side of what often appears elsewhere as a sturdy and Satanic affirmation of independence and resolution; here it becomes a somewhat more plaintive appeal to a lost and even feudal system of maintenance. The roles that Calvert and John Wordsworth played in the 1807 *Poems* and in the earlier drafts of *The Prelude* are still invoked. If Wordsworth (as narrator) is to continue to maintain his precarious posture of partial displacement or productive wandering, responding to the 'changeful breeze/ Of accident' and 'pausing at will' (2: 84–5, 108), he needs a supportive presence and a helping hand. The vocation of pedlar is no answer, since it is a dying trade, one 'deemed debasing now' (1: 327). The role of patron is now fulfilled by Lord Lonsdale, as the dedicatory sonnet makes clear. It is through Lonsdale's estates and 'fair domains' that the poet has wandered 'on youthful pleasures bent', and it is by Lonsdale that his energies have been disciplined and appreciated, 'by thy care befriended' (*PW*, 5: 1). The Wanderer became the person he is through a frugal upbringing in a remote part of Britain, but the poet cannot claim this of himself. Instead, he must acknowledge the uncomfortable (if yet acceptable) fact of dependence, which in one sense confutes and in another sense explains his Luciferic self-images. The '*excursive*' (4: 1263) or wandering powers of the poet's mind are not independent of Lonsdale's goodwill. This threatens or complicates his self-esteem, one result of which is, arguably, his adulatory attitude toward the Wanderer, who has made himself what he is. It also legitimates (by proxy) his claim to a disinterested moral judgement, announced in the promise 'to weigh/ The good and evil of our mortal state' (*PW*, 5: 3). Such a perspective on the world was traditionally held to be open only to those who could look upon it without feeling the pressures of their own vested interests. In 1818, Wordsworth would try to cast the Lowthers in this light, and it is of course the gentleman who can be most easily accommodated to this image of disinterested virtue. Having more than he needs, his opinions are not tainted by the insecure self-interest that afflicts those lower down the social and economic scale (see Barrell, 1983, 17–50). The case for Lonsdale was hard enough to make, as we have seen earlier in this study, but it could hardly have been made at all for Wordsworth, who confesses his dependence upon the local aristocrat – a dependence no less uncomfortable for being only partial. Wordsworth was never the figure that Coleridge wanted him to be, the 'man in mental repose, one whose principles were made up, and so prepared to deliver upon authority a system of philosophy' (*PW*, 5: 364). Among the reasons for this, we should never discount the economic facts of the poet's household, maintained as it was by the uneasy (even when unctuously acknowledged) sense of dependence upon the goodwill of the high and mighty. Like the archfiend himself, Wordsworth exercises freedom of choice under the eyes of an all-powerful, if not all-seeing, presence. Allowing him neither secure establishment nor unfettered freedom, it commits him to an uncomfortable and constantly adjusting vacillation between the two. We move now to a discussion of the end of *The Excursion*.

Postscript: 'The star of eve was wanting'

About half-way through the final book of *The Excursion*, the Pastor's wife responds thus to the Wanderer's presence:

> While he is speaking, I have power to see
> Even as he sees; but when his voice hath ceased,
> Then, with a sigh, sometimes I feel, as now,
> That combinations so serene and bright
> Cannot be lasting in a world like ours.
>
> (*PW*, 9: 465–9)

This echoes an earlier and longer speech by the Pastor himself (5: 485–557), in which all perception is described as a function of the person seeing: 'we/ Are that which we would contemplate from far' (lines 490–1). He proffers faith in providence as a working alternative (lines 515–22), but returns to expound at greater length the degree to which, as the Wanderer puts it, 'We see, then, as we feel' (line 558). This position is part of an ongoing debate, and not to be taken as simply authoritative; but it is important that a similar argument returns at a later point in the poem, as it is building towards its conclusion. Under the spell of the Wanderer's living voice, the Pastor's wife can convince herself that she sees and feels as he does; but without that living voice, even she has her doubts. The narrative of the poem does not explicitly confirm this threatened disjunction in the didactic ambition of the principal speaker; but neither does it lay our doubts to rest. The protagonists are not dispersed into any rampant solipsism of the postmodernist sort; but the precarious balance of their consensus is yet disturbed in various ways. After the Pastor's wife has made her point, the conversation is interrupted by the arrival of the children, upon which the whole party takes to the water in a passage that reads as a legitimated reminiscence of the famous episode of the stolen boat (*The Prelude*, 1: 372f.). The narrator's pleasure is here untroubled by stealth; he now has a community, a 'crew/ Of joyous comrades' (lines 486–7), and rows by invitation. The island in the lake upon which they alight is a place of limited wandering: 'we cannot err/ In this delicious region' (lines 503–4). Culture and nature, the beautiful and the sublime, all blend harmoniously. So too do the members of the little party, including even the Solitary:

> One spirit animating old and young,
> A gipsy-fire we kindled on the shore
> Of the fair Isle with birch trees fringed – and there,
> Merrily seated in a ring, partook
> A choice repast – served by our young companions
> With rival earnestness and kindred glee.
>
> (lines 526–31)

Reading beneath the poetic diction, we infer that a picnic is taking place, but it is one overcharged with telling allusions. Here again is the unbroken knot of human beings, sitting by a 'gipsy-fire', but this time the narrator is within the circle, not witnessing enviously and aggressively from outside. The communal spirit embraces ideological antagonists as well as young and old, but its existence is fragile and far from permanent. This is because of the passage of time, and because of the nature of human communities in themselves. There is a quiet but clear reminder of the environmental drama of 'Nutting' – 'Rapaciously we gathered flowery spoils' (line 537) – as if paradisal relaxation once again threatens to bring about a moment of transgression. The Solitary then meditates, in a 'plaintive note' (line 559), upon the emblem of the dying fire. But this in turn passes as the party beholds a splendid sunset, a 'rapturous moment' in which 'particular interests were effaced/ From every mind' (lines 588–90). This time, the narrator is neither stepping westward in an 'endless way', nor gazing puzzled at 'something far more deeply interfused'. He is reposing gratefully among his friends, and he has the Pastor to moralize the 'refulgent spectacle' (line 611) – two more items from the vocabulary of 'Gipsies' are here domesticated into a more stable context.

The Pastor's speech is one of 'fervent gratitude' (line 742) to the creator, but it is a prayer for rather than a prophecy of earth's harmony. The poem moves to its conclusion:

This vesper-service closed, without delay,
From that exalted station to the plain
Descending, we pursued our homeward course,
In mute composure, o'er the shadowy lake,
Under a faded sky.

(lines 755–9)

Significantly, 'the star of eve/ Was wanting' (lines 761–2). Vesper, the light that is ambiguously Messianic and Satanic, and disturbing in both these dimensions, has been rendered comfortably into its orthodox Christian afterlife, the vesper *service*. They cross the 'dewy fields' (line 769) that were so dark and cold in 'Stepping Westward', and head toward the Pastor's house. Before they get there, the Solitary takes his leave to return to his 'lonely dell' (line 775), but with the promise to come back tomorrow. Wordsworth commits the rest to 'future labours' (line 796) that were never to come to print.

These last pages of the poem are full of drama, or drama headed off. They are unusually dense in allusions to Milton, as de Selincourt's notes tell us (*PW*, 5: 474–5). The Wanderer's earlier promise, that those who dwell on earth might be 'Sons of the morning' (4: 232), has hardly been fulfilled, as perhaps it never could be in this life. In fact, the fulgent spectacle of sidereal immortality has been quietly domesticated. The 'exalted station' that the party obtains to view the sunset is abdicated willingly, not coveted forever, and they move down to the 'plain'. It is striking that Wordsworth uses that word again, for it suggests an undoing of the reversal of Milton's great epic that we have seen to mark the opening of Wordsworth's own poem. The descent to the plain thus offers the faintest intimation of the move *out* of Eden. We are left, in this sense, where we began, in a movement that suggests not only the frailty of the social and spiritual consensus that has just been achieved, but also the larger narrative irony of the projected great work itself, which has still to happen. There *is* an aura of contentment about the end of *The Excursion*, and the view from the 'exalted station' is not marked by the same giddying glimpse *down* into infinity as featured in its prototype (and post-type), the account of the ascent of Snowdon (*The Prelude*, 13: 54f.); but it is not unqualified by dissonant allusions. Wordsworth wanted his poem to have a 'star-like virtue', shedding 'benignant influence, and secure' (*PW*, 5: 6). But the final evening sky is one in which the 'inferior lights' have to do the job of celestial illumination that Hesperus has so often and so troublingly performed in Wordsworth's poems. Some do stand 'boldly forth' in 'twinkling lustre', but others are 'too faint almost for sight' (9: 762–5). The exemplary individuality that has consistently preoccupied Wordsworth, at times tempting him to extravagant gestures of self-assertion, at other times committing him to equally histrionic confessions of loneliness and displacement, is absent from the end of the poem as its emblem is absent from the evening sky. Wordsworth is not alone as a traveller under open sky, even if the terms of a consensus have yet to be worked out. But the moment of shared vision is a fragile and threatened one, and the cycle promises to begin again even as it comes to an end. The Satanic aspiration is quietly present in the very allusions that describe its appeasement, which are thus compelled, however peacefully, to regret its vanishing.

After *The Excursion*, did the light go out completely? It is tempting to pronounce, as so many critics have, some kind of epitaph upon the Wordsworthian imagination. While the terms of an answer to this question are beyond the scope of this study (and indeed beyond the present capacities of its author), I would caution against assuming that it did. If I have succeeded in making significant sense out of *The Excursion*, a poem little read and even less often enjoyed, then the same logic suggests the timeliness of a new interest in the poems written after 1814. My own experience with this study, which was at first intended to produce some 'total' vision of Wordsworth's career, but has resigned itself to writing in detail about a few poems, suggests that we should pursue this interest modestly, establishing small beginnings rather than aiming at grand summaries. This is, as has been explained often enough by now, an approach demanded by what I take to be the complexity of the relation between Wordsworth's languages and their history, both personal and objective. If we cannot imagine a totally incoherent poetic subjectivity that 'records' in some passive way the tides in the affairs of men with no critical continuity between one statement and the next, then we cannot rest content any longer with the opposite fiction, that of an intelligence continually evolving in ways that typify the life of a Coleridgean organic whole. When we accept that the most useful truths are to be found somewhere in between, then we are inevitably committed to a careful and detailed examination of particulars.

Certain guiding preoccupations and continuities do emerge after an inspection of minute particulars. But it is likely that an examination of the later poetry would need to establish different themes and priorities from those which have made (I hope) some sense of the poems discussed here. Property and labour, fixed settlement and wandering, and the Satanic encoding of the evening and morning stars are no longer in the later poetry the themes of crisis and tension that they are in the earlier. On these matters, there is little doubt that the maturing poet is much less anxious than he used to be, so that the terms devised for reading the earlier poetry will no longer bear interpretative fruit. It is striking, for example, that the various poems about journeying – memorials, itineraries and tours –

which continue to abound in the later work contain almost no reported encounters. These had often been fictional, or experienced by proxy (thus Wordsworth himself did not meet Alice Fell), but they were nevertheless worked into anxious meditations, for they positioned the speaker in a disputed space and brought about interpretative crises in which both self and other were called into question. 'The Solitary Reaper' was not written out of the poet's own experience of a highland woman; it was inspired by a passage in Wilkinson's manuscript *Tour in Scotland* (*PW*, 3: 444–5). But it was written from the perspective of such an experience, and its dramas depend upon our accepting the events as if they had happened. In 'The Gleaner' (*PW*, 4: 159), composed in 1828, no such fiction is created. The meditation is explicitly 'Suggested by a Picture', so that we need never test out the painterly terms of description against an encounter with which they might be in disjunctive relation. The poem has its complexities, but they are hardly those that result from the challenges of encounter or direct speech.

Again, in the poem 'I know an aged Man constrained to dwell' (*PW*, 4: 160), composed in 1846 and standing as the most obvious later analogue to 'The Old Cumberland Beggar', the element of personal confrontation is diminished to the point where it serves as little more than an enabling introduction. The imaging of the old man's posture is not troubled by any indication of a preconditioned or motivated observer of the sort that provides so many of the dramas of the earlier poems (and which we would do wrong to construe as merely egotism). All the awkwardness has gone. The criticism of the 'large house of public charity' is consistent with what Wordsworth published in 1800, though it is now considerably muted. But here, the old man is allowed precisely the empathic fellowship with nature that the Cumberland beggar was denied, with such complex results for the poem; and there is no attempt to poeticize the ambiguities and conflicts within the debate about charity and relief.

When we find in the later poems a repetition of one of the earlier poems of displacement, the echo is most often in a diminuendo voice. Here is a rewriting of the imagery of 'Gipsies', appearing now in 'The Labourer's Noon-Day Hymn' of 1834:

Look up to Heaven! the industrious Sun
Already half his race hath run;
He cannot halt nor go astray,
But our immortal Spirits may.

Lord! Since his rising in the East,
If we have faltered or transgressed,
Guide, from thy love's abundant source,
What yet remains of this day's course:

Help with thy grace, through life's short day,
Our upward and our downward way;
And glorify for us the west
Where we shall sink in final rest.

(*PW*, 4: 115)

There is here an unquestioned alliance between the poet and the subjects
of his poem, who no longer interrogate the image of the *labouring* writer,
as did the gypsies or the working figures in the 'Point Rash-Judgment'
poem. The ironies of Wordsworth's posture as speaking *for* the rural
labourers must have been as potentially uncomfortable in 1834 as they
had been in 1800, if not more so; for this was a period of considerable
unrest among country workers. But they are no longer expressed or
worked into the poem. The intersubjective dimension of this poem now
consists in an uncritical and even smug identification by its speaker of
working for hire (and for man) in the fields with working for salvation in
the afterlife: it is an exemplary synthesis of religious doctrine with social
and economic discipline and control. The schizophrenic allusions to paradisal unity and to Satanic displacement that marked the invocation of the
heavenly bodies in 'Gipsies' are quite absent here. The speaker never calls
into question the sufficiency of his own identity. Here, we are all humble
petitioners walking meekly in the sight of God. The 'fulgent west' has lost
both its appeal and its threat; it has been domesticated into a comfortable
theological metaphor.

In 'There is an Eminence' (*LB*, 222), the poem in which Wordsworth
describes the naming of a place after himself, he had imaged a self that was
at once located in the 'loneliest place we have among the clouds' and also
guaranteed a 'communion' with others such that 'no place on earth/ Can
ever be a solitude to me'. His social self walks *along* the 'public way', in
the company of others, *beneath* his attributed self, 'so distant in its height'.
This attributed self seems inaccessible and remote among the cosmic forces
– meteors, stars, and setting sun. But it sends down a 'deep quiet' to 'our
hearts'. The poem is built upon a double vision, projected to the point of
schizophrenia. The source of (poetic) power is not to be integrated into
everyday life or language; it subsists as an imagination and a name atop a
'lonesome Peak'.

After 1814, such double vision becomes much rarer, if it appears at all.
Wordsworth remains a wanderer; the sheer number of poems about journeying and touring alone testifies to that. But the passages are quieter and
more contented:

To muse, to creep, to halt at will, to gaze –
Such sweet way-faring – of life's spring the pride,

Her summer's faithful joy – *that* still is mine,
And in fit measure cheers autumnal days.

(*PW*, 3: 169)

The poet's 'divine vitality' (*PW*, 3: 52) now seems to have made its peace with the facts of mutability and decay. The hectic stride of 'Stepping Westward' and the over-confident treading forth of 'Gipsies', both inversely registering the problems of navigating an *un*authorized path through the world, have now been accommodated to a 'fit measure'. At the end of the 'Duddon' sequence of 1820, Wordsworth speaks of 'each tumultuous working left behind/ At seemly distance' (*PW*, 3: 260). The twilight is no longer a period of anxious self-interrogation, but an appropriate medium for contemplating the 'fallen grandeur' of old Bruges; the plea that darkness hold off awhile is related to little more than the tourist's desire for extra viewing time (*PW*, 3: 165). The planet Venus addressed in the 1838 sonnet (*PW*, 3: 59) is not a testing oxymoron of pagan and Christian, erotic and spiritual, demonic and divine. No longer tempting an improper self-projection, it is now a companionable form in the poet's quiet questioning of the failures of his generation. And the 'slowly-sinking star' of an 1819 sonnet (*PW*, 3: 22–3) now sponsors an acceptance of rather than a challenge to the facts of mortality. In the poem that Wordsworth chose in 1845 to stand at the head of his collected works, the comparison of poet to star is now a reminder to remain 'in thy place, and be content' (*PW*, 1: 1).

And yet ... in the preceding remarks on the later poems, I am uncomfortably aware of the degree to which I am repeating once again the standard position taken by almost all readers and critics: that there is a decline, a falling away in urgency and inspiration. A more truthful and sceptical verdict would be that we are not yet in a position to make such judgements. What I would say is that the terms in which I have tried to make sense of much of the poetry before 1814 do not appear to be so fruitful for the later work. But there may well be other terms, which we have not yet discovered. Much of the later writing seems to articulate a rhetoric of stability, rather than one of displacement. But it does employ its own forms of hyperbole, for example in its distrust of 'monstruous theories of alien growth', and in its Burkean (via Spenser) pronouncement that 'Perilous is sweeping change, all chance unsound' (*PW*, 4: 131, 129). The two poems titled 'September, 1819', composed just a few days after Peterloo (16 August) and at about the same time as Keats' 'To Autumn', are full of references and allusions to the crisis of which they do not directly speak, whether in the notice of the 'turbulence and heat' and 'quivering strife' of spring, or of the imagined better days when poetry alone, without violent action, was enough to make tyrants quake (*PW*,

4:98–9). Wordsworth's wanderings may have lost their anxious identifications with the great displaced figures of the cultural and literary past – Satan, Ulysses, Aeneas, Spenser's knights and Bunyan's pilgrim, all trying to turn crooked paths into straight and narrow ones, or glorying in their choice of error or indirection. He oscillates less painfully between open and closed space, between the wide and free life that promises communal innocence but threatens stability, and the shady groves that provide that stability but taint it with guilt and discomfort, and with the aura of worldliness. As Wordsworth becomes more comfortable with the bourgeois compromise, his stars shine less temptingly and more calmly. But there are hints, at least, that the genesis of settlement needs to be examined closely, rather than taken for granted, lamented, or ignored. As late as 1825, Hazlitt continues to speak of a Wordsworth whose poetry 'partakes of, and is carried along with, the revolutionary movement of our age', but which also bears the marks of a disappointed Luciferic spirit wherein 'native pride and indolence' is combined with a temper soured by the 'sense of injustice and of undeserved ridicule'. His observation of the poet's reading habits makes mention of an eye that continues to beam 'with preternatural lustre' (1930–4, 11:86f.). We have yet to rediscover the energies behind that light fallen, or falling.

Notes

Introduction: writing in history and theory

1 Fredric Jameson (1971) has, for example, made a strong case against 'preestablished categories of analysis' in maintaining that 'an absolute science of style is impossible', style itself being an 'historical phenomenon' (333, 335).
2 See Said (1983), 1–30, 54–89.
3 McGann (1983), 82–5. Cf. his remarks on the 'Intimations' ode, which is said to 'annihilate' its 'history' in order to become a 'record of pure consciousness' (90). The best parts of McGann's account themselves reveal that Wordsworth was not very good at such annihilation.

1 'Gipsies'

1 For an account of the argument and the reception of *The Deserted Village*, see Barrell (1980), 73–82, 87. Goldstein (1977), 95–112, offers a fine reading of the poem.
2 He also, inaccurately, identifies the gypsies as intruding into the Vale of Grasmere. The poem was in fact composed at Coleorton and was based on an encounter near Castle Donnington (*1807*, 419). For a brief discus-

sion of the poem in the context of current critical practices, see Simpson (1984–5).

3   Wordsworth quotes this very passage in a letter to Lady Beaumont of 21 May 1807 (*MY*, 1: 148).

4   See Douglas (1968), 27–39, for an account of Wordsworth's early economic circumstances.

5   For an account, see Simpson (1984), 58–9, 255, 266.

6   See also Parker (1979), 114–58, to which I am much indebted for my remarks on Milton. Hartman (1977) is continually eloquent about the Wordsworth–Milton relation.

7   By 1841, with the poem published as 'Guilt and Sorrow', the communistic pleasures of gypsy life are no longer transcribed, although their crimes remain (*SPP*, 255).

8   For another account of the conjunction of property, poetry and labour in Wordsworth, see Heinzelman (1980), 196–233, who astutely recognizes Wordsworth's preoccupation with poetry as a 'socially productive, economically pertinent labor' (199), and gives an insightful reading of the economics of the poet–reader relation.

9   Thus, by way of further example, Wordsworth's 'dewy ground' recalls the 'cold sudden damp' (*PL*, 11: 293) that comes upon Adam's spirits after Michael's explanation of his fate after the fall. In the final lines of Milton's poem, the avenging cherubim are likened to the 'evening mist' that 'gathers ground fast at the labourer's heel/ Homeward returning' (12: 629–32).

10   The first couple's 'blissful bower' was also constructed in 'thickest covert' (*PL*, 4: 690, 693), which thus both counters and forecasts their fall; and Satan's first access to paradise, like Wordsworth's to easeful composition, is blocked by a thicket:

> the undergrowth
> Of shrubs and tangling bushes had perplexed
> All path of man or beast that passed that way.
> (4: 175–7)

2   Wordsworth's agrarian idealism: the case against urban life

1   Arthur Beatty (1960), 169–92 has argued for an organic relation between the two, fancy giving way to imagination as youth passes into maturity. See also Scoggins (1966) and Ferguson (1977).

2   For a further account, see Simpson (1982a), 132–69; and (1982b), 20–38, and the bibliography there supplied.

3   At the same time, he does not endorse Rousseau's solutions. The idea of education set forth in *Emile*, for example, depends upon the continual supervision of the individual student by a private tutor, and could thus work only for the rich. Rousseau, furthermore, seems to have been ex-

tremely suspicious of the elemental passions whose development Wordsworth regarded as central to the ideal personality.

4 Cf. Shelley, *A Defence of Poetry*:

> To what but a cultivation of the mechanical arts to a degree disproportioned to the presence of the creative faculty, which is the basis of all knowledge, is to be attributed the abuse of all invention for abridging and combining labour, to the exasperation of the inequality of mankind? From what other cause has it arisen that the discoveries which should have lightened, have added a weight to the curse imposed on Adam?
>
> (1977, 503)

5 For details of Wordsworth's involvement in the 1818 election, see Wells (1940) and Douglas (1948), who suggests that Wordsworth's contribution consisted mainly in his willingness to put his name to the 'party line'.

6 See Simpson (1986) for a reading of 'Poor Susan' in this context. The theory of urban degeneration played a large part in the thinking of later nineteenth-century social commentators; see Stedman Jones (1984), 127–51, 281–314, 322–36.

3 Another guide to the lakes

1 Housman (1800) is similarly negative about the conservatism of Lakeland farmers, and about the obstacles to improvement that customary tenure entailed (see 65–6). Cf. also West (1805), 24; Hutchinson (1794), 1: 39.

2 Housman (1800) celebrates the well-being and civic virtue of some of the tenants and/or freeholders in the remoter regions in terms very close to Wordsworth's; see 64, 70, 104–5.

3 In the famous letter to Charles James Fox of 14 January 1801 (*EY*, 312–15) Wordsworth does seem to define the 'statesmen' quite strictly as those living upon 'their own little properties'. But the inhabitants of the 'perfect republic' later described in the *Guide* (*PrW*, 2: 196f.) were clearly customary tenants who lived *as if* they were freeholders. This 'republic' thus existed in appearance but not in fact, being determined by the condescension or indolence of the landowners.

4 J.D. Marshall (1972) has argued that the term 'statesman' was itself a picturesque innovation, not often found in parish records or local geographies, but belonging to 'middle-class myth and image creation' (272). G.P. Jones (1962) had sanctioned a somewhat looser usage.

5 On the pastoral element in Wordsworth, see Parrish (1973), 147–87.

6 See, for example, the Hammonds (1978a), 1–65; Chambers and Mingay (1982), 77–104.

7 The preface to West's *Antiquities* had also celebrated a harmonious relationship between masters and men:

> The line of right is drawn between the supreme lord and his free-homager and customary tenant. No oppression can be introduced by the one; nor default, under so light obligation, be made by the other.
> (1805, vii)

The same paean to 'British Liberty' appears in the first (London) edition of 1774.

8   See Johnston (1983); McGann (1983); and Levinson (forthcoming 1986/7). For related accounts of Wordsworth's fear of a modified landscape, see Goldstein (1977), 163–83; and Friedman (1979), 205–41.

9   See Beatty (1960), 169–222; also Scoggins (1966), Owen (1969), 157–87; and Ferguson (1977), 53–83.

10 See Barstow (1917), Owen (1969) and Heffernan (1969). However, Olivia Smith's (1984) fine recent account of the language theory of the 1800 preface is very much in the spirit of my own, which it anticipates at many points. Demonstrating the analogies between Wordsworth and Tooke, Smith shows that the preface *was* a radical text, and she understands Coleridge's disavowals in terms that are convincingly political. For an account of a possible philosophical background for Wordsworth's sociological idea of language, see Aarsleff (1982).

4   'In single or in social eminence'? The political economy of *The Prelude* and *Home at Grasmere*

1   I am drawing in the following paragraph upon the work of Johnston (1983), McGann (1983, 81–92), and Levinson (forthcoming 1986/7).

2   Lindenberger (1963), 53–7 reads the speaker's moments of inarticulacy as evidence of authenticity. Hartman (1977), 27–30 is more aware of the poem's ambiguities. But it is Onorato (1971), 29–87 who most fully prefigures the reading I have here proposed. Although he defines the poem's instabilities in psychoanalytic rather than social terms, Onorato perceives all the formal disjunctions that I have described. There is of course nothing mutually exclusive about social and psychological explanations. Quite the opposite. It seems convincing to assume that each reinforces and redetermines the other. Thus, Wordsworth's anxieties about poetry, property and labour are anxieties about the public symbolization of personality that could only have been more anxious thanks to the absence, for much of his life, of father and mother, also principles of a public (albeit intimately public) validation of selfhood. See also Douglas (1968).

3   The most influential example of the 'affirmative' reading of the poem is in Abrams (1971), 73–140. Sensing the effacement of the divine authority, Abrams relocates coherence in the Wordsworthian subject or selfhood, finding there a 'self-coherence, self-awareness, and assured power that is its own reward' (96). For Abrams, the imagination thus becomes 'redemptive' (117). This affirmative reading is given further historical specifica-

tion by McConnell (1974), who explains the poem's disjunctions within the conventions of confessional literature.

There are some precedents for a 'social' interpretation of the poem. Lindenberger (1963), 3–39, 99–129, notes the tension between private and public modes, both for the poet and for his audience. But he finally dismisses the 'social' books as aesthetic failures forecasting the 'heroic and triumphant' emergence of a new 'private sensibility' (269). He thus fails to explore the determining tensions that are written into *The Prelude*. David Aers (1981), 64–81, also finds, much more reductively, that Wordsworth gives no hints that 'the cult of desocialized but creative individualism might have social foundations' (75), and concludes that the poem 'easily transcends all social and historical pressures'. Chandler (1984), 184–234, has made a good case for the 'spots of time' as a traditionary (and Burkean) alternative to the historical–political modes of personality formation discussed by the French philosophers. He gives close and convincing evidence for Wordsworth's attempt to replace public by private history; but he misses the disciplinary and anxious nature of the rhetoric of these passages, which might indeed speak for a guilty recognition of exactly such an attempt at displacement. Chandler's point could yet stand, if we explain the rhetoric of discipline as that applied by a mature poet to his earlier public–philosophical infatuations. See also Simpson (1982a), 49–60, 122–69; Goldstein (1977), 163–83; and the fine reading of the 'crossing the Alps' passage by Alan Liu (1984), which offers convincing evidence of the degree to which Wordsworth's attributions of private experience are underpinned by political–historical allusions.

4   In his decision to read *The Prelude* in the vocabulary of *The Recluse*, Johnston (1984) senses the degree to which it is a social as well as a private poem. His awareness of the importance of the imagery of 'residences' does bring out the way in which Wordsworth strives for a sense of place while experiencing a reciprocally continual displacement.

5   See also McConnell (1974), 59–69, on *The Prelude* as Wordsworthian *Paradise Regained*.

6   See Simpson (1982a); and *Prelude*, 2: 415f.; 8: 598f.; 12: 1–14; 12: 285–98. The argument of 12: 145–278 is especially important as an explanation of the principles behind the 1800 preface.

7   On the 'tyrant eye', see McConnell (1974), 99–145.

8   Here I differ from Chandler (1984), 31–61, who offers Burke as the ideological begetter of *The Prelude*'s account of events in France. Burke never supported any version of republicanism in France or Spain. Wordsworth supported both, though not in any extreme Jacobinical incarnations.

9   For a more detailed account, see Simpson (1982a), 164–6.

10   It has certainly been exemplary for Wordsworth's critics, who have often found in it the conclusive achievement of a renewed selfhood. McConnell (1974), 148–90, finds in the event a 'new, Edenic language which acts out as well as asserts the power and blessedness he has learned through

memory' (183). See also Lindenberger (1963), 51–3. Hartman (1977), 60–9, finds the account conclusively inconclusive, a definitive *attempt* at the marriage of mind and nature.

11   Almost all readers have assumed that Wordsworth is able to reconstitute the features of this 'mighty mind' within his own; but this is just what the argument denies. Jonathan Wordsworth (1970), 467–74 has his doubts, but yet finds the poetry 'triumphantly positive' (474)! Onorato (1971), 287–94, again, closely anticipates my own account here.

12   Again, compare Satan, 'In this enclosure' (*PL*, 9: 543).

13   The function of this event as an admonition is played up in the 1850 text, which has the poet returning from a day spent in 'strenuous idleness' (4: 377).

5   'By conflicting passions pressed': 'Michael' and 'Simon Lee'

1   See Simpson (1986) for the relation between the city and moral decay (and hence perhaps shame) in 'Poor Susan'.

2   See also Fink (1958), 88–9, 134–5.

3   On the biblical allusions in the poem, see also Helms (1977–8); for a reading of the role of labour and proprietorship, see Heinzelman (1980), 215–33; and Sales (1983), 52–69.

4   See Woof (1970–1); J. Wordsworth (1971); Reed (1972).

5   See Sheats (1973), 188–93; Averill (1980), 162–6; Griffin (1977); and Danby (1960), 38–47. For a more general study of 'reader activation', see Simpson (1979).

6   In this context it is notable that the root that Simon is trying to sever is not attached to a flourishing (Burkean) tree but to a 'stump of rotten wood' (*LB*, 63). What is being swept away is thus a hollow or decaying growth; nor is the improver in any state of physical vigour. A more ingenious reader than myself might be able to find in this poem a place for the severed head of Louis XVI, and surely for a phallic motif in the incident itself, and in the identification of 'root' and 'stump'.

7   See Gilboy (1934), 80–2. Agricultural labour was notoriously irregular, so that most workers would not have had the chance to work for a full fifty weeks of the year.

8   Added evidence of Wordsworth's discomfort with the Alfoxden experience appears in 'Anecdote for Fathers', written during the same period. Pressured to choose between life at Kilve (perhaps Racedown) and Liswyn Farm (perhaps Alfoxden, and an apparent identification with Thelwall's new home in Brecknockshire), the boy bursts out 'At Kilve there was no weather-cock' (*LB*, 66). The 'broad and gilded vane' that catches the boy's eye may well be an image of the uneasy splendour of Alfoxden House, an awkward contradiction of the republican plainness wishfully intimated in the poet's calling his present residence (in the poem) after

Thelwall's. Wordsworth was not living on a farm, within a working economy, but renting a manor house.

9   In 'The Childless Father' (*LB*, 204) Wordsworth describes a man going out with the hunt in a gesture of rehabilitation after the death of his daughter. Bouch and Jones (1961), 231, suggest that such participation was often required by the squire of his tenants, as a boon service, at least in the Lake District. Wordsworth avoids specifying the degree of obligation, and thus may or may not be suggesting that the burdens of customary tenancy have a silver lining.

10 And to which may be added the sense of 'serve Ivor' in 'He is the sole survivor' (*LB*, 61). Praise or blame for this one goes to Fred See, to whom my gratitude.

6   Poets, paupers and peripatetics: the politics of sympathy

1   For an account of the second of these, see Simpson (1979), 72–6.

2   See, for example, Gill (1969) and Averill (1980), 127–30. On the theme of charity in contemporary thought, see Rodgers (1949). Friedman (1979), 163–203, discusses Wordsworth's attitudes to charity.

3   See Simpson (1979), 36–8, and other accounts there cited.

4   Bialostosky (1984), 125–9, argues for a high degree of conscious control on Wordsworth's part in this poem. Cf. Glen (1983), 225–30.

5   For a summary of Pitt's bill, see Poynter (1969), 62–76.

6   Langhorne (1774–7), 1: 17–19, offers good evidence of the antithetical sense of primal ideologies by suggesting that, of all people, vagrants were the most likely to be pressed into military service.

7   Similarly, in 'The Sailor's Mother' (*1807*, 77), the woman is as 'majestic' as a 'Roman matron'.

8   See *The Prelude*, 10: 835f., where the image of the butterfly is invoked to suggest the 'vanity' of the poet's philosophically-based optimism; and also its place in the deceiving rhetoric of Thomson's Knight of Indolence (1748, 5).

9   Bialostosky (1984), 139, seems to me to go too far in claiming that the speaker has no authority for his final claim because he has not seen Alice in her pride, having 'gone on with his journey or his business'. This was true for Robert Graham, who, according to Dorothy (1952, 1: 115), went his way having 'left money with some respectable people in the town'. But this is not the logic of the poem that Wordsworth made out of the incident, where the two have reached 'our journey's end' (line 49). There is nothing to negate the speaker's having seen Alice 'the next day'.

10 Simpson (1979) partakes not a little of the first extreme, though I did not mean to suggest there that conscious control outweighs historical compulsion. For a very good account of the element of 'artifice' in Wordsworth's poetry, see Parrish (1973), 1–33, 115–48 etc.

7   Structuring a subject: *The Excursion*

1   See also the special issue of *The Wordsworth Circle*, 9 (1978), devoted to *The Excursion*; Galperin (1980); and Johnston (1984), 237–329.

2   See Galperin (1980) for an account of the place of 'individuation' in the poem, in relation to the projected reader's struggle for a coherent perspective.

3   The 'Baker's Cart' fragment, never published by Wordsworth, further explores the way in which poverty and grief conspire to determine character in such a way that misery can 'become an instinct' (*RC*, 468).

4   See Lyon (1950), 113–19. Batho (1933), 234–311, argues that Wordsworth was always a moderate Anglican with latitudinarian impulses.

5   Ferguson's (1977, 223f.) reading of the first meeting of the Wanderer with the Solitary is a model of the detailed attention that much of *The Excursion* calls for. See also Alan Hill's (1974) argument for *Octavius* as a possible model for Wordsworth's use of the dialogue form; Annabel Patterson's (1978) essay on *The Excursion*'s allusions to classical retreat poems; and Stuart Peterfreund's brief (1978) account of the Miltonic element.

6   See Simpson (1982a), xii–xv, 20–1, 86–7. Burn (1800), 1:258–60, includes a discussion of the laws governing the murder of illegitimate children. Whenever a woman tries to conceal the death of such a child, 'there is no need of any proof that the child was born alive ... but it shall be undeniably taken that the child was born alive, and murdered by the mother'. But he also notes that this has been felt to be a rather harsh procedure 'of late years', so that 'some presumptive evidence' has tended to be required. See also Anon. (1777), 307.

Bibliography

Aarsleff, Hans (1982) 'Wordsworth, language, and Romanticism'. In *From Locke to Saussure: Essays on the Study of Language and Intellectual History*. Minneapolis. 372–81.

Abrams, M.H. (1971) *Natural Supernaturalism: Tradition and Revolution in Romantic Literature*. New York.

Aers, David, Cook, Jonathan and Punter, David (eds) (1981) *Romanticism and Ideology: Studies in English Writing, 1765–1830*. London, Boston and Henley.

Anon. (1777) *The Laws Respecting Women, as they regard their Natural Rights, or their Connections and Conduct*. London.

The Anti-Jacobin Review and Magazine; or, Monthly Political and Literary Censor (1799–1821) 22 vols. London.

Arnold, Matthew (1935) 'Wordsworth'. In *Essays in Criticism: Second Series*. Reprint of 1888 edition. London. 87–115.

Averill, James H. (1980) *Wordsworth and the Poetry of Human Suffering*. Ithaca and London.

Bailey, John and Culley, George (1794) *General View of the Agriculture of the County of Cumberland*. London.

    (1797) Second edition. Newcastle.

Barrell, John (1973) *The Idea of Landscape and the Sense of Place: An Approach to the Poetry of John Clare*. Cambridge.

    (1980) *The Dark Side of the Landscape: The Rural Poor in English Painting, 1730–1840*. Cambridge.

(1983) *English Literature in History, 1730–80: An Equal, Wide Survey.* London.

Barstow, Marjorie L. (1917) *Wordsworth's Theory of Poetic Diction. A Study of the Historical and Personal Background of the Lyrical Ballads.* New Haven and London.

Batho, Edith C. (1933) *The Later Wordsworth.* New York and Cambridge.

Beatty, Arthur (1960) *William Wordsworth: His Doctrine and Art in their Historical Relations.* Second edition. Reprint of 1927 edition. Madison, Wis.

Bell, Andrew (1807) *An Analysis of the Experiment in Education, made at Egmore, near Madras.* Third edition. London.

(1819) *The Wrongs of Children; or, a Practical Vindication of Children from the Injustice done them in Early Nurture and Education.* London.

Bentham, Jeremy (1812) 'Outline of a work entitled "Pauper management improved"' (1797). In *Pauper Management Improved: Particularly by means of the Panopticon Principle of Construction. Anno 1797. First Published in Young's Annals of Agriculture. Now first published separately.* London.

(1952) *Jeremy Bentham's Economic Writings.* Ed. W. Stark. 3 vols. London.

Bialostosky, Don H. (1984) *Making Tales: The Poetics of Wordsworth's Narrative Experiments.* Chicago and London.

Blackstone, William (1979) *Commentaries on the Laws of England.* A facsimile of the first edition, 1765–9. 4 vols. Chicago and London.

Blake, William (1982) *The Complete Poetry and Prose of William Blake.* Ed. David V. Erdman. Commentary by Harold Bloom. Revised edition. Berkeley and Los Angeles.

Bouch, C.M.L. and Jones, G.P. (1961) *A Short Economic and Social History of the Lake Counties, 1500–1830.* Manchester.

Brantley, Richard E. (1975) *Wordsworth's 'Natural Methodism'.* New Haven and London.

Brinton, Crane (1926) *The Political Ideas of the English Romanticists.* Oxford.

Brooks, Cleanth (1965) 'Wordsworth and human suffering: notes on two early poems'. In Harold Bloom and Frederick W. Hilles (eds) *From Sensibility to Romanticism: Essays Presented to Frederick A. Pottle.* New York. 373–87.

Brougham, Henry (1825) *Practical Observations upon the Education of the People, addressed to the Working Classes and their Employers.* London.

Burke, Edmund (1906) *The Works of the Rt. Hon. Edmund Burke.* 6 vols. London, New York and Toronto.

(1976) *Reflections on the Revolution in France.* Ed. Conor Cruise O'Brien. Reprint of 1968 edition. Harmondsworth, Middlesex.

Burn, Richard, Ll.D. (1800) *The Justice of the Peace, and Parish Officer. Continued to the Present Time by John Burn, Esq., his Son.* Nineteenth edition. Corrected and enlarged. 4 vols. London.

Burton, Mary E. (1942) *The One Wordsworth.* Chapel Hill.

Bushnell, John P. (1981) '"Where is the lamb for a burnt offering?": Michael's covenant and sacrifice'. In *The Wordsworth Circle*, 12, 246–52.

Butler, Marilyn (1982) *Romantics, Rebels, and Reactionaries: English Literature and its Background, 1760–1830*. New York and Oxford.

(ed.) (1984) *Burke, Paine, Godwin, and the Revolution Controversy*. Cambridge.

Carr, Raymond (1976) *English Fox Hunting. A History*. London.

Chambers, J.D. and Mingay, G.E. (1982) *The Agricultural Revolution, 1750–1880*. Reprint of 1966 edition. London.

Chandler, James K. (1984) *Wordsworth's Second Nature: A Study of the Poetry and Politics*. Chicago and London.

Christiansen, Jerome (1981) *Coleridge's Blessed Machine of Language*. Ithaca and London.

Clare, John (1963) *Selected Poems of John Clare*. Ed. Geoffrey Grigson. Reprint of 1950 edition. London.

(1979) *The Midsummer Cushion*. Ed. Anne Tibble and R.K.R. Thornton. Manchester and Ashington, Northumberland.

(1984) *The Oxford Authors: John Clare*. Ed. Eric Robinson and David Powell. Oxford and New York.

Cobbett, William (1906) *Cobbett's English Grammar*. Introduction by H.L. Stephen. London.

(1979) *Cottage Economy*. Preface by G.K. Chesterton. Oxford.

Coleridge, Samuel Taylor (1930) *Coleridge's Shakespearean Criticism*. Ed. T.M. Raysor. 2 vols. Cambridge, Mass.

(1957) *The Notebooks of Samuel Taylor Coleridge*. Vol. 1, 1794–1804. Ed. Kathleen Coburn. Princeton.

(1969) *The Friend*. Ed. Barbara E. Rooke. 2 vols. Princeton and London.

(1980) *Coleridge: Poetical Works*. Ed. Ernest Hartley Coleridge. Reprint of 1912 edition. Oxford and New York.

(1983) *Biographia Literaria*. Ed. W.J. Bate and James Engell. 2 vols. Princeton and London.

Colquhoun, Patrick (1806) *A Treatise on Indigence; exhibiting a General View of the National Resources for Productive Labour; with Propositions for Ameliorating the Condition of the Poor*. London.

Cooper, Lane (ed.) (1965) *A Concordance to the Poems of William Wordsworth*. New York.

Cowper, William (1787) *Poems*. Third edition. 2 vols. London.

Danby, John F. (1960) *The Simple Wordsworth: Studies in the poems 1797–1807*. London.

Dicey, A.V. (1917) *The Statesmanship of Wordsworth. An Essay*. Oxford.

Dickson, P.G.M. (1967) *The Financial Revolution in England: A Study in the Development of Public Credit, 1688–1756*. London.

Douglas, Wallace W. (1946) 'Wordsworth's political thought: a study in nineteenth-century conservatism'. Ph.D. diss. Harvard University.

(1948) 'Wordsworth in politics: the Westmoreland election of 1818'. In *Modern Language Notes*, 43, 437–49.

(1968) *Wordsworth: The Construction of a Personality*. Kent State University.

Dyer, George (1793) *The Complaints of the Poor People of England*. Second edition. London.

Eden, Sir Frederick Morton (1797) *The State of the Poor; or, an History of the Labouring Classes in England, from the Conquest to the Present Period*. 3 vols. London.

Erdman, David V. (1977) *Blake: Prophet Against Empire. A Poet's Interpretation of the History of his own Times*. Third edition. Princeton.

Evans, Evan (1764) *Some Specimens of the Poetry of the Antient Welsh Bards*. Translated into English. London.

Ferguson, Frances (1977) *Wordsworth: Language as Counter-Spirit*. New Haven and London.

Ferry, David (1959) *The Limits of Mortality: An Essay on Wordsworth's Major Poems*. Middletown, Conn.

Field, Barron (1975) *Barron Field's 'Memoirs of Wordsworth'*. Ed. Geoffrey Little. Australian Academy of the Humanities, monograph 3. Sydney.

Fink, Z.S. (1948) 'Wordsworth and the English republican tradition'. In *Journal of English and Germanic Philology*, 47, 107–26.

(ed.) (1958) *The Early Wordsworthian Milieu. A Notebook of Christopher Wordsworth with a few entries by William Wordsworth*. Oxford.

Fisher, Peter F. (1959) 'Blake and the Druids'. In *Journal of English and Germanic Philology*, 58, 589–612.

Floud, Roderick and McCloskey, Donald (eds) (1981) *The Economic History of Britain since 1700. Volume 1: 1700–1860*. Cambridge.

Friedman, Michael H. (1979) *The Making of a Tory Humanist. William Wordsworth and the Idea of Community*. New York.

Galperin, William (1980) '"Imperfect while unshared": the role of the implied reader in Wordsworth's *Excursion*'. In *Criticism*, 22, 193–213.

Garber, Frederick (1971) *Wordsworth and the Poetry of Encounter*. Urbana, Chicago and London.

Gilboy, Elizabeth W. (1934) *Wages in Eighteenth-Century England*. Cambridge, Mass.

Gill, Stephen C. (1969) 'Wordsworth's breeches pocket: attitudes to the didactic poet'. In *Essays in Criticism*, 19, 385–401.

(1972) '"Adventures on Salisbury Plain" and Wordsworth's poetry of protest, 1795–97'. In *Studies in Romanticism*, 11, 48–65.

Glen, Heather (1983) *Vision and Disenchantment: Blake's 'Songs' and Wordsworth's 'Lyrical Ballads'*. Cambridge.

Godwin, William (1797) *The Enquirer. Reflections on Education, Manners, and Literature. In a Series of Essays*. London.

(1976) *Enquiry Concerning Political Justice, and its Influence on Modern Morals and Happiness*. Ed. Isaac Kramnick. Harmondsworth, Middlesex.

Goldsmith, Oliver (1966) *Collected Works of Oliver Goldsmith*. Ed. Arthur Friedman. 5 vols. Oxford.

Goldstein, Laurence (1977) *Ruins and Empire. The Evolution of a Theme in Augustan and Romantic Literature*. Pittsburgh.

Griffin, Andrew L. (1977) 'Wordsworth and the problem of imaginative story: the case of "Simon Lee"'. In *Publications of the Modern Language Association* 19, 392–409.

Hamilton, Paul (1983) *Coleridge's Poetics*. Stanford.

Hammond, J.L. and Barbara (1978a) *The Village Labourer*. New edition, ed. G.E. Mingay. London and New York.

(1978b) *The Town Labourer*. New edition, ed. John Lovell. London and New York.

(1979) *The Skilled Labourer*. New edition, ed. John Rule. London and New York.

Hartman, Geoffrey H. (1972) 'Reflections on the evening star: Akenside to Coleridge'. In Hartman (ed.) *New Perspectives on Coleridge and Wordsworth: Selected Papers from the English Institute*. New York and London. 85–131.

(1977) *Wordsworth's Poetry, 1787–1814*. Reprint of 1964 edition. New Haven and London.

Hazlitt, William (1930–4) *The Complete Works of William Hazlitt*. Ed. P.P. Howe. 21 vols. London and Toronto.

Heffernan, James A.W. (1969) *Wordsworth's Theory of Poetry: The Transforming Imagination*. Ithaca and London.

Heinzelman, Kurt (1980) *The Economics of the Imagination*. Amherst, Mass.

Helms, Randel (1977–8) 'On the genesis of Wordsworth's "Michael"'. *English Language Notes*, 15, 38–43.

Hill, Alan G. (1974) 'New light on *The Excursion*'. In *Ariel*, 5, no. 2 (April, 1974), 37–47.

Himmelfarb, Gertrude (1984) *The Idea of Poverty: England in the Early Industrial Age*. London and Boston.

Hobsbawm, E.J. and Rudé, George (1973) *Captain Swing*. Reprint of 1969 edition. Harmondsworth, Middlesex.

Housman, John (1800) *A Topographical Description of Cumberland, Westmoreland, Lancashire, and a Part of the West Riding of Yorkshire*. Carlisle.

Hutchinson, William (1774) *An Excursion to the Lakes in Westmoreland and Cumberland, August 1773*. London.

(1794) *The History of the County of Cumberland, and some places adjacent*. 2 vols. Carlisle.

Itzkowitz, David C. (1977) *Peculiar Privilege. A Social History of English Foxhunting, 1753–1885*. Hassocks, Sussex.

Jacobus, Mary (1976) *Tradition and Experiment in Wordsworth's 'Lyrical Ballads' (1798)*. Oxford.

Jameson, Fredric (1971) *Marxism and Form: Twentieth-Century Dialectical Theories of Literature*. Princeton.

Johnston, Kenneth R. (1983) 'The politics of "Tintern Abbey"'. In *The Wordsworth Circle*, 14, 6–14.

(1984) *Wordsworth and 'The Recluse'*. New Haven and London.

Jones, G.P. (1962) 'The decline of the yeomanry in the Lake Counties'. In *Transactions of the Cumberland and Westmoreland Antiquarian and Archaeological Society*, vol. LXII, n.s., 198–223.

Jordan, John E. (1976) *Why the 'Lyrical Ballads'? The Background, Writing and Character of Wordsworth's 1798 'Lyrical Ballads'*. Berkeley, Los Angeles and London.

Keats, John (1958) *The Letters of John Keats*. Ed. H.E. Rollins. 2 vols. Cambridge, Mass.

Kiernan, V.G. (1975) 'Wordsworth and the people'. In David Craig (ed.), *Marxists on Literature: An Anthology*. Harmondsworth, Middlesex. 161–206.

Kramnick, Isaac (1968) *Bolingbroke and his Circle: The Politics of Nostalgia in the Age of Walpole*. Cambridge, Mass.

Land, Stephen K. (1973) 'The silent poet: an aspect of Wordsworth's semantic theory'. In *University of Toronto Quarterly*, 52, 157–69.

[Langhorne, John] (1774–7) *The Country-Justice. A Poem. By one of His Majesty's Justices of the Peace for the County of Somerset*. 3 parts. London.

Lea, Sydney (1978) 'Wordsworth and his "Michael": the pastor passes'. *English Literary History*, 45, 55–68.

Levinson, Marjorie (forthcoming 1986/7) *Wordsworth's Great Period Poems: Four Essays*. Cambridge.

Lindenberger, Herbert (1963) *On Wordsworth's 'Prelude'*. Princeton.

Liu, Alan (1984) 'Wordsworth: the history in "Imagination"'. In *English Literary History*, 51, 505–48.

Locke, John (1979) *An Essay Concerning Human Understanding*. Ed. Peter H. Nidditch. Revision of 1975 edition. Oxford.

Low, Donald A. (ed.) (1974) *Robert Burns: The Critical Heritage*. London and Boston.

Lyon, Judson Stanley (1950) *The Excursion: A Study*. New Haven and London.

McConnell, Frank D. (1974) *The Confessional Imagination: A Reading of Wordsworth's 'Prelude'*. Baltimore and London.

McGann, Jerome (1983) *The Romantic Ideology: A Critical Investigation*. Chicago and London.

Macherey, Pierre (1978) *A Theory of Literary Production*. Trans. Geoffrey Wall. London, Boston and Henley.

McKendrick, Neil, Brewer, John and Plumb, J.H. (1983) *The Birth of a Consumer Society: The Commercialization of Eighteenth-Century England*. London.

Mackenzie, Henry (1958) *The Man of Feeling*. Ed. Kenneth C. Slagle. New York.

MacLean, Kenneth (1950) *Agrarian Age: A Background for Wordsworth*. New Haven and London.

Malthus, Thomas (1970). *An Essay on the Principle of Population* (1798). Ed. Anthony Flew. Harmondsworth, Middlesex.

Manning, Peter J. (1977) 'Michael, Luke and Wordsworth'. In *Criticism*, 19, 195–211.

Marshall, Dorothy (1982) *Industrial England: 1776–1851*. Second edition. London, Melbourne and Henley.

Marshall, J.D. (1961) 'The Lancashire rural labourer in the early nineteenth century'. In *Transactions of the Lancashire and Cheshire Antiquarian Society*, 71, 90–128.

(1972) '"Statesmen" in Cumbria: the vicissitudes of an expression'. In *Transactions of the Cumberland and Westmoreland Antiquarian and Archaeological Society*, vol. LXXII, n.s., 248–73.

(1973) 'The domestic economy of the Lakeland yeoman, 1660–1749'. In *Transactions of the Cumberland and Westmoreland Antiquarian and Archaeological Society*, vol. LXXIII, n.s., 190–219.

Marshall, William (1818) *The Review and Abstracts of the County Reports to the Board of Agriculture; from the Several Agricultural Departments of England*. 5 vols. York.

Mayo, Robert (1954) 'The contemporaneity of the *Lyrical Ballads*'. In *Publications of the Modern Language Association*, 69, 486–522.

Mill, John Stuart (1969) *Autobiography*. Ed. Jack Stillinger. Boston.

Milton, John (1971) *Paradise Lost*. Ed. Alastair Fowler. London.

(1971) *Complete Shorter Poems*. Ed. John Carey. London.

Moorman, Mary (1968) *William Wordsworth, A Biography. The Later Years, 1803–50*. Reprint of 1965 edition. London, Oxford and New York.

(1969) *William Wordsworth, A Biography. The Early Years, 1770–1803*. Corrected edition. Oxford.

Morgan, Prys (1975) *Iolo Morganwg*. University of Wales.

(1984) 'From death to a view: the hunt for the Welsh past in the romantic period'. In Eric Hobsbawm and Terence Ranger (eds) *The Invention of Tradition*. Cambridge. 43–100.

Munsche, P.B. (1981) *Gentlemen and Poachers. The English Game Laws, 1671–1831*. Cambridge.

[Ogilvie, William] [1781] *An Essay on the Right of Property in Land, with Respect to its Foundation in the Law of Nature; its Present Establishment by the Municipal Laws of Europe; and the Regulations by which it Might be Rendered more beneficial to the Lower Ranks of Mankind*. London, n.d.

Onorato, Richard J. (1971) *The Character of the Poet: Wordsworth in 'The Prelude'*. Princeton.

Owen, W.J.B. (1969) *Wordsworth as Critic*. Toronto.

Ozouf, Mona (1976) *La Fête révolutionnaire, 1789–1799*. Paris.

Paine, Thomas (1976) *Rights of Man*. Ed. Henry Collins. Reprint of 1969 edition. Harmondsworth, Middlesex.

Parker, Patricia (1979) *Inescapable Romance. Studies in the Poetics of a Mode*. Princeton.

Parker, Reeve (1972) '"Finer distance": the narrative art of Wordsworth's "The Wanderer"'. In *English Literary History*, 39, 87–111.

Parrish, Stephen (1970) '"Michael" and the pastoral ballad'. In Jonathan Wordsworth (ed.) *Bicentenary Wordsworth Studies in Memory of John Alban Finch*. Ithaca and London. 50–75.

    (1973) *The Art of the 'Lyrical Ballads'*. Cambridge, Mass.

Patterson, Annabel (1978) 'Wordsworth's georgic: genre and structure in *The Excursion*'. In *The Wordsworth Circle*, 9, 145–54.

Peterfreund, Stuart (1978) '"In free homage and generous subjection": Miltonic influence on *The Excursion*'. In *The Wordsworth Circle*, 9, 173–7.

Pocock, J.G.A. (1975) *The Machiavellian Moment: Florentine Political Thought and the Atlantic Republican Tradition*. Princeton.

    (1985) *Virtue, Commerce, and History. Essays on Political Thought and History, Chiefly in the Eighteenth Century*. Cambridge.

Poynter, J.R. (1969) *Society and Pauperism: English Ideas on Poor Relief, 1795–1834*. London and Toronto.

Pringle, Andrew (1794) *General View of the Agriculture of the County of Westmoreland*. Edinburgh.

    (1797) Second edition. Newcastle.

Rawnsley, H.D. (1889) 'Reminiscences of Wordsworth amongst the peasantry of Westmoreland'. In William Knight (ed.) *Wordsworthiana. A Selection from Papers read to the Wordsworth Society*. London and New York. 79–119.

Reed, Mark (1967) *Wordsworth: The Chronology of the Early Years, 1770–1799*. Cambridge, Mass.

    (1972) 'On the development of Wordsworth's "Michael"'. In *Ariel*, vol. 3, no. 2 (April), 70–9.

    (1975) *Wordsworth: The Chronology of the Middle Years, 1800–1815*. Cambridge, Mass.

Reiman, Donald H. (ed.) (1972) *The Romantics Reviewed: Contemporary Reviews of British Romantic Writers*. 5 vols. New York and London.

Rodgers, Betsy (1949) *Cloak of Charity. Studies in Eighteenth-Century Philanthropy*. London.

Rose, Michael E. (1971) *The English Poor Law, 1780–1930*. Newton Abbot.

Rousseau, Jean Jacques (1767) *The Miscellaneous Works of Mr J.J. Rousseau*. 5 vols. London.

Ruggles, Thomas (1797) *The History of the Poor; Their Rights, Duties, and the Laws Respecting Them. In a Series of Letters. A New Edition, corrected and continued to the Present Time*. London.

Said, Edward W. (1983) *The World, the Text, and the Critic*. Cambridge, Mass.

Sales, Roger (1983) *English Literature in History, 1780–1830: Pastoral and Politics*. New York.

Scoggins, James (1966) *Imagination and Fancy: Complementary Modes in the Poetry of Wordsworth*. Lincoln, Neb.

Sekora, John (1977) *Luxury: The Concept in Western Thought, Eden to Smollett*. Baltimore and London.

Sheats, Paul D. (1973) *The Making of Wordsworth's Poetry, 1785–1798*. Cambridge, Mass.

Shelley, Percy Bysshe (1977) *Shelley's Poetry and Prose.* Ed. Donald H. Reiman and Sharon B. Powers. New York and London.

Simpson, David (1979) *Irony and Authority in Romantic Poetry.* London and Totowa, N.J.

    (1982a) *Wordsworth and the Figurings of the Real.* London and Atlantic Highlands, N.J.

    (1982b) *Fetishism and Imagination: Dickens, Melville, Conrad.* Baltimore and London.

    (ed.) (1984) *German Aesthetic and Literary Criticism: Kant, Fichte, Schelling, Schopenhauer, Hegel.* Cambridge.

    (1984–5) 'Criticism, politics and style in Wordsworth's poetry'. In *Critical Inquiry*, 11, 52–81.

    (1986) 'Making minor poems major: what bothered Charles Lamb about Poor Susan?' In *Studies in English Literature*, 24, 589–612.

Smith, Adam (1976) *An Inquiry into the Nature and Causes of the Wealth of Nations.* Ed. R.H. Campbell, A.S. Skinner, W.B. Todd. 2 vols. Oxford.

Smith, Olivia (1984) *The Politics of Language, 1791–1819.* Oxford.

Smollett, Tobias (1983) *Humphry Clinker.* Ed. James L. Thorson. New York and London.

Solkin, David H. (1982) *Richard Wilson: The Landscape of Reaction.* London.

Spence, Thomas (1793) *The Rights of Man, as exhibited in a Lecture, read at the Philosophical Society, in Newcastle (1775).* Fourth edition. London.

    (1797) *The Rights of Infants and Strictures on Paine's Agrarian Justice.* London.

Spenser, Edmund (1980) *The Faerie Queene.* Ed. A.C. Hamilton. Corrected edition. London and New York.

Stedman Jones, Gareth (1984) *Outcast London: A Study in the Relationship Between Classes in Victorian Society.* Reprint of 1971 edition. New York.

Sterne, Laurence (1967) *A Sentimental Journey Through France and Italy.* Ed. Graham Petrie and A. Alvarez. Harmondsworth, Middlesex.

Stone, Lawrence (1982) 'Madness'. In *The New York Review*, vol. XXIX, no. 20 (16 December), 28–36.

Tennyson, Alfred Lord (1969) *The Poems of Tennyson.* Ed. Christopher Ricks. London.

Thelwall, John (1793) *The Peripatetic; or, Sketches of the Heart, of Nature and Society; in a Series of Politico-Sentimental Journals, in Verse and Prose, of the eccentric Excursions of Sylvanus Theophrastus, supposed to be written by himself.* 3 vols. London.

Thomas, Gordon Kent (1971) *Wordsworth's Dirge and Promise: Napoleon, Wellington, and the Convention of Cintra.* Lincoln, Neb.

Thompson, E.P. (1969) 'Disenchantment or default? A lay sermon'. In Conor Cruise O'Brien and William Dean Vanech (eds), *Power and Consciousness.* London and New York. 149–81.

    (1976) *The Making of the English Working Class.* Reprint of 1963 edition. Harmondsworth, Middlesex.

Thomson, James (1748) *The Castle of Indolence. An Allegorical Poem Written in Imitation of Spenser.* Second edition. London.

Todd, F.M. (1957) *Politics and the Poet. A Study of Wordsworth.* London.

[Townsend, Joseph] (1786) *A Dissertation on the Poor Laws. By a Well-Wisher to Mankind.* London.

Trilling, Lionel (1965) 'The fate of pleasure'. In *Beyond Culture: Essays on Literature and Learning.* Reprint of 1955 edition. New York. 57–87.

Trotsky, Leon (1960) *Literature and Revolution.* Trans. Rose Strunsky. Ann Arbor.

Warton, Thomas (1762) *Observations on the Faerie Queene of Spenser.* Second edition. 2 vols. London.

Webb, R.K. (1955) *The British Working-Class Reader, 1790–1848: Literacy and Social Tension.* London.

Wells, John Edwin (1940) 'Wordsworth and de Quincey in Westmoreland politics, 1818'. *Publications of the Modern Language Association*, 55, 1080–128.

West, Thomas (1805) *The Antiquities of Furness.* New edition, with additions by William Close. Ulverston.

Williams, Edward [Iolo Morganwg] (1794) *Poems, Lyric and Pastoral.* 2 vols. London.

Williams, Raymond (1975) *The Country and the City.* Reprint of 1973 edition. London.

    (1977) *Marxism and Literature.* Oxford.

    (1983) *Cobbett.* Oxford and New York.

Woodring, Carl (1970) *Politics in English Romantic Poetry.* Cambridge, Mass.

Woof, R.S. (1970) 'John Stoddart, "Michael", and *Lyrical Ballads*'. In *Ariel*, vol. 1, no. 2 (April), 7–22.

    (1971) 'Mr Woof's reply to Mr Wordsworth'. In *Ariel*, vol. 2, no. 2 (April), 72–9.

Wordsworth, Dorothy (1952) *Journals of Dorothy Wordsworth.* Ed. E. de Selincourt. 2 vols. London.

Wordsworth, Jonathan (1969) *The Music of Humanity: A Critical Study of Wordsworth's 'Ruined Cottage', incorporating Texts from a Manuscript of 1799–1800.* New York and Evanston.

    (1970) 'The climbing of Snowdon'. In Jonathan Wordsworth (ed.) *Bicentenary Wordsworth Studies in Memory of John Alban Finch.* Ithaca and London. 449–74.

    (1971) 'A note on the ballad version of "Michael"'. In *Ariel*, vol. 2, no. 2 (April), 66–71.

Wordsworth, William (1940–9) *The Poetical Works of William Wordsworth.* Ed. E. de Selincourt. 5 vols. Oxford.

    (1959) *The Prelude.* Ed. E. de Selincourt. Second edition revised by Helen Darbishire. Oxford.

    (1967) *The Letters of William and Dorothy Wordsworth.* Ed. E. de Selincourt. Second (enlarged) edition. 6 vols so far. Oxford.

      (1967) *The Early Years, 1787–1805.* Revised by Chester L. Shaver.

(1969) *The Middle Years, Part I, 1806–1811*. Revised by Mary Moorman.

(1970) *The Middle Years, Part II, 1812–20*. Revised by Mary Moorman and Alan G. Hill.

(1978–) *The Later Years, 1821– *. 3 vols so far. Revised by Alan G. Hill.

(1974) *The Prose Works of William Wordsworth*. Ed. W.J.B. Owen and Jane Worthington Smyser. 3 vols. Oxford.

(1975–) *The Cornell Wordsworth*. General editor Stephen Parrish. In progress. Ithaca and Hassocks, Sussex.

(1975) *The Salisbury Plain Poems of William Wordsworth*. Ed. Stephen Gill.

(1977) *Home at Grasmere*. Ed. Beth Darlington.

(1979) *The Ruined Cottage and The Pedlar*. Ed. James Butler.

(1981) *Benjamin the Waggoner*. Ed. Paul Betz.

(1982) *The Borderers*. Ed. Robert Osborn.

(1983) *Poems, in Two Volumes, and Other Poems 1800–1807*. Ed. Jared Curtis.

(1984) *An Evening Walk*. Ed. James Averill.

(1984) *Descriptive Sketches*. Ed. Eric Birdsall.

(1976) (and Coleridge) *Lyrical Ballads*. Ed. R.L. Brett and A.R. Jones. Reprint of 1963 edition. London.

(1979) *The Prelude: 1799, 1805, 1850*. Ed. Jonathan Wordsworth, M.H. Abrams and Stephen Gill. New York.

Worthington, Jane (1946) *Wordsworth's Reading of Roman Prose*. Yale Studies in English, vol. 102. New Haven and London.

Young, Arthur (1767) *The Farmer's Letters to the People of England; to which is added, Sylvae; or, Occasional Tracts on Husbandry and Oeconomics*. London.

(1770) *A Six Months Tour through the North of England; Containing an Account of the Present State of Agriculture, Manufactures, and Population, in several Counties of this Kingdom*. 4 vols. London.

(1801) *An Inquiry into the Propriety of applying Wastes to the Better Maintenance and Support of the Poor*. Bury.

Index

Aarsleff, Hans, 220
Abrams, M.H., 220–1
Aers, David, 20, 221
Anti-Jacobin Review, The, 78
Arnold, Matthew, 9, 186
Austen, Jane, 46
Averill, James, 222, 223

Bailey and Culley, 84–5, 86, 141
Barrell, John, 20, 89, 208, 217
Barstow, Marjorie, 220
Batho, Edith, 224
Beatty, Arthur, 218, 220
Beaumont, Sir George and Lady, 34, 38, 40, 48–9, 74, 110
Bell, Andrew, 196–9
Bentham, Jeremy, 80, 168–72, 178, 197
Bialostosky, Don, 175, 223
Blackstone, William, 44, 47, 156, 178
Blake, William, 8, 181, 184
Bloom, Harold, 4
Bouch and Jones, 63, 82–3, 86–7, 88, 90, 93, 223
Brinton, Crane, 20
Brooks, Cleanth, 162
Brougham, Henry, 199
Brown, John, 68

Burke, Edmund, 14, 53, 58–9, 65, 66, 68, 73–4, 129, 138, 157, 167–8, 171, 172–4, 181–4, 188, 192, 221
Burn, Richard, 44, 167, 174, 224
Burns, Robert, 102–3
Bushnell, John, 147
Butler, Marilyn, 20

Calvert, Raisley, 35–6, 38, 118, 132, 147, 155, 208
Carr, Raymond, 156
Chadwick, Edwin, 82
Chambers and Mingay, 87, 89, 93, 156, 219
Chandler, James, 20, 68, 105, 172, 221
Clare, John, 45–6, 54, 90, 102
Cobbett, William, 20, 88, 92, 104, 198–9
Coleridge, Samuel Taylor, 3, 9, 27, 29, 38, 48, 54, 57, 97, 98–9, 107, 133, 150, 152, 164, 177, 183, 187, 189, 208
Colquhoun, Patrick, 199
Cooper, Lane, 30
Cowper, William, 45, 68, 69, 136, 180
Crabbe, George, 23

Danby, John, 158, 222
Dickens, Charles, 106

Dickson, P.M.S., 89
Douglas, Wallace W., vii, 87, 89, 90, 92, 93, 94, 142, 218, 219, 220
Dyer, George, 167

Eden, Sir Frederick, 90–1, 93–4, 167, 170–1
Engels, Frederick, 82
Erdman, David, 20
Evans, Evan, 152–5

Ferguson, Frances, 186, 201, 218, 220, 224
Ferry, David, 28
Field, Barron, 28, 57
Fielding, Henry, 45, 102
Fink, Z.S., 61, 222
Floud and McCloskey, 83, 89
Foucault, Michel, 81, 168
Friedman, Michael, 20, 28, 217–18, 220, 223

Galperin, William, 196, 224
Garber, Frederick, 162
Gilboy, Elizabeth, 222
Gill, Stephen, 223
Glen, Heather, 184, 223
Godwin, William, 73, 78, 102, 174
Goldsmith, Oliver, 22–5, 61, 69, 70, 71, 105, 146
Goldstein, Lawrence, 20, 25, 217, 220, 221
Gray, Thomas, 30
Griffin, Andrew, 158, 222
Gwilym, Dafydd ap, 152–3, 155

Hammond, J.L. and Barbara, 80–1, 88, 92, 156, 219
Hartman, Geoffrey, 4, 13, 19, 29, 41, 116, 129, 158, 177, 186, 218, 220, 222
Hazlitt, William, 27–8, 29, 33, 54, 117, 185, 187, 188–9, 190, 216
Heffernan, James, 220
Heinzelman, Kurt, 20, 218, 222
Helms, Randall, 222
Hill, Alan, 224
Himmelfarb, Gertrude, 178
Hobsbawm and Rudé, 89
Horace, 120
Housman, John, 219
Hutchinson, William, 86, 219

Itkowitz, David, 156

Jacobus, Mary, 20
Jameson, Fredric, 217

Jeffrey, Francis, 185, 186–7
Johnson, Samuel, 24, 135
Johnston, Kenneth, 162, 166, 185, 220, 221, 224
Jones, G.P., 219
Jordan, John, 20

Kant, 40
Keats, John, 7, 28, 34, 54, 60
Kiernan, V., 20
Kramnick, Isaac, 74

Lancaster, Joseph, 198
Land, Stephen, 100
Langhorne, John, 44, 223
Lea, Sydney, 147–8
Levinson, Marjorie, 20, 220
Lindenberger, Herbert, 220, 221, 222
Liu, Alan, 221
Locke, John, 111
Lyon, Judson, 186, 203, 224

McConnell, Frank, 221, 222
McGann, Jerome, 13–14, 20, 113, 217, 220
McKendrick, Neil, 89
Mackenzie, Henry, 165, 174
MacLean, Kenneth, 61, 86
Mallett, David, 31
Malthus, Thomas, 167, 194
Manning, Peter, 147
Marshall, Dorothy, 63, 82, 157
Marshall, J.D., 82–3, 88, 92, 93, 142, 219
Marshall, William, 84–5
Martineau, Harriet, 93
Marx, Karl, 17–18
Mayo, Robert, 20, 164
Mill, J.S., 9
Milton, John, 4–5, 31–4, 37–8, 41–3, 51–4, 59, 114–21, 130, 134, 180, 205–6, 211–12, 218, 222, 224
Mingay, G.E., 80
Moorman, Mary, 48–9, 150, 154, 155, 156, 188, 198
Morgan, Prys, 151
Morganwg, Iolo [Edward Williams], 152–5
Munsche, P.B., 154, 157

Ogilvie, William, 77–8
Onorato, Richard, 139, 220, 222
Owen, W.J.B., 220
Ozouf, Mona, 53

Paine, Thomas, 77, 129, 155

Parker, Patricia, 218
Parker, Reeve, 201
Parrish, Stephen, 9, 29, 148, 219, 223
Patterson, Annabel, 224
Peterfreund, Stuart, 205, 224
Pitt, William, 170–2, 223
Pocock, J.G.A., 61–2, 89, 112
Poynter, J.R., 161, 223
Pringle, Andrew, 85–6, 88–9, 90

Rawnsley, H.D., 93, 102, 145–6
Reed, Mark, 20, 35, 48, 150, 155, 222
Richards, I.A., 18
Rodgers, Betsy, 223
Rousseau, J.J., 65–6, 181, 218–19
Ruggles, Thomas, 171

Said, Edward, 12, 217
Sales, Roger, 20, 222
Savage, Richard, 31
Schiller, J.C.F. von, 40, 199–200
Scoggins, James, 218, 220
Sekora, John, 89
Sheats, Paul, 222
Shebbeare, John, 151
Shelley, P.B., 219
Simpson, David, 59–61, 101, 218, 219,
    221, 222, 223, 224
Smith, Adam, 65
Smith, Olivia, 220
Smollett, Tobias, 103, 164
Solkin, David, 151
Spence, Thomas, 77
Spenser, Edmund, 54, 97, 175–6
Stedman Jones, Gareth, 219
Sterne, Laurence, 164–5
Stone, Lawrence, 81

Tennyson, Alfred Lord, 51–2
Thelwall, John, 45, 150, 165, 174, 204
Thompson, E.P., 20, 84, 156
Thomson, James, 31, 114, 223
Townsend, Joseph, 167, 171
Trilling, Lionel, 64
Trotsky, Leon, 22, 55

Wales, image of, 151–9
Warton, Thomas, 97
Wells, John Edwin, 219
West, Thomas, 69, 219–20
Williams, Edward, 152–5
Williams, Raymond, 17, 20, 84
Woodring, Carl, 20
Woof, Robert, 222

Wordsworth, Dorothy, 110–12, 132,
    143, 147, 154, 160, 163, 165, 175,
    177, 179, 223
Wordsworth, John, 35–8, 133, 144, 208
Wordsworth, Jonathan, 162, 222
Wordsworth, William: Arnold on, 9, 186;
    and the Beaumonts, *see* Beaumont; and
    the 'beautiful soul', 39–40; and Burke,
    see Burke; and Calvert, *see* Calvert; on
    charity, 160–84; and civic virtue, 3,
    47, 56–107, 121–9, 185–208;
    classical figures in, 30; and Coleridge,
    see Coleridge; and dialect, 102–5;
    dramatic mode in, 7, 28–9, 159,
    182–4, 187–96, 200–8; on education,
    196–9; and the French Revolution, 2,
    31, 40, 43, 52–5, 58–9, 124–5, 181,
    222; and Goldsmith, *see* Goldsmith;
    and Gray, 30; Hazlitt on, *see* Hazlitt;
    and Keats, *see* Keats; and the Lowthers,
    48–9, 58, 72–4, 89, 91–3, 128–9,
    208; Mill on, 9; and Milton, *see*
    Milton; on pleasure, 63–4; poems of,
    see separate entry; on poetic diction,
    30, 42, 64–5, 66, 97–107; prose
    works of, *see separate entry*; and
    railways, 58, 75–7; on religion,
    199–200; and Rousseau, 65–6,
    218–19; and Spenser, 54, 97, 175–6;
    and Swift, 12; and Tennyson, 51–2; on
    theory and method, 57–8; and
    urbanization, *see* civic virtue
Wordsworth, William, poems of:
    'Adventures on Salisbury Plain', 191;
    'Alice Fell', 15, 177–84; 'Anecdote for
    Fathers', 29, 222–3; 'Beggars', 175–7;
    'Sequel' to 'Beggars', 176–7; 'Benjamin
    the Waggoner', 158; 'The Blind
    Highland Boy', 103; *The Borderers*,
    161, 191; 'The Brothers', 29–30, 101,
    105, 143–4, 149; 'The Childless
    Father', 223; *Descriptive Sketches*, 44,
    96; *An Evening Walk*, 96, 161; *The
    Excursion*, 8, 124–5, 136, 137,
    184–216; 'The Female Vagrant', 46;
    'Gipsies', 7, 8–9, 16, 18, 22–55,
    56–7, 74, 108, 110, 113, 130, 140,
    148, 157, 177, 210–12; 'The Gleaner',
    213; 'Goody Blake and Harry Gill', 58;
    'Guilt and Sorrow', 191, 218; 'To a
    Highland Girl', 103; *Home at
    Grasmere*, 34, 48, 70, 94, 96, 97,
    108–9, 120, 133–6, 186, 205, 207; 'I
    know an aged man', 213; 'The Idle
    Shepherd Boys', 34; 'Intimations of
    Immortality: Ode', 10; 'The Labourer's

Noon-Day Hymn', 213–4; 'The Last of the Flock', 192; 'The Mad Mother', 169; 'Michael', 48, 70, 93–4, 105, 118, 141–9, 169, 191, 192, 195; 'Nutting', 210; 'Ode to Duty', 39–40, 199; 'The Old Cumberland Beggar', 162–74, 213; 'Old Man Travelling', 162, 164, 165–6; 'Poems on the Naming of Places', 29, 30, 36, 101, 162, 214; *The Prelude*, 31, 34, 35, 42, 52–3, 97, 108–39, 162, 188, 200, 202–3, 210, 211, 223; 'Resolution and Independence', 38–9; 'The Ruined Cottage', 14, 164, 192–3; 'September 1819', 215–16; 'Simon Lee', 7, 16, 149–59, 207; 'A slumber did my spirit seal', 37, 164; 'The Solitary Reaper', 103, 213; 'Stepping Westward', 43, 50–2, 103, 104, 211, 215; 'The Thorn', 7, 29, 207, 224; 'Tintern Abbey', 10, 50, 96, 109–13, 133, 135, 146, 163; 'The Two Thieves', 207; 'When to the attractions of the busy world', 36–8

Wordsworth, William, prose works of, 56–107; *The Convention of Cintra*, 66–70; 'Essay on Morals', 57; *Essays Upon Epitaphs*, 41, 50–1, 102; *A Guide to the Lakes*, 69–71, 90, 94–5, 128; Llandaff, letter to, 73, 173; Preface to *The Borderers*, 57; Preface to *Lyrical Ballads*, 39, 57, 59–60, 62–7, 68, 98, 99–107, 203; *Two Addresses to the Freeholders of Westmoreland*, 72–4, 91–2; Postscript to *Yarrow Revisited*, 75, 173, 182

Worthington, Jane, 61

Yeats, W.B., 96
Young, Arthur, 44, 78, 90, 167, 168, 174